W9-ASK-166

THEOLOGICAL INVESTIGATIONS

Volume XVII

THEOLOGICAL INVESTIGATIONS

VOLUME XVII
JESUS, MAN, AND THE CHURCH

by
KARL RAHNER

Translated by
MARGARET KOHL

CROSSROAD · NEW YORK

1981
The Crossroad Publishing Company
575 Lexington Avenue, New York NY 10022

A translation of the second part of
SCHRIFTEN ZUR THEOLOGIE, XII
published by Verlagsanstalt Benziger & Co. A.G., Einsiedeln

This translation © Darton, Longman & Todd Ltd. 1981

Printed in the United States of America

Library of Congress Catalog Card Number: 61-8189
ISBN: 0-8245-0026-1

CONTENTS

PART THREE *The Ministry and the Spirit*

PART FOUR *Signs of the Times for the Church*

PART ONE

The Experience
of
Jesus Christ

1

CHRISTMAS IN THE LIGHT OF THE IGNATIAN *EXERCISES*

IT is easy to feel that to attempt to say anything to an audience trained in theology about the mystery of Christmas in our time – the real mystery of the holy night – is too difficult a task. This is especially true nowadays when the interpretation of the scriptural texts demands an exegetical knowledge and expertise to which only a few people can lay claim.[1]

Having hesitantly pointed to these difficulties, I should like here, as a dogmatic theologian, quite simply to make an attempt which may seem rather hazardous: I should like, in a few reflections, to try to show a connection between a basic approach characteristic of St Ignatius in the *Exercises*, and the mystery of Christmas. This connection may perhaps lead us into the Christmas mystery in a new way, making its *Sitz im Leben* – its situation in life – a little clearer. The attempt is a risky one, but I should like to make it all the same.

INDIFFERENCE

Jesuits will of course be convinced – and I hope they are right – that they know what indifference in the Ignatian sense means.[2] None the

---

[1] The present text is based on a Christmas sermon preached to a Jesuit community in 1974. Apart from slight stylistic revisions, the original character has been preserved. A few notes have been added for the sake of the reader who is less familiar with Ignatian spirituality.

[2] Cf. Ignatius Loyola, *Spiritual Exercises* no. 23, (London 1963). *See* in general G. Bottereau and A. Rayez, 'Indifférence' in *Dictionnaire de spiritualité ascetique et mystique (DSAM)* VII (Paris 1971), pp. 1688–708; also K. Rahner, 'Ignatian Spirituality and Devotion to the Heart of Jesus' in *Mission and Grace* III (London 1966), pp. 176–210, esp. pp. 199–210, and *Meditations on Priestly Life* (London 1973), pp. 30–8.

less, it may be useful, at the beginning of these brief reflections, to make sure that we are aware of the precise meaning of this attitude, and to say quite clearly and definitely what this key notion of Ignatian piety means.

It is probably correct to say that indifference is the same as what Paul calls the freedom conferred by the Spirit of God himself – freedom with regard to all the individual powers and forces in our human existence, both in our inner life and in our external situation. Indifference, that is to say, sees things from the point of view of the person who arrives at his decisions in freedom; whereas biblical freedom as we find it in Paul views them from the aspect of God's liberating grace. Paul sees freedom in the light of God, who gives himself directly and without mediation, and radically transforms our transcendental nature, directing it towards himself. In this way he liberates us – both inwardly and outwardly – from every individual thing in our existence to which we should otherwise be subject or enslaved, either with or without guilt. Indifference and freedom, seen as one and the same thing, signify the infinite and open space in which God becomes the event we encounter in our existence – God himself, not God represented by anything finite. Of course, here this event still takes place in a kind of emptiness and darkness, in dumbness and mute adoration of the ineffable mystery which shelters us namelessly in its infinity, without offering us any one resting place from which we can survey the whole.

ASSIGNMENT TO ACTION

But what does this freedom and indifference mean, this deathly reaching-out into the darkness of God[3] beyond the circumference of our own existence which we can name and mould in freedom? We can never know with certainty, by means of our own reflection or our own judgement about ourselves, whether we ourselves have achieved this result, or whether it is really conferred on us. No, this encountered event can only be the continuing object of our own wavering hope. But in the search for this experience should we not have become the mystics of an expressionless spirituality, or Buddhists, for whom

[3] On the question of the darkness of God, see 'The Hiddenness of God' and 'An Investigation of the Incomprehensibility of God in St Thomas Aquinas', both in *Theological Investigations* XVI (London 1979), pp. 227–43 and 244–59 respectively.

the world and history have dissolved, together with individual action and responsibility? Should we not be something quite other than Christians and men who know themselves to be sent on a mission for which concrete action is ultimately decisive?

In the face of this question it is essential to appeal to another fact of Ignatian spirituality; because for Ignatius Loyola 'indifferent' freedom for the tremendous mystery of God does not mean, simply and exclusively, we have found a home where we can abide, so as never again to have to return to the here and now of our everyday earthly life. On the contrary, it is an encountering event which, without itself disappearing, sends us back from itself into the concrete reality of our life for particular decisions and actions. For Ignatius himself, the event is truly conferred (and not merely in mystical ideology) only when we also let ourselves be sent back like this again and again into earthly existence. That is why for Ignatius indifference and freedom come into being only when people, out of this infinite freedom which, when it is experienced, he calls 'consolation', arrive at choice; when against this background they freely allow themselves to be given the specific assignment that is sent to them out of the freedom of God. But what is sent must at the same time be penetrated and reclothed, without adulteration and division, by that absoluteness, that eternal divine validity and glory out of which it is sent to us.

In this way Ignatian choice is, in unadulterated and undivided unity, the place at which divine freedom, the consolation of indifference and our earthly decision in freedom for something specific are simultaneously consummated. In Ignatius himself the mystery of this unity in the existential logic of decision may remain largely unexplained and continue to be a puzzling problem for theologians and philosophers.[4] But it seems to me all the same that in Ignatius Loyola we find that the experience of such unity is possible and is actually achieved. It lets us perceive how we can be, and must be, 'detachedly' lost in the incomprehensibility of God, in order in this very way to find the true reality of our unique existence in its own specific history. On the other hand, however, it also lets us discover how this world and the beyond, history and transcendence, can be bound into an

---

[4] Cf. K. Rahner, *The Dynamic Element in the Church* (London 1964), esp. 'The Logic of Concrete Individual Knowledge in Ignatius of Loyola', pp. 84–170; also 'Religious Enthusiasm and the Experience of Grace' and 'Modern Piety and the Experience of Retreats', both in *Theological Investigations* XVI (London 1979), pp. 35–51 and 135–55 respectively.

unadulterated and undivided unity, so that God is to be found in everything – or, better still: that he is to be found in the particular concreteness and uniqueness which is demanded of individual freedom in any given case, without any loss of identity. But this confronting event of infinite freedom takes place at the very point when in freedom we seize the specific, particular thing assigned to us – what God has provided for us, as distinct from other possibilities, because the Absolute only unites itself with this but not with that non-absolute, giving it its own eternal validity. In Ignatius indifference and choice of the particular possess an ultimate unity in diversity; freedom becomes concrete and what is concrete becomes free.

CHRISTMAS?

What I have said can only point to something in stuttering terms, without any theological and philosophical precision. Consequently we must go on to ask: what has all this to do with the mystery of Christmas? The answer can be summed up as follows: Christmas is the supreme instance of this unity of transcendence and concrete freedom, though of course it is unique, unsurpassable and exemplary. This unity, according to Ignatius, opens up a way of approach for us in our own experience to an understanding of what, for Christian faith, has happened in the birth and life of Jesus of Nazareth, and in the death he achieved. In saying this we are certainly not drawing Jesus down to the level of our own existence; on the contrary, we are merely establishing that human existence, in its unity of transcendence and historicity, is the potentiality of what theology generally calls the hypostatic union of God and an undiminished and untruncated humanity. But if we let the potentiality for this hypostatic union (which is what being man means) interpret and fulfil itself in the experience of that mysterious unity of indifferent freedom and specific decision, then we come to understand what being man is; and I am sure we are not acting incorrectly.

What is certain, however, is that here we have a particular access to the mystery of Christmas in the light of Ignatius' spirituality. In confessing the incarnation of the eternal divine Logos in our flesh, we certainly talk in faith about the 'ontological', 'substantial' unity of the Word of God and the full humanity of Jesus in unity and difference. Here nothing must be denied or repressed. But this unity of God and man reaches its own goal and essential perfection only when it is thought of in *completion*; when, that is to say, the divinely descending freedom of God (which wills each particular thing in its finitude) meets the freedom of man which it sustains; and when it frees this freedom for the absoluteness of God and for the obedient acceptance of that absoluteness – the absoluteness which therefore confers the freedom of God on the unique existence of the individual person.

If, now, this takes place in Jesus (as distinct from in us) to a comprehensive, exemplary and manifest degree, then this is itself an efficacious promise to us. For such unity also achieves fruition accordingly in the framework assigned to us as well – which is by no means a matter of course. And we experience what grace means as the act towards us of the divine freedom – an act on which we have no claim. In this way the correspondence and the difference between Jesus and ourselves is brought out so clearly that here we find a special starting point for an understanding of Christmas.

These suggestions remain highly theoretical and fragmentary, especially those of real christological significance. All the same, we may say that the practice of Ignatian indifference, as the freedom which loses itself willingly in the mysteriousness of God, and the finding a home in the specific existence uniquely given to every one of us, allows that unadulterated and undivided unity to grow in us. We then find God in that unity, even in the down-to-earth triviality of our everyday life; and we cease to be the slaves of that triviality. We cannot of course subjugate that unity to ourselves, but we can let it happen and lay hold of it, die and live. When that happens it is Christmas; Christ is born and the mystery of that birth lays hold of us as our own salvation.

2

ON THE SPIRITUALITY OF THE EASTER FAITH

P ROPERLY speaking, every truth of Christian faith has a relation to the Christian's spirituality, i.e. to the conscious and
(to some extent) methodical development of faith, hope and
love. For everything has been revealed for our salvation, and so aims
at man's perfection. This anthropological purpose of the whole of
revelation (as God's act and word) does not involve any anthropocentric narrowing down of revelation. It does not mean that revelation
is thought of according to the limitations of finite man.[1] For the man
of revelation is precisely the man who, through God's self-communication − or through 'God in himself', or through God in his
own glory − is to be pardoned and brought to perfection. Consequently the proposition that every tenet of faith can and must be
questioned with regard to its anthropological significance is absolutely
justified. And this means that every tenet of faith must also be questioned for its significance to the spirituality of the Christian.

What, then, does the Easter faith mean for the Christian's spirituality, if by the Easter faith we mean Christianity's acknowledgement that Jesus, the One who was crucified, lives, is risen, saved by
the power of the living God?

When we put this question to earlier text-books of dogmatic theology, we generally receive a very meagre and existentially unsatis-
fying answer which more or less evades the question as it affects the

---

[1] For another aspect of the subject cf. 'Dogmatic Questions on Easter',
Theological Investigations IV (London and Baltimore 1966), pp. 121–33. Recent
theological discussion seems to impute 'an anthropocentric narrowing down
of revelation' somewhat too carelessly and indiscriminately. It is not always
really clear what this imputation actually means, or whether it can be justly
and appropriately levelled against the statements of others.

here and now. The statements about Jesus' resurrection in our text books are generally made from the point of view of *fundamental theology*: the mission of Jesus, his teaching and the saving significance of his death are confirmed, sealed and made credible to us through the 'miracle' of Jesus' resurrection, seen in the light of fundamental theology and apologetics. The resurrection is the greatest of all miracles and can be effected directly by God alone.[2] But this establishes a merely indirect connection, at most, between Jesus' resurrection and our spirituality. In this view of the resurrection of Jesus, which belongs purely to fundamental theology, we do not perceive directly what this resurrection could have to do with the consummation of our own pardoned and deified existence. One might have the impression that, for our spiritual life as such, there would have been no real difference if the teaching of Jesus and the satisfaction for our sins made by Jesus on the cross had been authenticated for us by means of some corroboration other than the resurrection; or if the risen Christ had been snatched up into a dimension in which he had no relation to or meaning for us apart from the significance of his earthly life.

At all events, the meaning of Jesus' resurrection in terms of fundamental theology cannot offer any obvious *spiritual* relevance as long as the inner relationship between Jesus' death on the cross and his resurrection has not become clear as being the *single* event of our redemption. For if the resurrection really belongs to the redemption on the cross as an intrinsic aspect, not merely as an event that follows the cross in time and confirms it outwardly, then it is part of the spiritual significance of the event of the cross for us. But we must go on to discuss this from another starting point.

Beyond this aspect of Jesus' resurrection for fundamental theology, former text-book dogmatic theology concerned itself more or less only with the substance of the doctrine of the resurrection, in so far as it touches on Jesus' individual destiny and its accomplishment. In short: the resurrection as an actual 'mystery of salvation' which is

---

[2] As an example of the way of looking at things I have described, cf. thesis 34 on the resurrection of Jesus by M. Nicolau in *Sacrae Theologiae Summa* I (BAC 61), 4th edn (Madrid 1958), pp. 375–96. From the exegetical side, however, valuable attempts at finding an answer to our question have been made; cf. H. Schürmann, *Jesu ureigener Tod* (Freiburg 1975), pp. 66–96 ('Das Weiterleben der Sache Jesu im nachösterlichen Herrenmahl').

related directly to our Christian existence is not stated very clearly.[3]

If we look at the spiritual life of Christians themselves as we find it in traditional Catholic piety, then we can observe a curious phenomenon – or so it seems to me. If I try to make this clear here, I do not mean that in actual devotional life the relationship of the devout man or woman to Jesus Christ is found precisely and distinctly in the two forms that we are here distinguishing so sharply, so as to make them clear. But a difference of the kind I mean here does exist, and the unity of what is being divided forms precisely what we can call the spirituality of the Easter faith. For that reason it would seem justifiable to start with these contrasting models of the devout person's relationship to Jesus.

One kind of devotion to the person of Jesus is loving participation in the actual life of Jesus, in his earthly history, from the beginning of his life to his death and the crowning victory of that life in the resurrection. Even here, however, the resurrection is still seen as the final phase of this historical life, to which the believer turns in loving participation and personal involvement. This type of devotion can be found from the early Middle Ages onwards – especially since Bernard of Clairvaux – down to our own time. Of course the devout man or woman knows, in contemplating the life of Jesus as the norm of his or her own life, that this Jesus is the Son of God, the Word of the eternal Father, who appeared in history for our salvation. But their gaze still turns *backwards* into past history and is directly concerned with the historical details of Jesus' life. They undertake a pilgrimage back into history, so to speak, as one makes a pilgrimage to the Holy Land. The historical aspects of the life of Jesus have for this group of believers, as regards their immediate impression at least, a significance similar to other historical events which affect later people as a challenge or an example. This historical narrative may indeed differ from other historical material through its content, and thereby, of course, also through its existential meaning for us; but not through our mode of *access* to it.[4]

[3] On the idea of 'the mystery of salvation' or the mysteries of the life of Jesus, cf. K. Rahner, 'Mysterien des Lebens Jesu', *LThK* VII, 2nd edn (Freiburg 1962), pp. 721–2; 'Current Problems in Christology', *Theological Investigations* I (London and Baltimore 1961), pp. 149–200.

[4] One of the most highly developed examples of this viewpoint is to be found in the considerations of the life of Jesus in Ignatius Loyola's *Spiritual Exercises*. But these are always linked with the other aspect which is brought out here.

At the centre of the other type of devotion to the person of Jesus stands the invocation of the transfigured Lord, prayer to Jesus in his own blessedness and glory. But in this direct, trusting, loving and adoring relationship to the transfigured Lord there is still (purely descriptively, not fundamentally) no clear distinction between the relationship of the devout person to the eternal God as such (whether, in this religious relationship, he is explicit as the one or as the triune God) and his relationship to Jesus as the God-*man*; although, because of the unmixed duality of natures in Jesus Christ, the relationship to Jesus as the transfigured man must not be fundamentally and simply merged in the relationship of the devout person to God. In this relationship to the transfigured Lord, the earthly history of Jesus hardly plays a role any more; the believer turns to the now-ruling Pantocrator, who in his power and glory reaches new decisions (the hearing of prayer, the granting of grace etc.); or he may perhaps appeal to 'the bridegroom of the soul', to the all-ruling Logos of the Father, who forms the innermost centre of a person's own existence. Whether Jesus mysticism, or Logos mysticism, or the adoration of the heavenly Pantocrator is predominant in this second type of devotion is not here decisive. But there is, nevertheless, a danger that the history of Jesus may disappear from the field of vision of the person praying and meditating, as being 'something in the past'. Jesus' history may have been exemplary and of saving efficacy, but it is none the less a thing of the past, and has been replaced by God in himself and in his Spirit – the Spirit which has always sustained and ruled all history. Through this Spirit we have such direct access to God that in that access history is no longer to be found.

Even if we were to say (and of course we should, fundamentally speaking, be right) that these two types of Christian piety and religious relationship to Jesus are always present *together* in a living and unrestricted Catholic devotion, and in individual Christians, this would not really eliminate the difficulty which is meant and which we are discussing here. The gaze of the devout person would still have two different directions: backwards into a past which no longer exists 'now', and upwards into the eternity of God, which is ultimately outside history.

Of course the inward problem which is inherent in this double direction of vision in Christian devotion involves what is in fact the really basic problem of theology in general. We might characterise this basic problem briefly as being the question of the unity between transcendence and history. How can history have significance for salvation and achieve eternal validity, when man in his transcendental nature, radically altered through grace, has direct access to the infinite God in himself? And when this God lives as the infinite and unchangeable One, beyond all history, and in his infinite fullness of being holds in advance and from eternity everything that happens in history, in finite being and in particular events? How can a history made up of finite events and beings have a meaning that is absolute and ultimate in kind before an infinite God? Why does not history pass away, as something provisional and without substance, for the spiritual subject who has been raised by grace, once that subject has acquired a direct relationship to the God who is above all history? Of course we cannot treat this fundamental problem in detail here. It is a basic problem of the Christian faith, and hence of Christian devotion as well. But I wanted to touch on it at this point in order to indicate, at least, the deeper background to the question of the spirituality of the Easter faith.[5]

For this Easter faith postulates an indissoluble unity between transcendence and history. It demands that the Christian's devotional life should vividly realise this unity in its undivided and unadulterated nature. It demands, that is to say, that devotion should let the God of infinite, eternal and unassailed fullness of life be in truth the God of a history of abiding validity; and, conversely, that devotion should lay hold on the God of history (who – at least seen in the light of the eternal Logos – actually carries on his own history in his world and does not merely passively sustain it, being himself beyond the world) as being the God of fullness of life and reality, already possessed from eternity to eternity. In this unity of transcendence and history, the two aspects certainly cannot coincide for us in lifeless identity; the Chalcedonian 'unmixed' character of Christology applies here, too. But the Easter faith enjoins us – and especially in the light of Jesus Christ, the crucified and risen One – not to overlook this 'undivided' unity of history and transcendence, above all in the completion of history. It insists that we do not simplify it through a mere parallelism of the two aspects, but that we understand that the consummated

---

[5] On the problem of history and its significance for salvation, see among K. Rahner's more recent writings: 'Possible Courses for the Theology of the Future' and 'Experience of Self and Experience of God', *Theological Investigations* XIII (London 1975), pp. 32–60 and pp. 122–32 respectively; 'On the Concept of Infallibility in Catholic Theology' *Theological Investigations* XIV (London 1976), pp. 66–85.

encounter with God as he is in himself actually means encounter with the consummated history that is ours.

Seen in the light of the spiritual 'realisation' of the Easter faith, this means the following: when we turn to the exalted Lord in faith, in hope and in love, we find none other than the crucified Jesus, in whose death his *whole* earthly life is of course integrated. When we are told that that the crucified Jesus is to be found in the risen Christ, then this statement expresses considerably more than is clear from the duality of viewpoint on the part of the devout person which we mentioned earlier. The risen Christ is not merely the One who at some earlier time lived a human life, was crucified and died, but has now simply left all this behind him as the no-longer-existing past, and now leads a different, new life – a life which is linked with the earlier one only through the identity of the substantial bearer of both lives (or phases of life), beyond that claiming for itself only the moral qualities of that earlier life. No, the risen Lord *is* the One who was crucified. This 'is' does not merely indicate the identity of a substantial subject, who now sustains a different life from before. The 'is' states that this very earlier life itself is completed and has found eternal reality in and before God.

We must not trivialise the identity between the earthly Jesus and the exalted Lord – either through a mere recourse to the identity of the substantial subject, or through the notion that in the risen Christ the same 'character' is present as in the earthly Jesus. His eternal life is rather the ultimate form of his earthly life itself. What he leads in the 'Now' of eternity is not a new and different life (even though it exists in homogeneity with his earthly life). His life in eternity is the ultimate form of his history, so that when the devout person turns to the risen Christ, he finds the Jesus who was crucified, and vice versa. Of course much in the earthly life of Jesus is simply 'past and gone' and no longer exists. To deny that would simply be to assert that the history of Jesus is not *completed*. But for that reason this earthly life of Jesus is not after all simply past and gone: it *is*; it is completed and eternally valid; it has itself been accepted by God and acknowledged as real; from the human subjectivity of Jesus, it has been gathered out of the mere flux of earthly time into the Now of eternity, and taken into irrevocable possession.[6]

[6] On the whole subject, cf. K. Rahner and W. Thüsing, *Christologie – systematisch und exegetisch* (Quaestiones Disputatae 55) (Freiburg 1972), esp. 'Grundlinien einer systematischen Christologie', pp. 15–78.

Our understanding of history's consummation remains inevitably dialectical, allowing history to be truly 'passing', *while* preserving it as ultimately abiding; and we cannot of course transfer this to a unity which is in itself directly accessible to us. We have to come to terms with this dialectic. It is the same for us as for Paul, when in chapter 15 of the First Epistle to the Corinthians he describes the resurrection body as being totally different from the earthly body, and yet holds that it is this very resurrection body which signifies the concrete character of our earthly history.

We ought really now to go on to show, by means of biblical theology, that in the New Testament the exalted Lord is essentially understood as being one with the crucified Jesus, and vice versa. The evidence for this cannot be given here.[7]

We could also go on to show that the piety documented in the tradition of theology and spiritual writings has always tended towards a unity of the two viewpoints which we have described above in deliberately exaggerated form. When the devout person turns in prayer to the exalted Lord, he sees, like Stephen, the Son of man standing at the right hand of God (Acts 7:56); and when in his meditations he follows the paths of the earthly Jesus, he knows that what he contemplates so lovingly is now eternal reality, which has found its ultimate form in the life of the eternal God. When Jesus' 'resurrection' is correctly understood, as faith really believes it to be, then it does not mean the living-on of an identical subject, whose life, having gone through a past phase, now has a new content; the resurrection means the ultimate, God-given form of the earthly life belonging to history. And this history has an ultimate meaning because in the incarnation and cross of the eternal Logos it is the history of God himself.[8]

Of course we ought also now to go on to show that in history itself something eternal is already taking place as an encountering event and is to some extent already open to experience; and that this eternal happening 'takes place' through freedom, but is through that very freedom established as something final and irrevocable, not as

[7] I should like to draw express attention to W. Thüsing's questions and comments in K. Rahner and W. Thüsing, *Christologie – systematisch und exegetisch* (Quaestiones Disputatae 55) (Freiburg 1972), pp. 123–233. I am indebted to him for a number of points.

[8] Cf. K. Rahner, 'The Eternal Significance of the Humanity of Jesus for our Relationship with God', *Theological Investigations* III (London and Baltimore 1967), pp. 35–46.

something transient. So that eternity comes about *in* history and does not merely tack itself on *behind* history as something new and different. But here we can point only in the most cursory way to this more general problem of the relationship between freedom, time and eternity.

We have perhaps been talking about the spirituality of the Easter faith in very unspiritual terms, i.e. in merely abstract theological language. And even so, we have failed to mention many conclusions which might be drawn from the basic approach to an understanding of the risen Christ that we have indicated, and from the relationship of the devout person to this risen Christ. For example, we could go on to draw conclusions about the real nature of the heavenly intercession of the risen Christ with the Father; for this is not a new 'occupation' on the part of Jesus (*sit venia verbo*), provoked by us, but is identical with the validity of Jesus' earthly life and his cross, which he eternally possesses in knowledge and freedom. It is impossible to say any more here. My intention has been really only to encourage the devout man or woman to turn without reserve to the exalted Lord in prayer, because direct access to God also means direct access to the history which God has accepted as his own reality, finally confirming it as his own in the resurrection of Jesus.

3

JESUS' RESURRECTION

SOME OBSERVATIONS DRAWN FROM SYSTEMATIC THEOLOGY

IT is possible to enquire about Jesus' resurrection today (if we are to do justice to the facts and talk in a way that inspires confidence) only if we take into account the whole of what philosophy and theology have to say about man. Here we must start from the assumption that the hope that a person's history of freedom will be conclusive in nature (a hope which is given in the act of responsible freedom and which is transcendentally necessary) already includes what we mean by the hope of 'resurrection'. Whether this hope is accepted or rejected is initially unimportant in the context of a question of this kind. At all events this hope must include knowledge of what is really meant by resurrection.

It is only in the light of this starting point that a distinction which we can also observe in the history of revelation can be made comprehensible. I mean the distinction which exists between hope for the resurrection of 'the righteous', and the expectation that even the people who have finally, as part of their freedom, missed their calling will also 'be raised'.[1] The second 'resurrection', for the purpose of judgement, can be understood only as the presupposition and implication of hope for the resurrection of the morally perfect. It must consequently be essentially different in kind and can, so to speak, be only a borderline concept.

But hope for the conclusive nature of one's own history of freedom, because of its absolute responsibility, also includes the idea of 'the resurrection of the body', because the hoping person as such basically affirms his own unity and his own history in space and time; conse-

---

[1] Cf. I Cor. 15:12–58; John 5:29.

16

quently he is prevented from the outset from confining his hope merely to one part or excerpt of his reality. Of course such a hope can then always be differentiated, in the case of a particular individual; but it cannot be split up. That depends on the elements of his being and the particular interpretation which he gives to the quite natural differentiations of his single existence in its different aspects.

It is therefore quite possible (depending on the particular philosophical and anthropological interpretations of man's make-up we choose) to conceive of a considerable variation in the precise interpretation of what resurrection could mean for that particular aspect of man's being which we normally call his 'body'. Nor will this breadth of variation, philosophically speaking, be limited by the facts of the Christian revelation, as long as these facts themselves are carefully interpreted. Consequently, if we see the matter in the light of our own historical time, and judge it as belonging to the event of a person's being perfected in all the different elements of his being, we can leave the question open, theologically speaking, whether temporality is to be objectively included or not. In other words, it may remain an open question whether the perfecting of the individual person in his 'physical being' is an event which takes place 'later', as his personal perfecting, or whether it takes place when he dies; i.e. whether we have to expect the resurrection of the individual 'in the body' as part of a general resurrection of all men at the end of history, or whether it is 'co-existent' with historical time, which meanwhile continues to run its course.

At all events, we should be giving a temporal character to the perfection of man in a quite mythological way if we were perhaps to assume, with contemporary biblical scholars, that the one resurrection of men and women takes place *after* a period of complete non-existence on the part of the dead. This would make it impossible to talk seriously at all any more about a true identity between the person who has died and the person who is raised. On the contrary, we must cling to the fact that 'the resurrection' in its theologically valid sense refers primarily to the acquiring of a final and ultimate form by the whole, individual person in his own history of freedom; it applies to his 'body' only in a secondary and derivative sense.[2] But it is just this

---

[2] Cf. here 'Der Leib in der Heilsordnung' in K. Rahner and A. Görres, *Der Leib und das Heil* (Mainz 1967), pp. 29–44. The text is printed in the present volume, pp. 71–89.

which also corresponds to the facts of the Christian history of revelation. A doctrine of the resurrection 'of the body' which neglected
this or was not prepared to accept it as true would be subscribing to
mythological notions.

On the basis of what we have said, we might now formulate the
proposition that the knowledge of man's resurrection given with his
transcendentally necessary hope is a statement of philosophical anthropology even before any real revelation in the Word. But we
should have to counter this by saying that, at least initially, the
elucidation of man's basic hope as being the hope of resurrection was
in actual fact made historically through the revelation of the Old and
New Testaments. It was there that man was taught to take his existence in space and time and in the body really seriously. So at least in
actual fact and historically, this hope always remains theological.

Secondly, we should have to stress that – at least conceivably – the
actual and absolute hope for the ultimate consummation of our own
history of freedom – hope which is really lived as being actual and
absolute, and which finds the courage to express itself clearly – is
due, at least *sensu positivo*, to God's grace, which is always active in
men and women. For it is this which first gives human nature a claim
to finality of this kind; as 'pure nature' man simply could not have
it at all. This aspect of hope cannot be eliminated 'experimentally',
however. So the actual, specific hope of resurrection is founded on
grace and therefore remains theological, even in the light of its own
reality; although this is not a claim that it could be fundamentally
objectified and identified simply on the basis of the positive evidence
of Christian revelation (Scripture and tradition).

THE LORD'S RESURRECTION

We said at the beginning that belief in Jesus' resurrection is possible
only within this transcendentally necessary hope of resurrection. This
applies not only to the fact of Jesus' resurrection but also to its
meaning – if by meaning we understand, as we must, both 'meaning
in itself' and 'meaning for us'. This does not exclude – it expressly
includes – the fact that because of the circle that links all transcendental
and historical experience, the secure objectification of the transcendental hope of resurrection is brought about by the experience of
Jesus' resurrection. We therefore can and must say: *because* Jesus is
risen, I believe in and hope for my own resurrection.

For that reason we are now bound to interpret Jesus' resurrection as the final and conclusive form of this person and his actual history before God and with him. The statement 'he lives in the glory of God'[3] is therefore more primal and basic than the individual accounts of the visions and 'appearances' of the risen Jesus – in fact, and not only according to the biblical tradition.

Thus the fundamental experience of being saved and the enduring finality and conclusiveness of Jesus and his history are not simply identical with whatever can be reported directly and 'tangibly' in the experience of 'the appearances', in concepts drawn from time and space. On the contrary, what is really at stake is an experience of faith in the Spirit – the experience that Jesus is alive. And this experience is fundamentally open to every Christian. He has only to accept believingly and trustingly his own transcendental hope of resurrection and, therefore, also be on the look out, implicitly or explicitly, for a specific event in his own history, on the basis of which his hope can be believed in, as something that has been realised in another person. He has certainly also to hope for others just as much as for himself. But in view of Jesus and his history it becomes possible to believe that this Jesus has undergone an event whose liberating power can have an effect on the believer. In spite of this, the Christian experience of Jesus' resurrection remains bound to the apostolic testimony, because without that testimony our own resurrection could no longer be mediated to ourselves through Jesus, as an actual named individual. The search for the actual event towards which our own resurrection hope is directed, as its historical verification and mediation, would run into the sand without the testimony of the apostles. At the same time, faith in this testimony is not just the same as mere belief in a witness because he is competent and credible; for example, when we are told about an event whose facts we can no longer verify for ourselves.[4]

The *theological*, and not merely the philosophical, justification for the close link between our own personal existential hope of resurrection and the evidential character of Jesus' resurrection is to be found in the fact that the Lord's resurrection can of course be believed in

---

[3] Cf. here Matt. 22:44ff (following Ps. 109:1); Rev. 2:25 (following Ps. 16:9–11); Rom. 8:34; Eph. 1:20; Col. 3:1; Heb. 10:12; I Pet. 3:22; etc.

[4] Cf. here 'Theological Observations on the Concept of Witness', *Theological Investigations* XIII (London 1975), pp. 152–68 (which contains an extensive bibliography in n. 1).

only with the help of God's *grace*. This internal reasoning is admittedly really circular, as modern theology has understood ever since Rousselot's writings on the relationship between faith and credibility.[5] But this grace to believe must not be thought of as a purely neutral and colourless divine aid towards the act of faith; or as an essential 'supernatural elevation' of that act. It is in its very nature hope for *our own* 'resurrection' because it is God's eschatological communication of himself for our final salvation. It must therefore be attributed from within to the historical experience of a specific resurrection.

There is no doubt at all that the accounts of 'the empty tomb' belong to the oldest tradition in the New Testament. Yet we must not forget that this fact alone does not give us any real knowledge about Jesus' resurrection. The empty tomb ought rather to be judged as an expression of a conviction which had already spread for other reasons – the conviction that Jesus was alive. A secondary point is that we must also probably leave the question open of how the mention of the empty tomb is related to the accounts of the appearances, and what significance must be attributed to this report in view of the literary nature of the appearance narratives. This is simply a point to be mentioned here.

Finally, the 'facts' of Jesus' resurrection must simply be determined in the light of what we have to understand by our own 'resurrection'; and this must be decided first of all, quite apart from the significance for us of Jesus' resurrection in the context of salvation history. If we began by taking our bearings from the notion of the revival of a physical, material body, we should be bound from the outset to lose sight of the general meaning of 'resurrection'; but we should also no less miss the meaning of Jesus' own resurrection. For unlike everything which the Old and New Testaments report elsewhere about the raising of the dead, the Lord's resurrection means the ultimate deliverance of actual human existence by God and before him. This means that human history acquires its real validity for the first time; it neither simply goes on continuing into vacuity, nor is it simply destroyed. In view of this, death, without which this ultimate conclusiveness is impossible, is the essential and radical renunciation of every concept of the 'how' of this conclusiveness, whether it applies

[5] P. Rousselot, *Die Augen des Glaubens*. With intro. by Josef Trütsch. (Einsiedeln 1963); cf. E. Kunz, *Glaube, Gnade, Geschichte: Die Glaubenstheologie des Pierre Rousselot s.j.* (Frankfurt 1969).

to 'the body' or to 'the soul' of any human life.[6] From the very outset, the resurrection does not mean any kind of continuance on the part of a human existence which would be neutral towards man's salvation; it means that existence's acceptance and deliverance by God. That is why the person cannot be separated from the activity or 'cause' that animated his earthly life, when we are considering the resurrection and its interpretation. The real activity or 'cause' – if we do not give it an idealistic, ideological sense – is always whatever is brought to fulfilment in the actual existence of the human person. Consequently in saying that this is what has permanent validity, we are saying that what is permanently valid is the validity of the person himself. So when we say that the resurrection of Jesus means that his 'cause' did not come to an end with his death, then we must at the same time stress, positively and critically, what we have just said in the previous sentence, if we really want to exclude an idealistic mis-understanding of the cause of Jesus;[7] for otherwise the continuance of the cause would simply mean the validity and efficacy of an 'idea', which is continually engendered and wins ever-new acceptance.

We should also have to go on to ask why, when we talk about Jesus' cause, it still remains clear that – at least during the lifetime of the Lord – this cause remains indissolubly bound up with his person. He himself, after all, was deeply convinced of this, according to his own sayings and his own behaviour. But to talk about his cause seems to suggest that he himself could simply have perished, leaving his cause to live on – though this cause would then no longer really be *his* cause.

But if Jesus' resurrection continues to be the final, conclusive exist-ence of his person and his cause, and if this person-cause does not simply mean that some man or other and his history go on existing, but that the *victory* of his special claim to be the absolute mediator of

---

[6] Cf. K. Rahner, *On the Theology of Death* (Quaestiones Disputatae 2), 2nd edn, (London 1969); 'Ideas for a Theology of Death', *Theological Investigations* XIII (London 1975), pp. 169–86.

[7] The expression 'the cause' (*Sache*) of Jesus is taken from W. Marxsen, *The Resurrection of Jesus of Nazareth* (ET S.C.M. Press, London 1970). The present author has discussed the problem of the resurrection in the light of Marxsen's views in K. Rahner and W. Thüsing, *Christologie – systematisch und exegetisch* (Quaestiones Disputatae 55) (Freiburg 1972), Lehrsatz 25: 'Der Sinn von "Auferstehung" ', pp. 36–8. The following section is based on these earlier remarks, some of it word for word.

salvation is endorsed once and for all – then *faith* in his resurrection is an inner aspect of that resurrection itself. It does not simply mean registering a certain fact, which by its very nature could just as well exist even if we did not register it at all. The resurrection of Jesus is accordingly the eschatological victory of God's grace in the world. But for that very reason it cannot be conceived of without the free faith in it which actually exists; for it is only in this that its own essence is fulfilled at all. In *this* sense we can and may well say that Jesus is raised 'into' the faith of his disciples.[8] But this faith into which Jesus is raised is not really and directly faith in this resurrection; it is the faith which is experienced as liberty from all the forces of finitude, guilt and death. It is liberty brought about by God and it knows itself to be warranted by the fact that this liberty has come into being in Jesus himself and was revealed in him for us. If faith henceforth counts as being hope for our resurrection, then it must believe in *this* resurrection of Jesus' first of all, and cannot replace his resurrection by something different, without any specifiable 'content'. Of course in the last resort the *fides qua* (faith as personal act) and the *fides quae* (faith as object) are always indissolubly linked. But every *fides qua* as the subject's act of absolute freedom derived from and directed towards God, for him is already, at least implicitly, the *fides quae* of our own resurrection.

Jesus' resurrection, finally, takes on a unique salvation-history character because through faith we recognise it as being the eschatologically irreversible, historical appearance of God's promise of himself to the world. Of course this takes for granted that the disciples did not experience Jesus' resurrection merely as being the final and conclusive deliverance of a particular person, let alone as merely the revival of a dead person in our era of time and space, with its continuing history. It presupposes that they saw the Lord's resurrection as the final confirmation by God himself of the claim made by Jesus before Easter: the claim that the word, the fate and the person of the Lord means the nearness of the kingdom of God, and that this is a fact that cannot be rescinded. The disciples must have been conscious of this claim of Jesus' in some form or other, even though

[8] Cf. here K. Hollmann, 'Die Interpretation der Osterbotschaft durch Bultmann', *Existenz und Glaube* (Paderborn 1972), pp. 146–9; H. Häring, 'Der kirchliche Sinn der Auferstehung', *Kirche und Kerygma* (Freiburg 1972), pp. 48–50; 65–9.

we cannot define it more closely here. If this were not so the mere conviction 'he is alive' would have no meaning for us in the context of salvation-history. Of course to say this does not mean calling in question the fact that, against the background of contemporary Jewish theology, the resurrection could only be understood at all as an eschatological event – i.e. it was impossible to interpret it simply as just another event in history. Equally we are not overlooking the fact that the experience of the final deliverance of Jesus by God and with God also in retrospect facilitated and helped to sustain the radical interpretation of the claim made by Jesus before Easter. But at all events this kind of interpretation of the Easter experience is sufficient to make us see and hold fast to what Christian faith has to say and has to acknowledge dogmatically today about the soteriological significance of Jesus' death – if it is a faith that is consciously held and has been responsibly arrived at.

4

CHRISTOLOGY TODAY?

FOR Christians, questions about Christology are always topical. As believers, and also, it may be, as people in the service of the Church as proclaimers of the message of Jesus Christ, the crucified and risen One, the mediator of our salvation, we cannot be indifferent towards questions of Christology today; for we are at the same time people in a situation in life where this message is not simply a matter of course, but where it is controversial, doubted and rejected.

Of course there are innumerable questions of this kind. We cannot even list or name them here. How, for example, can a person outside definite 'committed' Christianity arrive at faith in Jesus Christ at all, in the sense in which the fellowship of believers acknowledge him? In the face of questions like these we must confine ourselves to a more limited subject. The only point we can and ought to discuss here is the following: how can a person who acknowledges Christ in principle (even if his confession of faith is perhaps somewhat vague and is still involved in a process of search) come to terms with things, when he is also convinced that his personal understanding of this Jesus cannot, and must not, be merely an individualistically isolated opinion, but has essentially to be related to the faith of the Church? For it is the Church, after all, which has passed the Gospel of Jesus Christ on to him in the first place.

TRADITIONAL CHRISTOLOGY

It must be said at once that contemporary Christology too must not simply emancipate itself from the classical position. Christology developed from the New Testament writings (especially Paul and John) down to the statements of the Council of Chalcedon (451).[1] Since that time this Christology has remained valid in the Eastern churches, in the Roman Catholic Church and – we may cautiously say – in the Reformed Churches, at least until the nineteenth century. It certainly cannot now be a question of simply deducing this classical Christology from its sources as being obligatory for our time and in the future too. And by 'sources' I mean, ultimately, a person's original experience with this Jesus of Nazareth (which is still open to us today) and, together with this experience and as part of it, the New Testament itself. At the same time I am quite convinced that this process is entirely possible, in spite of all denials by a liberalistic exegesis or by pamphlets such as that of Rudolf Augstein.[2] But it is a task that is primarily the function of proclamation and theology as a whole. It cannot be adequately summed up here in the space at our disposal.

First of all, however, a Christian who wants to lay claim to being 'a churchman' must note the following: we cannot simply leap over fifteen hundred years of classical Christology or push it aside as if it were a matter of indifference. We cannot do this if there is an enduring Gospel of Jesus Christ as the One who gives us an ultimate trust and an ultimate hope for the eternal significance and final validity of our existence; if we derive this ultimate attitude from the Church; and if we are convinced that this bond with Jesus Christ, in spite of all the history and historicity which surrounds it, is fundamentally valid for all future ages and therefore has a genuine continuity in the historical life and historical Word of Christianity. On the contrary, we must accept it as being binding on ourselves, too, fundamentally and as a whole. One reason is that for almost two thousand years Christianity has acknowledged this Christology and lived according to it. It is in this Christology – not through by-passing it – that Christianity has

---

[1] Cf. the formula Denzinger-Schönmetzer (Denz.), *Enchiridion Symbolorum* (Barcelona 1965), 301–2. For information about the background, development and significance of the Council's decision, cf. the now classic volume, A. Grillmeier and H. Bacht (eds), *Das Konzil von Chalkedon. Geschichte und Gegenwart*, I–III (Würzburg 1951–4). It has frequently been photomechanically reproduced.

[2] Cf. R. Augstein, *Jesus Menschensohn* (Gütersloh 1972). For criticism, cf. K. Rahner, 'Das Christentum – ein explosiver Irrtum?', *Frankfurter Allgemeine Zeitung*, 7 Oct. 1972 (No. 233), supplement; later printed in R. Pesch and G. Stachel (eds), *Augsteins Jesus* (Zürich 1972), pp. 40–9.

found Jesus Christ to be the mediator and Lord on which it has based its life and death.

Another reason is that this classical Christology still has a meaning and a message for us today. If it were simply no longer comprehensible because of the change in the boundaries of understanding (which is of course undeniable) then we should not even be able to talk about it at all or to reject it with apparent justification. Consequently we should also beware of cheap and hasty lamentations that Christology in its traditional form has become alien, and that 'it just doesn't appeal any more' because the presuppositions behind it, which are necessary for its understanding, no longer exist.

From many points of view a person who attempts today to assimilate this classical Christology must overcome greater difficulties. For instance, its historical pre-conditions and premisses (which are not simply self-evident to us from the start) may loom larger for us with our greater historical awareness. Nevertheless the meaning of this classical Christology can still be understood, and furthermore it can still be seen to be legitimately derived from a more primal experience of Jesus which is open to us now even though it is still historically mediated. Consequently we can come to recognise it as being authoritative and binding for ourselves also, provided we do not adopt the foolish idea that we can produce a new Christology of our own, as its 'only begetters', without the need for living bonds to connect our own Christianity with the history of the Christian faith itself.

Christology – like the Christian faith itself – is inconceivable without at least an ultimate continuity of genuine historical tradition, though this continuity is not something external to actual word or concept. Consequently the Christology of the early Church and the Fathers cannot be merely the object of an antiquarian historical interest; it must be binding on us. And this binding quality must not be opposed to the living and primal quality of faith in Christ today. If we were simply to declare that we could not make anything of classical Christology any more, this – if correctly interpreted at least – would not be a reproach to Christology. It would be a reproach to ourselves, and to our own spiritual and mental laziness, the stuntedness of our historical sense, and our bondage to a fashionable present which is not aware of its paltry limitations.

We can and must acknowledge today, too, that in Jesus the eternal divine Logos has entered our history, becoming man in time, the One who was pre-existent in the divine eternity, for whom it was no presumption to be equal with God. We can and must still confess with the Council of Chalcedon that the specific reality which meets us in Jesus (provided that we do not let it come to an end at a point determined by ourselves and our own arbitrary choice) was and eternally remains true man and true God in a unique and incomprehensible unity; so that we can and must talk about this one reality as being really and truly divine and human, without intermixture and division, in spite of the unmixed different elements that constitute it.[3] These Chalcedonian christological statements may sound strange to us at first. The road that leads to them from the simple Gospel may seem to us long and winding. But these classical christological formulations are binding and beneficial, if only because they continually face us with the inexorable question: do we ourselves meet Jesus at such a radical level that in him we meet God himself – and meet him in a unique and irreplaceable way, as he is in himself – the forgiveness of our guilt, our salvation, and our eternal life?

The classical formulations of Christology are one way (others are also perhaps conceivable) of compelling us, inexorably and inescapably, to take Jesus absolutely seriously – not simply to see him as just one religious genius among others, as a prophet who might be followed by others of the same kind, or perhaps even by greater ones who would supersede him; but to understand him as the unsurpassable and irreversible Word of salvation to ourselves – as the Word of God *per se*.

Any christological formulation which on the one hand allows Jesus to be quite objectively man, in the most radical sense, and which on the other hand allows him to be, in his life and death, the unsurpassable Word of God for us, could be enough; because it would then also be stating what is really meant by the classical christological formulations. But of course such a formulation was itself first given in this classical form. It does not exist anywhere else in such inexorable clarity, and at the same time in this generally adopted or received form.

That is why classical Christology still remains binding on us today, and is also irreplaceable. We have no reason to be ashamed of the Christology that has been passed down to us. Since today (in contrast to earlier more rationalistic eras) the feeling is growing that one can only talk very paradoxically, analogously or dialectically (or however

---

[3] Cf. Denz. 301–2 and the appropriate canon 303.

we may like to put it) about God and his redeeming relationship to us, we have no need to hide from our contemporaries the paradox which is also ultimately concealed in the apparently calmly ontological phraseology of classical Christology; for we have no need to feel that these formulations, even though they may be necessary, are somewhat old fashioned.

THE LIMITATIONS OF CLASSICAL CHRISTOLOGY

But are we therefore also compelled to overlook, forget or ignore the limitations of classical Christology today? These limitations were certainly not so clearly seen earlier, and were not so clearly thought about; for that was, largely speaking, impossible at the time. In our own period, at all events, we should quite freely indicate what these limitations are.

First of all, classical Christology clearly stresses that Jesus Christ was true and perfect man, without any curtailment, except for actual sin (i.e. a real 'no' to God's grace and love). But as it developed, this Christology did in fact tend so to idealise this true man – and to idealise his human dimension especially – that *even here* he appeared as a kind of semi-god,[4] instead of being the Word of God for us *just because* he shared in the very reality and fate of a real historical person, including his death. So in actual fact classical Christology not infrequently strayed unintentionally into a monophysitism which was basically criticised for the emphatic distinction it made between the divine and the human. Instead of this distinction there was a mingling of the two in a curious deification of the man, in place of a radical acceptance of the bitterly finite character of the person in whom God appeared among us. The fact that Jesus also believed, hoped, searched and was tempted, and unavoidably capitulated before the incomprehensibility of God may not have been obscured in the loving devotion of believers to the One who was crucified; but it was to some extent obscured in textbook theology.[5] Today's sober exegesis, which em-

---

[4] The present author has already complained of this in a number of earlier essays, cf. K. Rahner, 'Current Problems in Christology', *Theological Investigations* I (London 1961), pp. 149–200.

[5] Here something might be said about the importance of living piety for textbook theology; for influence by no means flows only in the reverse direction. As the other essays in the present volume make clear, my main intention is not only to discover what theology has to say, but to quicken it

phasises the historical dependency of Jesus and his doctrine, also makes us clearly aware of the limitations of classical Christology, as this was actually expounded, when it did not always remain true to its own principles; and it enjoins us to take Jesus' historicity seriously. A vertical Christology of descent,[6] which was the approach of classical Christology, must today no longer overlook the fact that what the Logos who descended from the glory of God desired to take upon himself was precisely the sombre facts of historical existence with its limits, dependency and baseness, without which there can be no true and full humanity. Today classical Christology certainly has to go on considering what has to be added to Christ's human reality as well, so that it can fulfil its function in salvation-history. With this in mind Christology can, for example, certainly not avoid, even in our period, talking with the Epistle to the Hebrews about Jesus' sinlessness as a man.[7] But what it can and must avoid doing is so to transfigure Jesus even in his earthly life that it is no longer evident that he took our human, poverty-stricken and sombre fate on himself, fully and completely, redeeming us through that very fact.

Classical Christology presents a doctrine of the descent of the pre-existent Logos through his assumption of a human 'nature'; it is an incarnational Christology. For that reason it is further limited by the fact that it does not sufficiently and directly make clear the connection between the incarnate Logos and his function as the mediator of salvation. Of course it established this connection. It attempted to do so either by talking about the sending of the eternal Son into the world for its salvation in the way that Eastern theology did, seeing the taking-on of flesh (i.e. of human nature) as being in itself the saving and deifying acceptance *of* human nature, or man as a whole; or it proceeded as Western theology did, understanding the Incarnation as the establishment of a divine-human subject who, by obediently accepting the death for which he was destined, can offer God

---

in the light of the experience of lived faith, as this mediates actual salvation, or fails to do so. As an example, I should like to draw attention to an earlier essay on this subject: *Heilige Stunde und Passionsandacht* (Innsbruck 1949, Freiburg 1955).

[6] Cf. here K. Rahner, 'The Two Basic Types of Christology', *Theological Investigations* XIII (London 1975), pp. 213–23; the beginnings are already to be found in the New Testament, cf. the christological hymn in Phil. 2:5–11.

[7] Cf. Heb. 5:1–10; 7:22–28.

in his holiness expiation and satisfaction for the guilt of mankind. But a connection that is conceived of in either one of these ways will either work very platonically and speculatively, taking as its presupposition a unity of divinity and humanity in one and the same nature (a platonic train of thought which it is difficult for us to follow today); or it will make use of the solution that adopts the categories of Germanic legalistic thinking in the theory of satisfaction. In this case it will draw on the postulate of the divine decree by which the incarnate Logos is appointed to be the atoning representative of sinful mankind. Today these patterns of interpretation come up against considerable difficulties, which we cannot go into here.

But above all a vertical incarnational and 'descent' Christology of this kind, considered in isolation, involves a limitation and a danger. For it first talks only about the adoption of a human nature which remains abstract. It does not simply begin from the very outset with the actual, specific reality of Jesus' life and death. Yet after all it is this which we experience first of all, and it is this that we grasp in faith and hope as what is saving and liberating for ourselves.

The vertical Christology of the incarnation and a horizontal Christology of salvation-history are generally insufficiently related to each other.[8] One might also say that in traditional incarnational theology there is too little Christology in the sense of 'fundamental' theology. That is to say, too little weight is given to the experience of Jesus which grasps him as being the saving Word of God to us which cannot be superseded, and which finds him in the specific reality of his life and his redeemed death. This is not clearly enough incorporated from the very outset in the incarnational Christology we have described. Up to a certain point it has even been replaced by a doctrine which looks from God to us and not from us to God. This is supported only by some sayings of Jesus about himself, which are historically and exegetically difficult to interpret, and not by his death and resurrection. We might also say that in classical Christology there is too wide a gap between the substance of the doctrine and its function. 'Christ for us' does not lead on to 'a Christ in and for himself'. Instead a Christ-in-himself, conceived of in a doctrinaire

---

[8] For one particular attempt to relate the two for the whole of Christology, see the doctrinal statements 'Grundlinien einer systematischen Christologie', in K. Rahner and W. Thüsing, *Christologie – systematisch und exegetisch* (Quaestiones Disputatae 55) (Freiburg 1972), pp. 15–78.

way, is made the starting point for what might be called an attempt to arrive retrospectively at a Christ for us, by way of connections set up in the way we have indicated.

But in our time at least it must be clear that we have to find our faith in a living encounter with Jesus the Christ – an encounter which is of course sustained by the Spirit.

NEW APPROACHES

Today a whole number of new approaches to Christology are crystallising. These neither deny nor mean to call in question what classical Christology is aiming at. The point at issue is not even to dispute the permanently normative character of classical Christology, although these new approaches for their part are also absolutely necessary today if access to faith in Jesus as Christ and Lord is not to be made unduly difficult for modern men and women.

To state that these new christological approaches exist does not of course also mean that the new approaches are absolutely novel or that they could or must be developed into a full systematic Christology, which would then stand parallel to classical Christology as something completely fresh and utterly different. It is rather a question of something more modest: the fact that the statements of classical Christology can also be formulated in simpler statements which we find more accessible today and yet which underlie those of classical Christology. But if we are to take this assertion seriously in a really radical way, then these statements already incorporate the whole of classical Christology in themselves. On the other hand they also preserve classical Christology from its intrinsic danger of being misunderstood in a monophysite sense – the danger, that is, of thinking of Jesus simply as God, who merely appears on earth in a human livery.

New approaches of this kind are not to be rejected just because there have already been a number of attempts in this direction since the Enlightenment – attempts which have come to grief because of their rationalism. Of course, no one will expect these to be followed up here in systematic accounts of the Christologies of Protestant[9] or Catholic theologians. That would take us too far and involve the risk

---

[9] Cf. one of the author's earliest essays, 'Die deutsche protestantische Christologie der Gegenwart', *Theologie der Zeit*, Theologische Beihefte zum 'Seelsorger' 1 (Vienna 1936), pp. 189–202.

of simplifying through brevity or of distorting these attempts at a Christology. Neither are we saying here that behind all these modern attempts there is *only one* Christology, either Catholic or Protestant, of the kind which we have indicated under the somewhat too portentous title 'new approach'. On the contrary, we can also find very modern christologies, with considerable intellectual and religious power, which are radical Christologies of descent, to such an extent that the death to which Jesus was destined threatens to become the inner destiny of God himself, in an almost gnostically monophy- sitic way. But I do not intend either to describe or to criticise all that here.

What I mean here by 'new approaches' is really something very simple: quite plain statements about the meaning of Jesus and what he did for us, statements which give us the impression that, in spite of their *relatively* easy accessibility, they still contain in full the classic, essential Christology. This requires that on the one hand they are taken really seriously, in a thoroughly radical way; and that, on the other, people do not again interpret them in a monophysitic sense (even, it may be, unintentionally and non-thematically) and then claim that these new functional approaches must support and provide evidence for this latent misunderstanding.

In order to make the precise intention and real meaning of these 'new approaches' clear, let us begin with the quite simple experience of faith in Jesus. Jesus is a person who loves, who is faithful, who serves others, and who does not evade – either inwardly or outwardly – the death for which he is destined. In his death he experiences the ultimate God-forsakenness, and in that very situation yields himself and his fate into the Father's hands.

We now believe that the abyss of death in which he was swallowed up is the blessed fullness of divine life; that he lives, and that his history of failure was accepted and ratified by God; that it is now valid for ever; and that he is the risen One. We experience this redeemed destiny of Jesus as God's answer to us, since we are the absolute question which we ourselves cannot answer. It is God's answer to us because Jesus has identified himself with us to the ultimate degree, and because, on the other hand, we cannot do anything else than see our own fate in the fate of our neighbour. Otherwise we would be merely isolated monads, not people who can only find themselves in others by loving them.

This answer for us is Jesus as the One who died and is risen.[10] That is what remains the definitive and irrevocable Word of God to us. God may indeed say many things to us through creation and through history. The history of revelation even shows that a second word of God, which moves into a certain place in our history, can supersede a first word and reduce it to provisional status. Indeed it may itself remain provisional, seen against the incalculable number of possibilities in which God will encounter us in the course of history. But when the whole of our existence and history is all at once withdrawn from us and struck out by what we call death – when such an all-annihilating 'nay' is heard and this, just this and nothing else, becomes the divine 'yea' – then such a divine Word must necessarily be irrevocable and definitive.

God can doubtless, therefore, say something else to us before this, though not afterwards; even if that 'before' may undoubtedly occur in a still current history and although the definitive death-word of God, which means his victory, has already been uttered in that history. This word has been uttered in the death and resurrection of Jesus. It is definitive because after death no history continues and no new possibilities offer themselves.[11] But it is irrevocable because in death, if it is really taken seriously, only God can offer himself unless nothingness is to engulf us. Jesus was crucified and is risen into the incomprehensible darkness of God. This means that he is *the* Word of God to us, not simply *a* word. But if in this Word-for-us God promises himself to us irrevocably, then that Word has a unique relationship to God himself. It is a relationship that is specifically different from the ones that speak through the many words of God within the course of our history, which do not irrevocably promise God himself but simply some gift and task which is provisional in comparison with him.[12] This irrevocable and *real* Word of God to us

[10] Cf. K. Rahner and W. Thüsing, *Christologie – systematisch und exegetisch* (Quaestiones Disputatae 55) (Freiburg 1972), pp. 15–78, esp. IV: 'Die Theologie des Todes und der Auferstehung Jesu', pp. 35–50.

[11] Cf. K. Rahner, *On the Theology of Death* (Quaestiones Disputatae 2) (2nd ed., London 1969) and the essays in the present volume, 'The Liberty of the Sick, Theologically Considered', and 'The Intermediate State', pp. 100–13 and pp. 114–25 respectively.

[12] For a brief summing up of the author's ideas, see 'God's Self-Communication', *Sacramentum Mundi* V (New York and London 1970), pp. 353–5 (bibliography).

(real because it is given with Jesus' redeemed destiny to die) could, abstractly considered, naturally have been uttered in some other person. But in fact it let itself be heard in its primal quality and non-derivability only in Jesus. At the demarcation line of death, all other words fall back on the question of man. But it is only in Jesus and nowhere else that we hear this irrevocable Word of God's blessed promise of himself in the absolute calling in question of death; if all other promises of prophets and sages turn into questions in the face of death; if even the doctrine of the immortality of the soul (which is in itself quite rational) can really only offer the continuance of the subject and the limitless question he represents, but not the comprehensive answer to the question which makes everything else questionable; if all this is so, then an absolute relationship to Jesus is our right and duty, in spite of his impenetrable facticity in the midst of possibilities of thought which remain empty. Unless we want to miss encountering him from the very beginning, then we can only accept him as the absolute Word of God's promise of himself to us, in which God himself is involved, which has a history and does not simply sustain that history as if it were a foundation beyond history.

Unless it is untrue to itself, the simplest experience of faith with Jesus, the crucified and risen One, therefore leads inescapably to statements which in actual fact include an ontological Christology of descent and incarnation, but which also from the very beginning simultaneously include, seriously and effectively, the horizontal Christology of salvation history and fundamental theology.

This modest indication of what we mean by 'new approaches' is by no means intended as a claim that everything has undoubtedly been said in a sufficiently express and clear way, though this is essential and indispensable for new approaches too, if they are really to stand up to examination. These new approaches are based on faith's experience of Jesus, his destiny, his death and his resurrection; and we are convinced that it is only this resurrection (the proof of his destiny's enduring validity before God) which lends his testimony to himself and interpretation of himself in the proclaimed Word as its ultimate meaning and ultimate importance. But this does not mean that the experience of Jesus that is meant here has been achieved or can be bestowed on the basis of the bare fact of the resurrection of just anyone; for this fact is necessarily constituted in part by the self-understanding of Jesus as a specific person, the specific Jesus who has himself interpreted himself through his Word in the life he lived.

After all, this resurrection of the Lord is not merely to be understood apologetically as an external verification of his self-testimony. We must see it as the inner, essential element of Jesus' testimony to himself, which can only arrive at complete fulfilment in his history.

A person's basic experience of Jesus and his history as we have indicated it ought perhaps to be clarified by even more explanations of this kind, or by similar ones. Of course we could also describe this basic experience under quite different aspects and against the background of quite different horizons of understanding. What seemed most important first of all in this brief essay was only to show that it is possible to make a statement about the experience of Jesus which is ahead of (or perhaps behind) the ontological Chalcedonian Christology of descent and incarnation. Classical Christology still provides, and will go on providing, the norm for us. But, when all is said and done, it belongs from the very beginning within a much wider field of possible christological statements. It, too, belongs to a system of co-ordinates allowing viewpoints and critical questions which go beyond it, though this does not mean that it can really be superseded. To say this is certainly important and involves many consequences; but in spite of that it is really a matter of course, because even in the New Testament, among the many and varied Christologies there, the statements which led to the classic Christology of Chalcedon do not always provide the foundation and beginning. Moreover, the important thing here was also to stimulate the conviction and insight that those christological statements which derive from the original experience of Jesus, the crucified and risen One, lead to Chalcedonian Christology through an inner correspondence and equivalence. The only presupposition is that both the experience and the statements should be taken seriously and that their claims should be pressed without any rationalistic omissions or trivialisations. At the same time, we still do not need to fear that classical Christology will founder in these statements, as something that was merely provisional. Nor, conversely, do we need to suppose that these statements are really no more than an ultimately dispensable preparation for the ancient ones.

It would now be useful, and indeed necessary, to work out more precisely and in more detail this mutual correspondence between a new Christology, deriving from the experience of the Lord in salvation-history, and classical Christology. But that is impossible here.[13] I hope, however, that even the indication of these new approaches has been clear enough for us to discover through it (if we look carefully) the contours of Chalcedonian Christology as well. One observation, however, may give a little extra depth to the subject at this point. It would be pointless to try to see essential, ontological Christology and functional, existential Christology as being from the outset mutually exclusive alternatives, between which we have to choose. Of course when classical Christology talks about hypostasis and person (in the earlier sense of what subsists individually and as a whole, but not in the modern sense of a subjectivity whose liberty has been given it by God), about nature and substance, about unity, unification and difference, it is employing terms and categories which can ultimately be traced to the experience of being *in general*, but not to an experienced subjectivity and its fulfilment. But wherever existentially ontological terms are drawn on in order to describe the relationship of the human reality of Jesus to God – and that seems absolutely possible – an ontological Christology is really also being pursued. Nor does this necessarily involve falling victim to a rationalistic Christology of the consciousness, which would interpret Jesus merely as a particularly good and devout person. For the terms used here are onto-logical in a radical sense, even more than those which are first derived from some arbitrarily chosen objective being.

In addition, every statement which sees itself as 'functional', 'existential', 'actualistic', etc. (if it is not simply to be merely the senseless self-utterance of the speaker) is inevitably related to something in itself, which even the most functional thing must refer to and speak about as its own reality, in the conviction that it is saying something *about it*. All christological terms, correctly understood, have ultimately an ontological sense. The essence is recognised by its function. That is why a statement about function is always basically a statement about essence. If we talk in any Christology whatever about the existential relationship of the man Jesus to God as something not arbitrary but unique, understanding by this that this unique relationship to God is of course based again on the act of God for this person, then we are pursuing ontological Christology. If in a similar way we then express the relationship of Jesus to man as being also unique and as being the foundation *per se* of our salvation, then we again have onto-logical Christology – whether this is the result of deliberate

[13] But see reference in n. 10.

reflection or not. For the terms which are unavoidably used in the process are basically more ontological than the ones which underlie classical Christology, even if they are not derived directly from the being which is 'onto-logical' because in spirit and freedom it opens on to the absolute being of God, and this direction constitutes its essence.

In addition, classic terms such as 'hypostatic union', for example, can really be made comprehensible only if one explains them by going back to a predicative communication of idioms*; and this ultimately also involves going beyond a merely ontic Christology.

Moreover in classical Christology the 'is' in statements of communication of idiom such as 'Jesus is God', 'God is man', does not mean *identity* between subject and predicate, as it does in our other 'is' statements.[14] It only means a unity and a link. If we held the contrary to be true, we should be denying the 'unmixed' character asserted by the Chalcedonian view and should be holding a heretical opinion. The statement that God is 'in' Jesus at least means neither a heresy nor necessarily a truncation of orthodox Christology, provided only that we are aware that God's being 'in' Jesus, in the sense in which it is meant here, indicates a unique relationship which makes the Lord the unsupersedable Word of God for us, and which involves God himself, bringing him into our history.

We may sum up what we have been saying as follows: We must acknowledge classical Christology and yet see that it is not the only possible one, in the sense that there could be no other orthodox statements of a christological kind. For there are in fact statements which also lead to classical Christology and which protect it better and more effectively from misunderstandings than it can protect itself today simply by means of the history of its interpretation. Indeed the

---

* *Editor's note:* The term 'communication of idioms' (idioms = properties) 'primarily means that because of the hypostatic union the properties of both natures can and must be predicated of the one Person Jesus Christ'. Cf. Karl Rahner and Herbert Vorgrinder, *Concise Theological Dictionary* (London 1965), p. 90.

[14] On this subject, cf. the author's controversy with Cardinal Höffner, 'Karl Rahner antwortet Kardinal Höffner', *Münchener Katholische Kirchenzeitung* 64 (1971), 31 Jan. 1971, pp. 12–13; also 'Über die Gottheit Jesu Christi und über die Unauflöslichkeit der Ehe. Ein Briefwechsel zwischen Joseph Kardinal Höffner/Köln und Professor Dr. Karl Rahner s.j./Münster', *Kirche und Leben* 26 (Münster 1971), 24 Jan. 1971, p. 6, ET *The Month*, April 1971, pp. 104–7.

usual interpretation of classical Christology urgently and imperatively needs true deepening and supplementing. So the new approaches today would seem useful above all because the monophysitic mis-understanding of Christology is still a real and indisputable danger, both for believers who misunderstand the Church's dogma, and for unbelievers who presuppose that this misunderstanding of the dogma is the doctrine of the Church, and therefore reject it. But every concept of the incarnation which views Jesus' humanity, either overtly or implicitly, merely as the guise God takes upon himself in order to signalise his speaking presence, is and remains a heresy.[15]

[15] For further development, cf. 'On the Theology of the Incarnation', *Theological Investigations* IV (London 1966), pp. 105–20.

5

JESUS CHRIST IN THE NON-CHRISTIAN RELIGIONS

WHAT do we mean precisely and specifically when we say that Jesus Christ is to be found in non-Christian religions as well? That is the question we shall be considering here.[1] First, it must be said in introducing the subject that we shall be considering the question dogmatically, not in the light of the history or phenomenology of religion. In this matter the Christian dogmatic theologian cannot be a substitute for the religious historian, who works *a posteriori*. After all, his own sources of faith, which are binding on him, are derived from the Old and New Testaments, and even from the Church's doctrinal explanations, which were based on those Testaments; they have developed without any direct contact with most of the non-Christian religions (though we may perhaps except here the Declaration on the non-Christian religions made by Vatican II). Consequently the material drawn from the history of religion which is germane to our question has not been assimilated in these sources at all. In addition, if these sources do deal with the non-Christian religions at all, even from afar, they do so, for understandable reasons, in a rather dissociating and defensive way. Consequently they are highly unfruitful for our question. A dogmatic

---

[1] The ideas developed here are of course closely connected with what the author has already said under the familiar heading of 'the anonymous Christian' and in connection with a transcendental Christology. Consequently some of the material may well be familiar, though for details the reader should turn to the relevant essays themselves. Cf. 'Observations on the Problem of the "Anonymous Christian" ', *Theological Investigations* XIV (London 1976), pp. 280–94, where references to earlier work are also given. Cf. also *Christologie – systematisch und exegetisch* (Quaestiones Disputatae 55) (Freiburg 1972), pp. 15–78.

theologian has to think *a priori* here, unlike the religious historian, whose task is to discover Christ as far as possible *a posteriori* in the non-Christian religions. This means that the dogmatic theologian's reflections can provide only something like a provisional indication for the religious historian, which may perhaps guide and sharpen his seeking glance in a task of which the dogmatic theologian cannot relieve him. The question here is, therefore, simply this: what dogmatic principles and reflections have we to postulate prior to a historical investigation, with regard to the question to be formulated and the probable result, when we are considering whether Christ can be present in the non-Christian religions? Whether the religious historian can then himself fulfil this expectation *a posteriori*, whether he falls short of it in the facts he discovers, or whether he perhaps goes even further – that must remain an entirely open question here.

There are two presuppositions to be made in answering the dogmatic question which we have narrowed down in this way. First of all, we are presupposing a general supernatural divine will to salvation which is really efficacious in the world.[2] This makes possible a belief in supernatural revelation everywhere, i.e., in the whole length and breadth of human history. This presupposition is also expressly taught by Vatican II.[3] Vatican II is certainly extremely reserved with regard to the question of how such a redeeming faith in a real divine revelation in the strictest sense can come about outside the sphere of the Old and New Testaments. But this does not forbid the theologian's asking in what way there can be such a universal opportunity of faith; and it cannot, either, really release him from asking a question of this kind. The answer to this question – or at least one possible answer to it – does not really have to be given here but may be presupposed (even if, somewhat in the style of Heb. 11:1–40, it still does not clarify the christological character of redeeming faith of this kind). We may just briefly observe that the elevation by grace of man's 'transcendental nature', with a supernatural formal object (*objectum formale*) which is thereby given (even if this is not objectified and the object of reflection), already crystallises the concept of a supernatural rev-

---

[2] This general will to salvation was emphatically stressed by Vatican II. Cf. *Lumen gentium* (Church), n. 16; *Nostra aetate* (non-Christian religions) n. 1; *Ad gentes* (mission), n. 7.

[3] Cf. n. 2 above, but also the general statements in *Gaudium et Spes* (the Church in the world), n. 2; 10; 22; etc.

elation, and (if accepted freely) the concept of faith, into the question,[4] what historical and objectifying mediation the acceptance of such a supernatural and revelatory elevation really has.

If it is permissible to assume that this question can be positively answered and that it is already more or less clarified, then we really only have to ask whether and how such a redeeming faith in revelation can and must reach out to Christ even outside the sphere of an explicit Christianity; or whether, since this is impossible, it is unnecessary; so that in this respect impossibility and good-will release the non-Christian from the christological character of a faith which is in other respects possible everywhere.

The question also remains whether or not the non-Christian religions as specific historical and social phenomena have a positive importance in the coming into being of such an act of faith, interpreted in either the one way or the other – i.e. christologically or non-christologically. The question whether Christ is present in the non-Christian religions or not must then be answered accordingly.

There is a second presupposition too. When a non-Christian wins salvation through faith, hope and love, the non-Christian religions cannot be thought to have played no part, or only a negative one, in this winning of justification and salvation.[5] This statement does not mean asserting a particular Christian interpretation and evaluation of any specific non-Christian religion. Nor is it a question of putting a religion of this kind on a par with the Christian faith as regards its importance for salvation. It is no denial of its vitiated character or its provisional place in salvation-history. Nor does it deny that any such specific religion may also have a negative influence on the genesis of the salvation event in an individual non-Christian.

But having said this, we must go on to say the following: if a non-Christian religion could have, from the outset, no positive influence at all on the supernatural event of salvation in the individual

---

[4] For a more detailed explanation of this idea, cf. K. Rahner, 'The Existential, B. Theological, in *Sacramentum Mundi* II (New York and London 1967), p. 306; also Existence: II 'The Existential, B. Theological', *Encyclopaedia of Theology. A Concise Sacramentum Mundi* (London 1975), pp. 494–5.

[5] Not only is this notion contradicted by Vatican II's declaration on the relationship between the Church and the non-Christian religions (*Nostra aetate*); the basic attitude reflected in the declaration is also opposed to any such viewpoint. This basic attitude goes far beyond the declaration itself, and we are attempting to develop some important aspects of it here.

Christian – or if, from the outset, no such possible influence is conceded to it, then the salvation event in a given individual would be seen in completely non-social and unhistorical terms.[6] But this fundamentally contradicts the historical and social character of Christianity itself. The possibility of private revelations, extraordinary visions (especially at the hour of death) and so forth has certainly been envisaged, in order to bring the divine revelation to the non-Christian who has not been reached by the Christian proclamation. But these are arbitrary and improbable postulates, and one cannot see why they should be permitted to take place only in extraordinary and special cases. And quite apart from that, these expedients contradict the basic character of the Christian revelation and the nature of man. For even in his most personal history man always remains a social being, whose innermost decisions are mediated through the specific form of his social and historical life. They do not take place in some special reserve, cut off from the rest from the very outset. In addition, in a theology of salvation history, which takes God's universal will to salvation seriously and remembers the tremendous distance in time between 'Adam' and the Mosaic revelation in the Old Testament, the whole intermediate period between the two points (which even Vatican II's constitution *Dei verbum*[7] passes over somewhat too quickly) cannot be conceived of as empty of divine revelation. And this cannot simply be cut off *per se* from the whole history of specific religions. For if one simply imagines the world without all these religions, there is no way of saying at all where God and his history of salvation and revelation can be found in the world.

If we want to bridge this intermediate period by postulating a tradition, a 'primitive revelation',[8] then it must once more be said

[6] So Vatican II's declaration about religious freedom, *Dignitatis humanae*, also says (n. 4) that the freedom from compulsion in religious matters which is due to the individual must also be conceded to people who are acting as a group. For the social nature of man, as well as the social nature of religion itself, demands the existence of religious groups.

[7] Cf. the dogmatic constitution on divine revelation (*Dei verbum*), n. 3., where, however, the initial development of revelation is described in somewhat too uniform and unilateral terms.

[8] Cf. here H. Fries, 'Primitive Revelation', in *Sacramentum Mundi* V (New York and London 1969), 355–8 and 'Primitive Revelation', in *Encyclopaedia of Theology. A Concise Sacramentum Mundi* (London 1975), pp. 1468–71. Also K. Rahner, 'Revelation; B. Theological Interpretation' in *Sacramentum Mundi* (New York and London 1969), 348–53, and 'Revelation: I B. Theological Interpretation', *Encyclopaedia of Theology*, pp. 1460–6.

that a postulate of this kind is highly problematical in view of the immense duration of human history. Above all, only the historical and socially constituted religions can really be considered as being the bearers of such a tradition, which is supposed to reach the individual, for it is these which awaken and keep alive the possibility and obligation of man's relationship to the mystery of existence which challenges him, however particular religions may interpret this primal mystery of existence, and whatever concrete form they may give to man's relationship to it – perhaps even vitiating it in the process.

This would suggest that, even allowing for a universal and efficacious divine will that all men since the fall should be saved (with the concomitant universal possibility of a redeeming faith in revelation), we cannot get along without conceding a positive saving function to the pre-Christian religions, at least in this interim period. There would seem to be no prior reason in principle, therefore, why we should (even if we could) deny the non-Christian religions a similar and at least partially positive function for people who have not yet been reached by the Christian message in a way which is directly binding on them. We do not have to discuss here the specific ways in which a non-Christian religion can have a positive function for the possibility of a real faith in revelation. That may remain an open question.

Having made these assumptions let us now turn to the real question at issue. How can Jesus Christ be understood as being present and efficacious in the non-Christian religions, in the light of Christian dogmatics – which is to say *a priori* to an *a posteriori* description drawn up in response to this question? We must first of all state quite openly and soberly that the answer is directly related to the question: how is Jesus Christ present and efficacious in the faith of the individual non-Christian? Other considerations, such as the social and institutional aspects of the non-Christian religions cannot come within our scope, in view of what we pointed out at the beginning, however regrettable this may seem. Anything that may perhaps be said about the presence of Christ in the non-Christian religions apart from his presence in the redeeming faith of the non-Christian, is a matter for the theologians who are concerned with the history of religion, and who work *a posteriori*.

With the presuppositions and qualifications we have mentioned, Christ is present and efficacious in the non-Christian believer (and therefore in the non-Christian religions) through his Spirit. An assertion of this kind is first of all a matter of course, dogmatically speaking. If the non-Christian can have a redeeming faith and if it is permissible for us to hope that this faith really exists on a wide scale, then such a faith is, of course, made possible and sustained by the supernatural grace of the Holy Spirit.[9] And this is the Spirit who proceeds from the Father and the Son, so that as the Spirit of the eternal Logos he can and must, at least in this sense, be called the Spirit of Christ, the incarnate divine Word.

But although this is a matter of course, dogmatically speaking, the statement we have just made has not yet been really taken in, in its meaning and its justification. For the question is simply whether the Holy Spirit's supernatural grace, which confers faith and justification, can be called the Spirit of Jesus Christ when it is active in the person who has not been baptised; and if so, what this really means. Every Catholic textbook of dogmatics will doubtless give an affirmative answer to the first question, and try to make it comprehensible by declaring that this Spirit which makes faith possible and which justifies is given everywhere and at all times *intuitu meritorum Christi*;[10] and that it can, therefore, rightly be called the Spirit of Jesus Christ. This statement is initially certainly justified and will also be deemed comprehensible (more or less, at least); and it can, therefore, serve as the starting point for our further reflections. But the statement certainly does not answer all the questions which can be raised here. First of all, the connection between the grace of the Spirit on the one hand (which is given everywhere and at all times) and the historical event of the cross on the other (which constitutes a point in space and time) is not after all as comprehensible and clear in this statement as might appear at first sight. Is (we may ask) the connection between these two realities made only via the knowledge and the will of the

[9] This can already be deduced from the statements of the First Vatican Council's dogmatic constitution *Dei Filius* (cf. Denz. 3008 and 3009) even though this is principally concerned with the way the Christian arrives at faith.

[10] This expression is to be found in the papal Bull *Ineffabilis Deus* (cf. Denz. 2803), in a context which can seem surprising at first glance. But the definition of the Immaculate Conception is also important for our question, because this is a matter which must be placed *before* the historical-categorial saving work of Jesus Christ, although it is related to and founded on that. One might also point to the event of justification, which is always an individual event in each given case (cf. Denz. 1530, etc.), but which cannot come about without express knowledge of the historical appearance of Jesus Christ.

God who transcends even salvation-history, so that there is after all no true connection between the two realities themselves? Can the event of the cross be thought of as exerting an influence on God, 'physically' or 'morally'? So that as a result of this influence, which in a certain sense proceeds from the world and has its effect on him (even though it is always foreknown), he has always poured out the Spirit's grace on the world? But if this cannot be said in the real sense, because God in his sovereignty cannot be influenced and is unmoved and unalterable, what does it mean when we say that he gave this Spirit because of Jesus Christ's merits, as the morally meritorious cause of this Spirit? If we say that the statement in question does not link Jesus' sufferings (as God's motivation) with God himself, but with the grace of the Spirit (just as one must say of a prayer of intercession, for example, that it is not the cause of God's decision to hear the prayer, but is the moral cause – with which God freely associates himself – of the reality of God's hearing of prayer), then we must ask what this is really supposed to mean. Especially since this inner-worldly moral cause, which is not supposed to 'influence' God himself, is much later in time than its effect.[11] It might be pointed out that in the case of the second example (intercessory prayer) it would probably not occur to anyone to intercede with God for some reality in the world that had already taken place; although this ought also to have a point if the commonly accepted interpretation of *intuitu meritorum* makes sense.

We must also add the following to these questionable points. We can and must see God's free will to salvation as the *a priori* cause (a cause conditioned by nothing outside God himself) of Christ's incarnation and cross as well; so that from this point of view, too, it is not easy to see how the cross of Christ could be the reason for God's saving will towards other people, if this saving divine will after all precedes the cross of Christ, as its cause and not as its effect, and must then be viewed as being related to all men. For a saving will related solely to Christ would be meaningless from the beginning and would contradict the fact that through the saving will of God Jesus Christ is meant from the very beginning to be the redeemer of the world.

[11] For the author's further ideas on this point, the reader should turn to K. Rahner and W. Thüsing, *Christologie – systematisch und exegetisch* (Quaestiones Disputatae 55) (Freiburg 1972), pp. 47–50.

We can only emerge from these difficulties (and others which we have not mentioned) if we see the incarnation and the cross as what scholastic terminology calls the 'final cause' of God's universal self-communication to the world, given with God's saving will, which knows no reason outside itself and which we call the Holy Spirit; and if we view the incarnation and cross in this sense as the cause of the imparting of the Holy Spirit at all times and in all places in the world. This Spirit is always, everywhere, and from the outset the entelechy, the determining principle, of the history of revelation and salvation; and its communication and acceptance, by its very nature, never takes place in a merely abstract, transcendental form. It always comes about through the mediation of history. Consequently this communication is from the beginning directed towards a historical event in which this communication and its acceptance, in spite of their freedom, are irreversible and can be grasped historically even in this triumphant eschatological form. But this comes about in what we call the incarnation, cross and resurrection of the divine Word. Since the universal efficacy of the Spirit is directed from the very beginning to the zenith of its historical mediation, which is the Christ event (or in other words the final cause of the mediation of the Spirit to the world), it can be truly said that this Spirit is everywhere and from the very beginning the Spirit of Jesus Christ, the incarnate divine Logos. The Spirit communicated to the world has itself, as such, an inner relation to Jesus Christ (not merely in the divine intention which transcends the world, which would be external to the Spirit). Jesus is the 'cause' of the Spirit, even if the reverse relationship is equally true, as is the case in unity and difference, and the mutually conditioning relationship between efficacious and final causes. Since the efficacious cause of incarnation and cross (i.e., the Spirit) has its goal within itself, as inner entelechy, and fulfils its own being (as communicated to the world) only in the incarnation and cross, the Spirit is from the outset the Spirit of Jesus Christ. Since this Spirit always and everywhere sustains justifying faith, this faith is from the outset, always and everywhere, a faith that comes into being in the Spirit of Jesus Christ, who is present and efficacious in all faith, through this Spirit of his.

Jesus Christ is always and everywhere present in justifying faith, because this is always and everywhere the seeking *memoria* of the absolute bringer of salvation, who is by definition the God-man, who arrives at his consummation through death and resurrection.[12] We cannot discuss this statement more exactly in all its aspects here, because that would take us too far. Above all, we cannot go on to explain in more detail that the historical bringer of salvation (who makes God's gift to the world an irreversible event and as such brings it to manifestation) is necessarily the incarnate divine Logos, whose earthly reality is fulfilled through his death and resurrection.[13] Nor can we show the precise connection between the first proposition and the second. The two are of course closely connected; but we shall not go into that in detail here. In the context of what we are considering at present, the only important thing is to clarify to some extent what is meant by the proposition that the seeking *memoria* of every faith (wherever it comes into being) moves towards the absolute bringer of salvation; though again we cannot consider here the question of how far the goal of this seeking *memoria* has to be explicit, or whether it need only be implicit. (Indeed we do not even have to differentiate according to whether the sense of faith is meant collectively or individually.) When we talk about *memoria*, this concept seems from the beginning to contrast with the special character which we ascribe to it when we say that *memoria* 'seeks'. In the common interpretation of the word, *memoria* always seems to be related only to what has already been discovered in the past. It does not apply to something which has still to come, generally or for the individual – something which still has to be found, and is therefore still to be sought for. But if we think of Plato's doctrine of anamnesis,[14] or Augustine's doctrine of *memoria* (though we cannot go into these here), we see immediately that the matter is not so simple. This is indicated, ultimately, by the whole problem about the relationship between transcendence and history, and between the *a priori* and *a posteriori* nature of knowledge. Man can only find and retain what he encounters in history if there is an *a priori* principle of expectation, seeking and hope in man's finding and retaining subjectivity. And – following a tradition that

[12] On the following ideas, which are somewhat sketchily outlined here, cf. J. B. Metz, 'Erinnerung', in *HphG*. Munich 1973. Here *memoria* is considered in more detail, especially in its more comprehensive function.

[13] In this connection let me remind the reader of the remarks at the beginning of this essay.

[14] Cf. here C. Huber, 'Anamnesis bei Plato', *Pullacher Philosophische Forschungen* VI (Munich 1964).

can be traced through the whole history of Western thought – we may call this principle *memoria*.

Memoria in this sense must not be understood as if it were the mere capacity for receiving everything and everyone. It is not the simple, empty space into which the chances of history indiscriminately and arbitrarily gather everything which may have happened. *Memoria* has itself *a priori* structures, which certainly do not simply anticipate what is free and unexpected in history, but which first of all offer possibilities of perceiving something in this history, of distinguishing it and of assigning it a certain place. *Memoria* is the *a priori* possibility of historical experience *as such* (as distinct from the *a priori* conditions for the possibility of the *a posteriori* knowledge of things, which we find in the natural sciences). This general doctrine of *memoria* can of course only be touched on here.

The really important thing is the following: *memoria* is (or is also – or is indeed above all) the anticipation of the absolute bringer of salvation. It seeks him and is on the watch for him in history (though it leaves open the possibility of formal experience and consequently suffers history without anticipating it in its specific form). In his transcendental nature as spirit and liberty, man always experiences his dependency on the incomprehensible mystery which we call God.[15] He experiences in himself the hope that this dependency is so radical that it will find its fulfilment in the direct self-communication of God, and will be freed, given radical form and sustained by supernatural grace; though this is not a hope he can claim by right. But this transcendental nature of man's to which grace gives radical form is always a matter for reflection, at least at the beginning, and is freely accepted or rejected. Consequently it is communicated through historical experience; for it is through the content of historical experience that man becomes conscious of his own transcendental nature.

This historical experience which mediates his own transcendental nature, elevated by grace, can certainly be of the most varied kind. It does not even always and everywhere necessarily have to be religious, as long as it mediates man to himself as the one who disposes freely over himself, as an individual and a whole. But as history (which is not merely an amorphous mass of things, lying side by side

[15] The author has already repeatedly discussed this experience under different aspects, cf. 'The Experience of God Today', *Theological Investigations* XI (London 1974), pp. 149–65.

in space or time) it has a structure in which all its individual aspects have their particular place in space and time, and do not all have the same significance. The seeking anticipation of this structure belongs to the nature of this *memoria*. History is a history of freedom, and freedom is not simply the capacity continually to make new, arbitrary choices; it is the capacity to decide for what is ultimate and final.[16] Consequently those decisions belong to the structure of history expectantly anticipated by *memoria*, through which history is brought, partly or wholly, to freely realised finality from the open plurality of indifferent (or equally valid) potentialities. If we once presuppose that in still continuing history the finality that has to be achieved in history can as a whole arrive at all at historical manifestation and tangibility, and that this does not simply have to be identical with the abolition of history in general, then we can say that the *memoria* of man's transcendental nature, raised by grace, seeks hopefully and in anticipation for that event in history in which the free decision for a saving end of all history is made and is within our grasp; and where this decision is made in the light of the liberty of God and man alike, and for the one history of mankind as a whole. This event, which is sought for and expected by *memoria* in this way, is what we call the absolute bringer of salvation.[17] This is the anticipation of *memoria* which is present with every faith.

It is, of course, another question (a question which can ultimately be answered only *a posteriori*, by the history of religion) whether and how far, how explicitly or how implicitly, in mythology or history, this anticipation of the absolute bringer of salvation by the *memoria* of faith is demonstrable. As we have already said, at this point the dogmatic theologian must pass the question on to the religious historian and to Christian interpretation of that history of religion.[18] Here it seems to me ultimately a secondary question, dogmatically

[16] Cf. K. Rahner, 'Freedom; III Theological' in *Sacramentum Mundi II* (New York and London 1968), 361–2, and 'Freedom: II. Theological' in *Encyclopaedia of Theology. A Concise Sacramentum Mundi* (London 1975), pp. 544–5.

[17] Cf. the account of transcendental Christology in its basic features in '13. Lehrsatz' in K. Rahner and W. Thüsing, *Christologie – systematisch und exegetisch* (Quaestiones Disputatae 55) (Freiburg 1972), pp. 21–4.

[18] The division of labour between the dogmatic theologian and the religious historian which is described here must not of course be misunderstood: there is no suggestion that we should draw back from the scientific treatment of the positive material of systematic and dogmatic theology, as if the end of positive theology were even being heralded. The point at issue is rather the

speaking, whether the seeking expectation is objectified in myths about a saviour, or whether it is projected on to historical figures to whom the character of saviour is ascribed – whether the saviour be provisional or final. From his own presuppositions, the dogmatic theologian can say only that religious history must be asked in kindly but precise terms whether saviour figures of this kind are to be found in it, and how. He will say that from the dogmatic point of view there is no reason to exclude such discoveries from the outset, or to write them off contemptuously, as if they stood in such contrast to faith in Jesus, as the eschatological, unsupersedable saviour, that they can only be judged negatively. Saviour figures in the history of religion can certainly also be viewed as signs that – since man is always and everywhere moved by the Spirit – he gazes in anticipation towards that event in which his absolute hope becomes historically irreversible and is manifested as such.

With these two theses about the presence of Jesus Christ in justifying faith (which is made possible everywhere by God's grace and, consequently, is possible in the non-Christian religions, too) we have of course no intention of saying that in view of these theses *all* aspects of the one presence and efficaciousness of Jesus Christ can be seen and expressed in the faith of the non-Christian, and of non-Christian religions. Perhaps one might even have the impression that everything that has been said about our question is a matter of course anyway. But it seems to me, first of all, that simply from the standpoint of Christian doctrine we cannot easily go further than this answer to the question we have raised. It appears to me that the main task here has to be performed by the religious historian, who interprets history in Christian terms. If this interpretation were carried out more clearly and precisely, it could well be that this *a posteriori* religious history of the presence of Jesus Christ in all religions would draw the dogmatic theologian's attention to implications in his own doctrine of that presence which he had hitherto overlooked.

---

attitude of the Christian dogmatic theologian towards positive facts about the non-Christian religions. In any case, the proposed attempt is only to be understood as one possibility among others.

PART TWO

Man in the Spirit

6

THE THEOLOGICAL DIMENSION OF THE QUESTION ABOUT MAN

THE subject which we are going to be discussing in the following pages – the theological dimension of the question about man – might also be put differently: we might call it the theological dimension of anthropology. But from what aspect can we begin to deal with a subject of this kind? Let us first of all define our points of departure by means of a few preliminary remarks which are essential – or at least useful – both for our understanding of what follows, and for our method of approach.

POINTS OF DEPARTURE

If we are to talk about the theological dimension of the question about man (or anthropology), then this presupposes that there really is something like an anthropology – a question about man that can be asked with some prospect of an answer.[1] This premise is by no means a matter of course.

Of course there is a whole series of sciences which tell us something about man, and whose statements we may here assume to be correct. But to say this is by no means to declare that the question about man is a possible one, or one that makes sense as such. It might very well be said with some justice that the human sciences (i.e., the sciences dealing with man) as well as contemporary criticism of 'humanisms' in our present culture are seemingly bringing man to the point of

---

[1] For a concise survey of theological anthropology (with bibliography), cf. *Sacramentum Mundi: An Encyclopaedia of Theology* III (London 1969), art. 'Anthropology (theological)', pp. 365–70. For a more comprehensive account cf. K. Fischer, *Der Mensch als Geheimnis – Die Anthropologie Karl Rahners* (Freiburg 1974); also K. Rahner's letter on the subject, ibid., pp. 400–10.

dissolution. Today human sciences, whether ethnology (Lévi-Strauss), sociology, social psychology or depth psychology, are displaying the tendency so to formalise everything about man, and to trace it back to abstract structures that the actual, specific person, as someone who is always unique and bestowed on himself, is disappearing. Modern philosophical anthropology tends to suggest that the interpretation of man as *animal rationale* has a merely *limited* character and is purely *Western*; while in structuralism it allows man as subject to disappear altogether. Modern criticism of the different 'humanisms' and different patterns of culture call in question both the ideal of the *honnête homme* (which belongs to the tradition of the Enlightenment) and the tragic humanism of the existentialist pattern, as well as Marxist humanism of the Promethean type. They want to make man so sceptical and so bare a figure that he knows that he is poised 'over nothingness', as Augstein's book puts it.[2]

The presupposition that there is such a thing as anthropology is therefore not as self-evident as our theme would at first seem to suggest. We shall, therefore, at least implicitly, have to consider at the same time why and how there really is something for which we seek to find a theological dimension.

Another preliminary remark which has to be made is this: if in our reflections we seem to be considering methods rather than content, at least at first sight, this is no cause for criticism. For on the one hand we have to answer the question: where precisely the question about man (which has inevitably to be asked and re-asked) definitely offers a point of contact for a theological enquiry. That is to say, it is a methodological question that has to be put. And on the other hand it is a matter of course that we cannot present a full Christian anthropology here.

There is yet another, third, preliminary point. I do not believe that what I have to say is peculiar to any one Church, or that it cannot equally well be said to Protestant *and* Catholic teachers of religion, and to other teachers as well.[3] Perhaps I am deceiving myself, and

[2] Cf. R. Augstein, *Jesus Menschensohn*. Gütersloh 1972; also the present author's discussion of the book, *Das Christentum – ein explosiver Irrtum?* in R. Pesch and G. Stachel (eds), *Augsteins Jesus* (Zürich 1972), pp. 40–9.

[3] The present essay was originally a lecture delivered on 9 Sept. 1972, in Dortmund, on the occasion of the 25th anniversary of the '*Religiöse Schulwochenarbeit*' in Westphalia. It was published in Donauwörth the same year, under the same title as our present essay.

am too little consciously aware of my own theological background. But if my remarks should seem to be too rational and philosophical, and too little based on the Scriptures, perhaps I may ask you to consider the following.

We cannot confront the people we have to do with today with the Scriptures, assuming, simply and from the very outset, that these have formal authority as the Word of God. What the Bible says, what it tells us about ourselves, what the truly central thing is in this statement and promise about us men and women must convince us through its *inner* truth. *This* is what must convince us of the authority of Scripture. But it is just this unique content of Scripture which, if we are to put it clearly and succinctly, can also be expressed even without a directly biblical method of exegesis and theology. And it is this, and the preliminary reflections that are required for it, which are what we have been and are still engaged in here.

QUESTIONING MAN

There is no need for a lengthy exposition of the proposition that the question about the theological dimension in anthropology is a fundamental one.

Today above all, the Christian proclamation must appeal to a person who is concerned about himself. This fundamental concern of man with himself does not have to be suspected of being un-Christian from the outset; for after all, Christianity sees itself as a message about *man's* salvation. If we really come down to fundamentals, a theocentric theology (which we must always have) is not opposed to what one might call an anthropocentric theology.[4]

For the whole point of the message of Christianity is that God, in his own unrelated sovereignty and glory, can be the content and centre of human existence, and in the liberty of his grace actually desires to be so. We, therefore, by no means have to do with a God who 'really' has nothing to do with us. So theocentricism, rightly understood, is, therefore, transformed into anthropocentricism through the grace which God himself communicates. And conversely

---

[4] Here and for what follows, cf. 'Reflections on the Unity of the Love of Neighbour and the Love of God', *Theological Investigations* VI (London and Baltimore 1969), pp. 231–49. It should be noted that this essay develops ideas drawn from spiritual theology, on the possibility of the veneration of the saints; cf. ibid., p. 231, n. 1.

man can find himself only when he gives himself up in adoration and love into the free incomprehensibility of God, i.e. when he himself transforms his anthropocentricism into theocentricism. An anthropocentric question, as it is put to us here, therefore, has no need to by-pass the essence of Christianity. It is no contradiction of Christianity's essence when we view this anthropocentric question as being a fundamental one and – if one may so put it – enter unabashed and quite 'naïvely' into the fundamental interest which man has in himself, in order to try to understand what God and Christianity mean from that standpoint.

If we are to discuss the theological dimension of the question about man – the theological dimension of anthropology – then we must immediately register a fundamental reservation with regard to this formulation of the subject.

We can certainly talk initially about different dimensions of the question about man, or anthropology. That seems obvious enough, if only because on the one hand there are a number of different human sciences, while on the other these human sciences (today at least) do not see themselves as mere handmaids of a metaphysical anthropology – a philosophy which is recognised as the sole spokesman of man as such. Nor do they recognise a clear relationship of super-ordination and sub-ordination among themselves, even though each of these empirical human sciences tends to set itself up, by a process of extrapolation, as the sole and universal one.

The actual and insurmountable pluralism of the human sciences is enough to show that man is a being with many dimensions, and that these dimensions cannot adequately be traced back to one another, or to a single systematic starting point, which could be arrived at by means of scientific and empirical reflection.[5] So it seems at first a matter of course, or at least harmless, for us to talk about a theological dimension too, in the question about man (or anthropology), and in man himself.

It cannot be denied that, whenever a Christian anthropology based on revelation allows the validity of the other human sciences as at

---

[5] On pluralism in science and theology, and on theology's relationship to the multifarious sciences, cf. the following essays in *Theological Investigations* XIII (London 1975): 'Possible Courses for the Theology of the Future', pp. 32–60; 'Theology as engaged in an Interdisciplinary Dialogue with the Sciences', pp. 80–93; 'On the Relationship between Theology and the Contemporary Sciences', pp. 94–102.

least partial and limited anthropologies, it often puts itself too naïvely and innocently on the same level with these other sciences, as if it were just another of the same kind. At the most, it cherishes the conviction that in this group of human sciences it has the most important and ultimately decisive thing to say about man.

This self-understanding on theological anthropology's part is a limited interpretation of its own role. It is essentially encouraged by the fact that, although theological anthropology sees itself as founded on revelation, it views this revelation as one individual, particular source of knowledge alongside others belonging to secular empiricism and the philosophy of man. From this standpoint it seems to it a matter of course that it – theological anthropology itself – should assert particular facts about man which can be known only through its own source of knowledge and which differ from what the secular human sciences have to say.

But it is not really as simple as this. Christian anthropology, if it interprets itself properly, is not one 'limited' human science among others, differing from these others simply through its source and perhaps also because what it says is more important.

In justifying this assertion, we shall dispense (for reasons of brevity) with a consideration of the exact character of theological talk about man, compared with the kind of statements made by the secular human sciences.[6] Nor shall we consider what precisely theological anthropology says about man, and whether what it says can simply be added to the statements of the secular anthropologies. For it could well be that a consideration of what theological anthropology has to say will itself make its comprehensive character clear, and will make it evident that (as we shall see later) theological anthropology does not just add something new (even if it is something of the greatest importance) to the statements of the secular anthropologies. It actually bursts these secular anthropologies radically apart, thereby making access possible, for the first time and finally, to the one mystery which we call God.[7]

[6] On the question of the importance of the human sciences for theology, cf. the essays cited in n. 5; also 'Reflections on Methodology in Theology' and 'The Future of Theology', *Theological Investigations* XI (London 1974), pp. 68–114 and 137–48.
[7] On the possible part to be played by a metaphysical anthropology in the eyes of the theologian, cf.' The Current Relationship of Philosophy and Theology', *Theological Investigations* XII (London 1975), pp. 61–79.

In justification of this proposition, we shall first say only one thing here. If we understand a *theological* anthropology as one limited anthropology among others, parallel to the secular, empirical anthropologies and perhaps (if these are still prepared to put up with such a thing today) parallel to a metaphysical anthropology, we are making this theological anthropology unconvincing for people today – something into which they cannot enter at all. For this inevitably means presupposing *a kind* of divine revelation which the modern man or woman does not find (or no longer finds) in the realm of his own experience.

A particular factor called God, who makes himself felt as one reality among others but who influences these others, so creating a present which is cut off from other realities in our world of inner or external experience – this simply does not exist. Or at least a factor of this kind is merely the notion, reduced to a number of categories, of what is really meant by God.[8]

We cannot substantiate this proposition any further here. We can only support it by appealing to the feeling about life shared by contemporary men and women. The proposition is not denied by the Christian conviction that God and the world are not identical; we must be clear about this once and for all. For the non-identity in itself, and our recognition of it, still do not make God one special, individual reality, *parallel* to the realities of the world. It means a difference of a completely unique kind; and to state and bring out this difference truly is one of the most difficult tasks of a Christian theology. It is a task which we cannot, of course, follow up here and now as a separate theme.

If we presuppose this interpretation of the relationship between God and the world, then it is also clear that a revelatory self-manifestation of God in the *ultimate* resort cannot be thought of only as a particular event in time and space, within the world and its history. We can also no doubt understand without more ado that an interpretation of revelation as being *initially* and *solely* historical is opposed to modern mentality, which thinks 'regionally'.[9]

[8] We have frequently discussed the modern question about God and the possibility of talking about God today, cf. especially 'The Experience of God Today', *Theological Investigations* XI (London 1974), pp. 149–65. P. Weß attempts to discuss this point in *Wie von Gott sprechen? Eine Auseinandersetzung mit Karl Rahner* (Graz 1970).

[9] At the same time this observation is not simply intended to mean that

Such a proviso with regard to a common understanding of revelation naturally does not mean a denial that a revelation which (being God's self-communication) already takes place in the most fundamental structures of the world and the spirit, and always constitutes their radical depth, takes objective form; and that it necessarily arrives at objective reflection in what we describe in Christian terms and in our usual vocabulary as revelation. Nor do we deny that the original essence of revelation really has a 'limited' and particular history.

The basic point at issue in these suggestions is this. If we regard theological anthropology simply as a 'limited' anthropology, even though furnished with new, factual content, but numbered among the other anthropologies, with which it is then bound (necessarily and inevitably) to exist in a situation of confrontation, competition and conflict, then we should inevitably be presupposing a concept of God and revelation which would be deeply opposed, at least, to contemporary mentality. We must remember this when in our reflections we talk about the theological *dimension* of the question about man (or anthropology), and ultimately the theological dimension of man himself. There cannot really be a *special* theological dimension of this kind within a pluralism of other empirical secular dimensions.

MAN'S EXPERIENCE OF GOD

But then what can talking about a theological dimension possibly mean? In the first place the problems associated with discourse of this kind leave one fact unconsidered: the fact that the Christian and Christian theology are convinced that the reality which we call 'God'

---

history is always and solely a science restricted to a particular area. We cannot consider the problem of history in detail here. We have also discussed it in connection with the question of the development of doctrine; cf. K. Rahner and K. Lehmann 'Geschichtlichkeit der Vermittlung' in *MySal* I, 2nd edn (Zürich 1975), pp. 527–91. For an initial survey, cf. the relevant articles in *Sacramentum Mundi* III (New York and London, 1969); A. Darlap and J. Splett, 'History and Historicity', 31–9; P. Hünermann, 'Philosophy of History', 39–43; W. Kasper, 'Theology of History', 43–47; see also A. Darlap, 'Faith and History' in *Sacramentum Mundi* II, 326–9. These articles may also be found in *Encyclopaedia of Theology: A Concise Sacramentum Mundi* (London 1975) under the following titles: 'History and Historicity', pp. 618–27; 'Philosophy of History', pp. 627–32; 'Theology of History', pp. 632–5; and 'Faith and History', pp. 514–18.

exists; that there is a quite particular relationship between man and God; and that consequently statements can and must be made about man which include the word 'God'.

How to reconcile this Christian conviction about a theological anthropology with the rejection of a particularist and 'limited' theological anthropology, of course, depends ultimately on a more precise, and really primary, understanding of the relationship between God and man. If we really come down to it, therefore, it depends on the answer to the question: can a place be found in man's self-understanding for the experience of God which will allow this relationship and this God himself to become after all more than a particular individual fact? For that would mean that theological anthropology itself would become a limited human science, and we should then today be bound to have the impression that its earlier object had long since become secularised and had been taken over by the secular human sciences.

We originally asked: 'where is the theological dimension in the question about man – a question which has other dimensions as well?' In order to progress more rapidly in what we are trying to say, let us now ask instead: 'How and why can and must all questions about man (irrespective of the legitimacy of all provisional anthropological questions) be given so radical a form, and be pinned down so firmly to that form that they themselves all turn into *the one theological question* which by itself offers the answer for man's free affirmation of faith?'

Perhaps this re-formulation still does not make the question itself properly comprehensible. It will, or would, probably become more or less clear only through its answer. But I hope that it is already evident now that this re-formulation takes us, at least methodologically, out of the predicament we talked about. What we are seeking now is not a reality *parallel* to the human realities with which the secular human sciences are concerned. It is the radical form of these human realities themselves. The theological dimension of the question about man is identical with all the dimensions of man which the secular anthropologies contemplate, provided only that these dimensions are seen and accepted in their whole radical depth and are consciously considered as such, becoming a theme of their own.

This thematisation of the question about man in its ultimate, radical form – the question which is ultimately man himself and which he does not arbitrarily ask or cease to ask – is not a limited or an additional anthropology, if only because this radical form of the question is nothing other than man's initiation into the incomprehensible mystery which we call 'God'. So that all statements made by a theological anthropology can be read as – and are only correct if they are read as – warnings not to stop in an anthropological statement at any point short of the one where these statements in an apophatic anthropology are dropped into *the incomprehensibility of God*.[10] Theological anthropology is only truly anthropological when it really sees itself as *theology* and loses itself in that. But theology is theology only when it becomes the acknowledgment of God's incomprehensibility, before which we can only fall dumb in adoration; before which and towards which we exist, whether we wish to or no; being able only to choose whether to accept this exposure to the mystery *per se*, entering into it in believing liberty, or whether to repress it sceptically.

Really this understanding of a theological anthropology is a matter of course for a Christian theology, if we start from the fundamental facts of such a theology.

What else could a Christian theology of revelation say about man (if it is not to be made superfluous by the secular anthropologies) except to assert the free relationship of God to man, which cannot exist in a finite reality different from God (and hence a reality explorable by man himself) but which has to be identical with God himself, if we are to be able to think of it as the first and last and unsupersedable object of divine revelation?

But how would God really be understood as God if he were thought of, not as the incomprehensible mystery, which cannot be carried over into the system of co-ordinates of our intellectually penetrating and dominating understanding as one, individual reality, but as if he exists as the incomprehensible ground of an understanding that comprehends everything? An understanding which is always and everywhere already present, sustaining and revealing, at the point where man begins to set up the system of co-ordinates of his understanding of things, where he begins to assert things in science and,

---

[10] The present author's recent reflections here may be found in *Theological Investigations* XVI (London 1979): cf. 'The Hiddenness of God', pp. 227–43, and 'An Investigation of the Incomprehensibility of God in St Thomas Aquinas', pp. 244–54.

in a continual process, increasingly to perfect them or to call them increasingly in question.

But if man is comprehensible theologically only in his dependence on God, and if apart from this relationship (of course with all its presuppositions, implications and consequences) nothing more can be said theologically about man at all;[11] and if this means that God is truly taken seriously as God – i.e. is accepted as the eternally incomprehensible mystery – then the interpretation of a theological anthropology we have proposed is really a matter of course.

But it must be taken seriously. It must not finally disappear again after all, behind the multiplicity of theology's anthropological statements, which are put forward as if they were additions that can simply be made on top of the statements of the secular anthropologies. For to do this is ultimately to misunderstand them.

We should have to examine all the statements of a Christian theological anthropology one by one, showing in each case that every assertion is the radical, critical form of a secular anthropological statement, in which this secular statement is broken up and cast into its own incomprehensibility. In the incomprehensibility of the statement the incomprehensibility of God comes to be experienced, and every secular statement of this kind is forbidden, as if in a court of law, to interpret itself as final, as wholly understood, or as the basis of an absolutely unequivocal self-manipulation on man's part.[12]

When the individual secular anthropological statements are given this radical form, so that they enter into the mystery of God, these statements are set in a certain relationship to one another. It is a relationship which forbids every individual secular anthropology to see itself as self-sufficient, and as the mistress of all other secular anthropologies, capable of bringing man as a whole under control in the light of this particular, individual point of departure.

The nature of theological anthropology as the apophatic, radical form of secular anthropology will perhaps be most easily grasped by the average Christian mind if we try to see the dialectical relationship

---

[11] Cf. 'Man (Anthropology): Theological' in *Sacramentum Mundi III* (New York and London 1969), 365–70, with extensive bibliography; also *Encyclopaedia of Theology: A Concise Sacramentum Mundi* (London 1975) 'Man (Anthropology): III. Theological', pp. 887–93.

[12] This of course also applies to statements about man as such. In fact it applies to these especially, because their relative nature allows man's dependency on God to find expression.

of the various theological statements to one another. We then see clearly that there is no theological anthropology which could really be seen as a system in the true sense, i.e., as a complex of statements which could be built up from any other axiom except this: that man is the being who loses himself in the incomprehensibility of God and can accept this as his innermost salvation without being identical with it. But it is precisely this single fundamental axiom of a theological anthropology which prohibits a real anthropological system.

This emerges, however, as we have already said, in the definitive dialectic in which the individual statements of theological anthropology are related to one another. It is this which causes the lack of system (even to the point of seeming contradiction) and the obscurity of a theological anthropology.

For this Christian anthropology, therefore, man is a being of temporal and spatial history, even to the point where his salvation is concerned, which is to say always and everywhere. And yet he is not totally absorbed by space and time. He is the subject of a liberty that is unique in each case. And yet in that liberty he is a person who lives in a collective history of salvation and is also *as such* partly determined by it in his individual, unique history of freedom, which he cannot transfer to anyone else. For Christian anthropology, man is essentially the historical being for whom divine revelation and salvation are encountered through his specific history. At the same time he is the being who is always already endowed by what we call the Holy Spirit of grace with the saving reality of God himself, as offer made to his liberty, which can be realised in *all* history. He is always the sinner who cannot justify himself before God and who is yet surrounded by God's self-communicating love, so that he really always already stands beyond death's demarcation line, which distinguishes God from finite creation.[13]

One could go on for a long time making statements of this kind about theological anthropology. The dialectical relationship in which the statements stand always points beyond these statements themselves into the mystery of God, which cannot be reduced to a system;

---

[13] We have followed up the dialectic of statements like these in a number of essays, trying to bring out differences and contrasts, without falsely trying to relate them or − something that would be equally false − to divide them. This seems to have been overlooked by some critics. Essay titles in all the volumes of *Theological Investigations* point to this dialectic, which not infrequently provided the starting point for the treatment of a particular question.

and without this self-transcendence the statements would neither be true nor theological.

If we could analyse the meaning of these individual statements of theological anthropology more closely, it would emerge that they are really only the radical form of secular anthropological statements. And it would, of course, also be possible to do the same thing in the reverse direction: what are apparently merely secular anthropological statements prove to be secretly theological assertions, if they are only taken seriously in the radical form which is implicit in them.

Thus it could be shown, for example – and shown in both directions – that what we call faith, even in the strictly Christian meaning of the term, is nothing other than the freely accepted, radical form of man's rational nature. The provision is only that this faith should really be understood as being sustained and empowered by the transcendental nature of this very rationality, in which the latter is merged into the incomprehensible mystery we call 'God' with which we inevitably have to do in this experience of our transcendental nature, whether we consciously define that dependency or not.[14] So it might be shown that the experience of human liberty and responsibility, without which man cannot live, ultimately has its foundation of reconciliation towards all inexorable necessities, absurdities and futilities only if this freedom from a responsibility which cannot be transferred and is yet in need of redemption knows itself to be safely cherished in the forgiving and self-communicating mystery which gives itself as eternal peace in all – but also beyond all – irreconcilabilities and contradictions in man's history of freedom. The doctrine of the incarnation of the divine Logos and his act of reconciliation on the cross is the radical form of the conviction that even man's most radical subjectivity is realised historically; and that it again reaches its final form only when it also takes tangible and irrevocable form in historical happening.[15] The doctrine of the Church merely gives radical form to the doctrine of the social nature of man, and allows this

[14] The author already developed these ideas in detail before the war in his well-known book on the foundations of a philosophy of religion, *Hearers of the Word* (London 1969). Later an attempt was made to carry the ideas further in reflections on man's freedom and responsibility.

[15] For the basic principles of the author's attempt at a 'transcendental Christology', cf. K. Rahner and W. Thüsing, *Christologie – systematisch und exegetisch – Arbeitsgrundlagen für eine interdisziplinäre Vorlesung* (Quaestiones Disputatae 55) (Freiburg 1972), pp. 15–78.

social nature to have continuing importance even in the history of man's most personal uniqueness.[16]

One might go on in this way and see all theological statements about anthropology as the radical form of secular anthropology, which forbids these seemingly merely secular statements to take themselves absolutely seriously and also enjoins them, as individual disciplines, not to set themselves up in such absolute terms that a system is built up which allows man to rule over himself in what is ultimately a cynical way, since it means that he sees himself as being transparently futile and null.

THE LOSS OF REVELATION

When we say that Christian anthropology is 'only' the radical form of secular anthropology, in our sense of the phrase, then the Christian has no need to fear that this statement means the dissolution of a theological anthropology based on revelation and its transformation into a secular anthropology based on rationalism and science, or into a mere secular humanism.

For to give radical form to all the dimensions of anthropology and of man himself means recognising that man is not comprehensible simply in himself alone; but that the experience of his own incomprehensibility and the incomprehensibility of the world and, as part of that, the incomprehensibility of experience means what we call 'God'.[17]

If we give anthropology this radical form, man is to be understood as the being who – at least in the form of the offer made to his freedom – is always and everywhere inescapably endowed with God's self-communication – the Holy Spirit of grace. It is in this that he already experiences the fundamental event of what we call Christian revelation. To see revelation in this way as fundamentally taking place in God's self-communication does not contradict the traditional concept of revelation. For it is a matter of course that this grace which communicates God and so reveals him, which always comes into being in man's transcendental dependency on God (which it elevates)

---

[16] For the author's ideas on 'the Church', cf. the essays gathered together under the heading of 'ecclesiology' in *Theological Investigations* X (London 1973).

[17] Cf. 'Experience of Self and Experience of God', *Theological Investigations* XIII (London 1975), pp. 122–32.

can – and indeed must – for man become a self-given fact which he reflects upon only in the context of mankind's history. It is in history, wherever this reflection authentically takes place, arriving at its zenith in Christ, that we can talk about Christian revelation in the traditional sense of the word.

After all, man in his innermost nature is a historical being, and consequently the radical form of the dimensions of his being, which are merged by the grace of God into the history of God himself, also means that his history takes on the radical form of salvation-history. For it is precisely that which is the history of man's free acceptance of the transcendental gift of grace, which leads him into the incomprehensibility of God himself.

If we consider these three facts, then it is impossible to say that the radical form of the secular dimensions of man which are open to experience cannot lead to his supernatural destiny, to theology, and to a real theological anthropology. Grace simply means giving radical form to man's being. It is not a new, additional storey planted on top of what is really a self-contained sub-structure known as the nature of man.[18] Consequently a secular anthropology in its radical form is already theological anthropology. Of course this is not based primarily on the arbitrary private reflections of the single and non-historical individual. It develops in the event which we call the history of mankind, which is ultimately the history of man's being as it is in grace. It is not simply some merely static being, lingering behind and beneath history.

What we have tried to indicate up to now are really only hints about the direction in which secular and theological anthropology must move if they are to discover their unity (which does not mean

---

[18] Cf. 'Grace: Theological' in *Sacramentum Mundi II* (New York and London 1969), 412–22, with extensive bibliography; also *Encyclopaedia of Theology: A Concise Sacramentum Mundi* (London 1975), 'Grace: II. Theological', pp. 587–94. B. van der Heijden takes the present author's earlier essay *De gratia* for the starting point of his account in *Karl Rahner – Darstellung und Kritik seiner Grundpositionen* (Einsiedeln 1973). This is not the place to discuss this, but a historical comment on the essay *De gratia* may put some of van der Heijden's comments in a different light. As p. 3 shows, he evidently knew only the fifth edition of 1959–60, not the third. For reasons of space the foreword to the earlier editions had to be left out. But this shows that the essay was written in 1937–8 under the pressure of difficult circumstances, while much of it is indebted to H. Lange, *De gratia* (Freiburg 1929); cf. also and especially the preface to the third edition of 1951.

uniformity), and if they are to ensure that a theological anthropology is not seen as something supplementary to the secular anthropologies. It must be seen as their innermost centre, which has found itself, and in this conscious reflection gives man a task of his own once more: the task of an explicit religion.

INSIGHTS AND PROCLAMATION

But even if we grasp these ideas and believe that they are correct, what do they mean for the proclamation of the Christian message today?

First of all they allow orthodox Christian teaching to start unabashedly with man, with his experience of himself, with his existence. And – understood correctly – they allow us to end with man, too. Today this ought not (or ought not any more, at least) to give the impression that things about man which are additional to his own experience and indeed are quite simply beyond what he experiences in his own existence are to be taught. The Christian message which is to be conveyed to men and women does not mean conveying something alien and external. It means awakening and interpreting the innermost things in man, the ultimate depths of his existence's dimensions.

We certainly must not presuppose that man in all the dimensions of his existence is no more profound than he appears to be in the shallowest head and the most superficial heart. We must certainly not expect that the interpretation of his own existence which gives it its most radical and objective form will be actually understood by a process of reflection and accepted by every individual, in every phase of life. Even the most objectively correct and the subjectively most human proclamation will often fall on deaf ears because of the private and collective situation of the listeners; and this is a difficulty which is often practically unsurmountable. But all this does not affect the right and the duty to present the Christian message in such a way that it is really nothing other than the interpretative call of the reality which is experienced and present in the listener himself, even if it is not understood.

This is not intended to be the propagation of a shallow humanism or a secularization of religion;[19] because in asserting this we are after

[19] On the question of humanism, cf. K. Rahner, 'Christian Humanism', *Theological Investigations* IX (London 1972), pp. 187–204; and on the problem of secularisation, 'Theological Reflections on the Problem of Secularisation', *Theological Investigations* X (London 1973), pp. 318–48.

all convinced – and have to be convinced, if we want to be Christians – that what is preached from the outside has been present as a reality in every man and woman, long before our preaching, in the form which we call the Holy Spirit. It is present at least in the sense of being an offer made to man's liberty. We are convinced, too, that the historical content of our message is simply this: that in Jesus we have the firm historical and revealed assurance that this inner endowment with the Spirit conferred on man's existence is and remains, finally and victoriously, the innermost entelechy or determining principle of mankind's history.

If in the actual history of theology in all denominations this approach by way of man's own understanding of himself has often failed to lead to an orthodox theology, or to a theology whose content is sufficiently differentiated, this is not because starting from man's experience of himself was basically wrong or inadequate, or was bound to stick fast in a rationalistic humanism or horizontalism. It is because this approach is not carried through radically and courageously enough. Moreover, individual efforts in that direction do not sufficiently take their bearings from the way this approach has been carried out in the past – for it has always existed, if we take the history of Christianity and the Church as whole.[20]

Today more than ever, it is impossible simply to begin with the formal authority of Scripture or the doctrinal authority of the Church, if only because, when all is said and done, even the acknowledgement of this authority as source or norm of a Christian theological anthropology also needs a reason and justification. But this legitimation is ultimately simply dependent on man's recognition that the essence of his own existence comes to meet him clearly and convincingly through the agency and authority of Scripture and Church – something which he has always already experienced but which he cannot by himself clearly enough objectify through the processes of reflection, and from which even his own liberty recoils because of the uncanny mystery with which it is faced.

If this means that we are maintaining the thesis that the theological dimension of the question about man is nothing more than the radical depth of all other, seemingly merely secular dimensions of anthro-

[20] On 'horizontalism', cf. 'The Church's Commission to Bring Salvation and the Humanization of the World', *Theological Investigations* XIV (London 1976), pp. 295–313.

pology, we may and should start from just that proposition, without fear of being unorthodox.

It is undoubtedly possible to arrive at the Christian faith by way of the Jesus of history, the sole proviso being that we do not distort the Jesus of history through an abbreviated presentation of him; and that we do not interpret the Christ of faith monophysitically, either openly or in a concealed but implicit way, regarding this misinterpretation as being the very height of orthodoxy.[21] In the same way, even a seemingly secular anthropology leads to a theological one, always providing that we really face up to the incomprehensibility of man's existence, do not avoid it out of embarrassment, and do not think that because we can only stammer over this incomprehensibility, we can let it alone. And always presupposing, too, that we understand the content of the Christian message in that unity and sublime simplicity which belongs to it, in spite of an unavoidable two thousand years of reflective differentiation.

Of course I realise that to lay down a proposition and postulate of this kind is not much more than to formulate a formal and abstract imperative.

We ought now to analyse the individual dimensions of human existence, showing how all of them – each for itself, and all of them because of their common incalculability – together pull man into the incomprehensibility of God and offer this incomprehensible God of inexpressible mystery as the One who in giving himself provides the goal and content of human existence from within. We ought to show how all dimensions point to the history of man and mankind, in which the irrevocable victory of this promise is manifested in Jesus, the crucified and risen One.

We should have to call upon the dimensions of man as the being of an absolute truth (at least in the form of a limitless, critical question) and the radical responsibility conferred by liberty; the dimension of the private and political existence of man with man; the dimension of man's origin and his futurity. And we should have to show that all their unfathomable depths really conceal in themselves the mystery of God in his turning to man.

All these dimensions could, if we liked, provide brief formulations of the Christian faith in which the radical nature of these dimensions

---

[21] Cf. 'Current Problems in Christology', *Theological Investigations* I (London 1961), pp. 149–200.

and the traditional content of the Christian faith are defined, and in which the radical nature of these dimensions and the traditional content of the Christian faith reflect each other and make each comprehensible.[22]

But of course all that is impossible here. Nor have we the space to answer the question of how all that we have said can be translated into statements which are more easily accessible to the mind that is less well trained theologically. Another problem we cannot consider here is how far the different anthropological points of approach to which we have referred each have their different importance and their greater or lesser accessibility, according to the point in the history of thought at which they are advanced, and according to the affinity they have to a particular phase of human life.[23] Here we must simply point to other work in which we have tried to provide an answer to these questions too.

---

[22] In this question I am indebted to R. Bleistein, *Kurzformeln des Glaubens* (Würzburg 1971). An accompanying volume of texts offers specific illustrations. The present author has also considered this question since 1966, cf. also 'The Need for a "Short Formula" of Christian Faith', *Theological Investigations* IX (London 1972), pp. 117–26.

[23] This would be the problem of a 'mystagogy' in the Christian faith, which we have repeatedly discussed. For the most detailed consideration of the subject, cf. 'Die Notwendigkeit einer neuen Mystagogie', *HPTh* 2/1 (Freiburg 1966), pp. 269–71, and 'Die Rücksicht auf die verschiedenen Altersstufen in der immer erneuten Glaubensmystagogie', ibid., 3, 2nd edn (Freiburg 1972), pp. 529–35.

7

THE BODY IN THE ORDER OF SALVATION

W E shall be dealing with this subject here from the dogmatic point of view.[1] But what can Christian dogmatics contribute to this question? Not very much, it would seem at first sight; for it is a very general discipline to which we are looking for an answer, a discipline unavoidably somewhat remote from the specific needs and anxieties of everyday life. But let us recall some theological statements about the body, and from that basis try to work out some theological principle for the elucidation of the particular truths of faith. Let us try, that is, to bring out what all these statements of Christian faith have in common, and to form a theological concept of the human body.

REVELATION BY WAY OF THE BODY

In recalling some theological statements which are part of Christian belief and underlie any subjectively coloured theology, the fundamental thing for us to remember is that *the body is created by God.*[2] God is the creator of the human body as well as of everything else.

That is to say, the God who is pure spirit, the ineffable mystery, who is incomprehensible and nameless, who dwells far off in unlocated majesty, has also created this body – this actual, visible body

---

[1] This essay was originally based on A. Görres' remarks in 'Der Leib und das Heil: Caro cardo salutis' in K. Rahner and A. Görres, *Der Leib und das Heil* (Mainz 1967), pp. 7–28. The present writer has discussed the subject in detail in *Geist in Welt: Zur Metaphysik der endlichen Erkenntnis bei Thomas von Aquin*, 3rd. edn (Munich 1964).

[2] Cf. Denz. 3896 (*Humani generis* v. 12. VIII 1950 'de humani corporis origine').

that we see, with which we have to cope, whose pleasures and pains we experience. It has been directly willed by God. This body is not just something that came about by chance; nor was it fortuitous in the sense that God really intended something different. It is not merely a by-product. It is not only something which came about by way of man's history – for example, because the spirit turned away from God in some history that took place before the foundation of the world, acquiring this concrete form as a result. Space and time – and therefore history – and therefore the human body – and therefore human sexuality – are not things which God did not *really* desire. All of them are created by the One whom we call the creator of heaven and earth. Even if it is not a truth of faith, we Christians can and must supplement this today by saying that somehow this specific bodily nature of man's, as it actually is, owes its existence to God's direct, creative intervention. (At least this is what follows from doctrinal statements of the Church which, though they are not properly speaking definitions, are still largely valid, according to a ruling of the Biblical Commission.) This has nothing to do with the question of evolution, for the statement can quite well be made in an evolutionary context too; but I do not need to go into that here. I should only like to emphasise the fact so that we can see how much the Church's teaching authority stresses the fact that man's bodily nature was created, willed, by the one, eternal, holy, just and incorporeal God, and puts this in the foreground of faith's consciousness.[3]

Secondly, this body is made out of the dust of the earth. The vivid account at the beginning of Genesis, which tells us how God formed man from the dust of the earth, like a potter, and breathed life into him, may seem childlike, primitive and pictorial, but it is fundamentally a tremendous and moving story. It is tremendous and moving not only because man, as a specific reality, stands in an immediate relationship to the eternal God, but also because we are told again that God takes what he makes in this way from the dust of the earth.[4]

---

[3] On this question, cf. the present author's article 'Monogenism', *Sacramentum Mundi* IV (New York and London 1969), 105–7 (with bibliography); also 'Monogenism', *Encyclopaedia of Theology. A Concise Sacramentum Mundi* (London 1975), pp. 974–7. Cf. also 'Theological Reflections on Monogenism', *Theological Investigations* I (London and Baltimore 1961), pp. 229–96; 'The Sin of Adam', *Theological Investigations* XI (London and New York 1974), pp. 247–62; 'Evolution and Original Sin', *Concilium* 3 June 1967.

[4] Cf. Gen. 2:7.

That is stated about the God who can in principle make things with a free, creative 'let there be'. We are told that this independent God (who in his creative activity is not dependent on any presupposition in the way of matter) made man from the dust of the earth. We are not told that he made man's *body* out of dust – though that is our modern, platonic interpretation. He made *man* out of the dust of the earth. And that means that from the very outset he took him and set him in the whole world in its totality, by creating him to be his direct partner in a dialogue with himself. The Scriptures let us feel this tremendous tension and the problems involved, even in this simple story, in which God acts as the direct creator, who makes something out of the dust of the earth. It lets the tension and the problem remain, without softening them or trivialising them – the tension and the problem that are involved in the fact that man is created out of dust and is yet created by God.

There is a third point which we must remember about this fact of theology. *Original sin is transmitted through procreation.*[5] Not, of course, because there is anything sinful or interior about the act of procreation. But because it is the plain, simple fact that everyone belongs to this one, particular human race, where everyone is related to everyone else by blood; and this makes a person a member and sharer in what we call original sin. We may briefly remark here that original sin simply means that man, because he is a descendant of Adam, belonging to this historical, human family, ought to possess divine grace but does not do so. Grace is conferred on him only if he is also one who has been redeemed by Jesus Christ. But both things are based on this bodily community of shared descent: the fact that according to God's plan man was to be endowed with sanctifying grace, divine life, divine nearness and divine glory; and the fact that he does not actually have all this.[6]

[3] In addition to the articles cited in n 3, cf. 'Original Sin', *Sacramentum Mundi* (New York and London 1969), 328–34 (with bibliography); also 'Original Sin', *Encyclopaedia of Theology. A Concise Sacramentum Mundi* (London 1975), pp. 1148–55; P. Overhage and K. Rahner, *Das Problem der Hominisation*, (Quaestiones Disputatae 12/13) (Freiburg 1961).

[6] For a summing up of the results of the present author's numerous essays on the theology of grace, cf. the articles 'Zur Theologie der Gnade', 'Gnadentheologie' and 'Gnade und Freiheit', *Sacramentum Mundi* II (Freiburg 1968), 450–65, 465–9 and 469–76 (with bibliography); also 'Grace: II. Theological', *Encyclopaedia of Theology. A Concise Sacramentum Mundi* (London 1975), pp. 587–95.

The fourth thing we must remember in this connection is the saying in the first chapter of the Gospel of John, 'And the Word became flesh.' We do not need to describe in detail here the whole depth and breadth of the Johannine concept of *sarx*. That concept is a more complicated and more subtle one than we need here.[7] But at all events the sentence states that man – and hence the divine Word as well – is truly flesh. We are, therefore, told that the eternal Word of God, by uttering himself into what is not God out of the inner divine silence in which he is with the Father, becomes just what we call *sarx* – man; but truly physical man, man indeed who bears the marks of death, suffering man, man in his tribulation. We cannot consider all these things here. Let us simply hold on to one thing: that it is a fact of faith that when God desires to manifest himself, it is as man that he does so.

I admit that the formulation I have just used really goes beyond what is defined in faith and is an interpretation which the individual theologian has to justify. But I should like to put forward this interpretation here, because it is of great importance for a real understanding of what we are concerned with. If we really want to understand the saying 'And the Word became flesh' in its total depth, then we simply must not assume that we already know what flesh is, or what man is, or – to put it theologically – what human nature is. If we knew all these things, in saying that 'the Word became flesh' we should only virtually be saying: 'We have long since known what the eternal Logos of the Father became; it is something of which we have our own personal experience.' We must go about things in exactly the opposite way. If we want to know what man is, or what flesh means, then we must, so to speak, choose this theological definition of the statement 'And the Word became flesh,' saying: flesh, man as a bodily, concrete, historical being is just what comes into being when the Logos, issuing from himself, utters himself. Man is therefore God's self-utterance, out of himself into the empty nothingness of the creature.

Of course this does not make what man is, or what man as a bodily

---

[7] On the concept 'flesh' in John, cf. E. Schweizer in *ThW* VII (Stuttgart 1964), esp. 138–41; cf. also R. Bultmann, *Theologie des Neuen Testaments*, 2nd edn (Tübingen 1954), pp. 386–96, ET *Theology of the New Testament*, (London 1965), vol ii, pp. 227–46; R. Schnackenburg, *Das Johannes Evangelium* I, 2nd edn (Freiburg 1967), pp. 241–9, ET *The Gospel According to St John* I (New York and London 1968), pp. 371–3.

creature is, any clearer. For all those exact definitions and ways of expression which we have acquired as a matter of course through the sciences and through metaphysical anthropology, etc., are left behind and what man is, is thrust into the absolute mystery of God. For if it is true that what we are is just what comes into being when the eternal Logos utters himself, then it is clear that we ourselves are the absolute mystery. We might say: if an anthropology that sees itself not merely as provisional but as absolute fails to talk about God, it is a heresy. It is not, and cannot be, a Christian anthropology. So when we have to talk, and want to talk, about man in the ultimate, most radical and absolute sense – not about man's spirituality, but about bodily man, man in the flesh, about the *sarx*, which always means the whole man, but in his actual, bodily nature – then we really have to talk about God. So when as Christians we ask what bodily man is, in the ultimate meaning of the word, then – if we want to give a final answer, not a provisional one – the only answer we can give is, 'And the Word became flesh.' The *sarx* is what comes into being when the Logos becomes something which it is not already in itself, in its divine nature. It is what comes into being when the Logos desires to be less and to become less than it is of itself. It is what comes into being, what is present, when the Logos manifests itself in the sphere in which it does not desire to be the infinite, blessed, intrinsically luminous Word of the Father, but issues from itself and speaks whither only the finite, creaturely Word can be heard. The flesh which is man is the self-utterance of God himself.

In order to avoid misunderstanding, let me stress that here I am going beyond the clear, simple facts of Catholic teaching in so far as they are binding on Catholic Christians. I am doing so in the consciousness that I am not saying anything heretical, though I am equally aware that in giving this interpretation I am not – so to speak – covered by the explicit teaching of the magisterium. But I think that my interpretation is correct. And I think that it is necessary to say this today. The being of man is what comes into existence when God utters himself into the otherness of nothingness; and that means man, in so far as he is *sarx*.

A fifth thing must be said at the same time as we state these theological facts. *As human beings we are all redeemed through Christ's death.* That is a statement which directly affects the body too. This means that if we were only to say what Scripture *also* says – we have been redeemed by obedience, through the obedient love of the incarnate One – then we should certainly have said something that is true; but we should not have stated this true fact in its concrete, bodily form. When we say that we have been redeemed through the blood of Christ, through Christ's death, through his sufferings on the cross, then we must not mean by this that a spiritual event of love and obedience was unfortunately or strangely accompanied by rather unpleasant circumstances. (That has been a danger in standard Catholic scholastic theology ever since the Middle Ages.) We must not consider that it was really a matter of chance or externals, which has nothing to do with what was really intended, nothing to do with the obedience and love of this incarnate Word of the Father's. The statement that we have been redeemed through the death of this Son of God, and through the shedding of his blood (i.e. a bodily event) is the concrete, bodily form of what we express in abstract and formalised terms, as it were, when we merely say that we have been redeemed through the Son's obedience and love, and his readiness to sacrifice himself.[8] We have been redeemed through an event which is, of course, spiritually free and personal in its nature. But according to the Father's will, it took place, and could only take place, in this entirely concrete, bloody reality, given over to death. The place where this love and obedience are to be found is therefore this bodily existence, if love and obedience are what they are intended to be – i.e. redemptive. And this event could be redemptive for us only because it took place as the love of the Son and the obedience of the Son in his actual, specific bodily nature, which we called his death, or his Passion, in which we from the outset communicate with him and are united with him through the unity of the human family.

Let us suppose for a moment – in a kind of hypothetical theology – that the Logos had become an angel. He could then also, of course, have loved God, have trusted him, have obeyed him in this angelic, created and creaturely nature; but he could not have redeemed us through it. This event would not be one which would by its nature take place in a dimension which touches us from the very beginning. In other words, we have been redeemed through Christ's suffering and death, because this event by its nature, as a redemptive act, took

[8] A. Grün has recently attempted to express this idea in his monograph, *Erlösung durch das Kreuz. Karl Rahners Beitrag zu einem heutigen Erlösungsverständnis* (Münsterschwarzach 1975). But this book is somewhat diffuse and is not entirely satisfactory.

place in an actual bodily existence; and we were able to be redeemed through this bodily event, because what takes place in this sphere is from the outset a *patrimonium commune*, a common heritage for all those who belong to one another in this community of the body, this blood-relationship which binds them in Adam to a common destiny.[9] We may remember the Epistle to the Hebrews, 'He who sanctifies and those who are sanctified have all one origin.'[10] Here we can perhaps see most clearly what Tertullian already said 1600 years ago, 'The flesh is the hinge of salvation – *caro cardo salutis*.'[11]

Another article of faith is *the resurrection of the flesh* (not the body, as we shall see). The basic Christian acknowledgment of man's perfecting, his absolute validity before God, is not expressed by saying that we save our souls, but by affirming that we believe in the resurrection of the flesh. Again flesh here, of course, means the whole person. There are also doctrinal statements made by the Church which talk about the resurrection of the body. But the resurrection of the flesh is the statement which means precisely body *and* soul, in that very unity in which man is flesh. For if he were simply body, then he would not be flesh at all in the Biblical sense. Flesh means *that* person who is on the one hand the frailty, the threatenedness, the inexplicableness, the weakness, the obscurity of this individual, concrete, specific entity, and who at the same time knows this and is afraid. In other words, flesh means the one person – it is almost impossible to say 'who is made up of spirit and flesh'. We shall see later that although this formula is a common one, and is quite justifiable, and although it also corresponds to what the catechism says, it, too, really fails to bring out clearly enough the facts of the true reality of the Christian view of existence. At all events we must say that in as much as Christianity confesses the resurrection of the flesh

[9] We cannot give separate consideration here to the important problem of monogenism and its relationship to original sin, but cf. K. Rahner, 'Erbsünde und Monogenismus' (published as an appendix) in K.-H. Weger, *Theologie der Erbsünde* (Quaestiones Disputatae 44) (Freiburg 1970), pp. 176–223. This expressly supersedes some of the work cited in n. 3. Unfortunately the author was unable to complete for publication the more considerable monograph on the subject which had already been announced in some quarters. Other commitments and reasons of health prevented him from carrying this project through.

[10] Cf. Heb. 2:11.

[11] Cf. Tertullian, *De carn. resurr.* VIII (CSL 47) 36, 27–8 and (CCL 2) 931, 6–7.

– and confesses it as a central article of its faith, which expresses in this single formula the whole of man's future hope and the acknowledgement of his one, total, final validity – it has included from the outset in man's unity what we, in our modern Western way, call the body, and really acknowledges only this single person.[12]

A seventh point which we deduce from these facts about the Church's teaching is that *man is a unity made up of body and soul*. The doctrine of the Church – its express, defined doctrine, – does not merely state that man consists of body and soul. It also obliges us to maintain the real, true, radical, substantial, original unity of body and soul.[13] Not, of course, in the sense of identity or uniformity, and not, of course, in the sense that the one can simply be deduced from the other. (We cannot simply derive what we call the body from its spirituality, in the spiritualistic sense; and even less can we deduce man's spirituality from his bodily nature, in a materialist sense.) But although that is impossible; and although the Church has made doctrinal statements – e.g. at the Fifth Lateran Council – about human spirituality and about the immortality of the human soul; and although the Vatican Council of 1870 condemned the people who were not ashamed to say (as the Council put it) that nothing exists but matter – yet the real, true, original unity of body and soul is an article of the Catholic faith, and was particularly defined at the Council of Trent in the sixteenth century.[14]

THE CONSEQUENCES OF A THEOLOGY OF THE BODY

We need only briefly point here to the results of the theological facts we have discussed, for the aspects that suggest themselves are in any case so numerous that we cannot mention them all. So we must first understand why the Church as a concrete, bodily, sociologically constituted community sees itself as the Church that is necessary for salvation. And this is understandable if the Church teaches that sacraments consisting of physical elements are necessary for salvation. (Why and in what sense, in spite of this statement about the necessity for salvation of certain sacraments, other people may none the less

---

[12] Cf. 'Jesus' Resurrection' in the present volume, pp. 16–23.

[13] Cf. the constitution 'Fidei catholicae' of the Council of Vienne (1312): 'De anima ut forma corporis', Denz. 902.

[14] Cf. 5th Lateran Council (1513), Denz. 1440; Council of Trent (1546), Denz. 1512; 1st Vatican Council (1870), Denz. 3002 and 3022.

expect to be saved who do not belong in actual bodily terms to this visible Church – e.g. are not even baptised – is a question that need not concern us here.)

At all events, we see that from this theology of bodily existence (which runs through the whole of Catholic dogma) it also follows that the Church cannot merely be a spiritual power of conviction or opinion, and that it does not merely begin at the point where we pass beyond what is sociological, social, earthly and tangible into a pure spirituality of the mind. This bodily existence also asserts itself in the doctrine of the Church and the sacraments.[15] We might put it paradoxically and say that the average Christian almost has the impression that the world is concerned with the body, with visible tangible realities; while the Church and its pastoral care is concerned with that strange thing called the soul, which is so difficult to grasp. To put it even more paradoxically and in perhaps exaggerated terms, we might almost say that the exact opposite is true. Christianity is continually concerned with the body. It is a bodily, concrete, shaping, speaking, acting, organised, ecclesiastical, sacramental religion, a religion which concerns itself in its dogmas with concrete things, and expresses something through these dogmas. And it leaves entirely to God, and God alone, whatever elements of this spirit-endowed body go beyond the purely physical.

We might point to a whole number of things here. Even though the Church allegedly deals only with the soul, it does not judge the innermost heart. It sticks to what is tangible. It says: this or that formulation is correct. But what you have thought in your ultimate, deepest, innermost, most subjective heart of hearts – that I neither know nor have any control over. And if you want to think something new and clever and deep in your theology, or in metaphysics and philosophy, then you must express it in such a way that it fits into this community, so that it sounds comprehensible to other people, and so that it can be written into a catechism. We might say, even the teaching authority of the Church is concerned with what is bodily. And this is true of pastoral care and the sacraments too. The same

---

[15] The present writer has already expressed his views on the theology of the sacraments several times, cf. *Kirche und Sakramente* (Quaestiones Disputatae 10) (Freiburg 1961); 'Die Sakramente als Grundfunktionen der Kirche', *HPTh* I (Freiburg 1964), pp. 323–32; *Die siebenfältige Gabe. Über die Sakramente der Kirche*. Munich 1974.

may be said about the truths of faith: there are none which do not also touch on man's bodily nature.

But then we might well ask: what about the mystery of the Holy Trinity? Of course God does not have a body in our sense. I am not attempting to conjure something bodily into God by some subtle means or other. But the fact remains that we have heard about the Holy Trinity and we are concerned with it only in so far as, and because, the Logos has become flesh, since he uttered himself to us in bodily form. He did not even do so merely in a human word – although that too would have been something bodily. He uttered himself in the human concreteness of a fleshly, bodily history. That is the reason, and the only reason, why we have anything to do with the mystery of the Holy Trinity.[16] And I believe – though this again is more of a theological statement than a directly expressed truth of faith – that we must also say that the beatific vision, the direct contemplation of God, is based on a grace which would not exist, and probably could not exist, unless the divine Logos had taken, and remained, flesh. We must never forget that the Christian, authentically Catholic truth of faith about the Incarnation of the Father's eternal Word does not mean that God put on some kind of overall called humanity, because his world had somehow broken down, contrary to his original plan, so that he had to repair God the creator's original plan down here in this world of ours. It means that God is man to all eternity, so that to all eternity we cannot think rightly about this God or express him properly unless we add to our thinking what we men and women all are as well. There is no longer any theology, to all eternity, which is not anthropology too.

a) The Fundamental Concept of the Body

The doctrine we have described, with all it has to say, obliges us to make a distinction, but also to realise that this distinction excludes the possibility of an existential cleavage between body and soul. People have reproached Greek (which is to say Western) theology, to some extent unjustifiably and in too wholesale a way, with having broken up the ancient biblical anthropology of unified man (which belongs to the New Testament as well as the Old) into a Greek

[16] Cf. the brief remarks under the heading 'The Mystery of the Trinity', *Theological Investigations* XVI (London 1979), pp. 255–9.

duality of *anima* and *corpus*, soul and body, thus distorting or even corrupting the original biblical message.[17] This is certainly an exaggeration. We do not need to agonise in this connection as to whether what we have to understand theologically by body and soul can really be made to coincide entirely with what Graeco-scholastic philosophy understands by the same words. Let us confine ourselves to theology. If we do, I believe, in view of normal theological usage and the teaching authority of the Church, that we can and must say that it is undoubtedly legitimate to go on making a distinction between body and soul. To say this is by no means simply to state the obvious – what everyone knows and accepts. If we start from the anthropology of the Old Testament and the New Testament too, the distinction is correct, but by no means an absolute matter of course. When the New Testament talks about the soul, it means something which does not have very much to do with what we understand by the term. According to biblical theology it is quite possible to hold that the whole anthropology of the New Testament is still entirely the same as the biblical theology of the Old; and in Old Testament theology there is really only the one, bodily person who – since he is God's partner – is of course what we call 'spirit' as well, but in such a way that the Old Testament never really distinguishes between the body and the spiritual soul in our philosophical (platonic), scholastic sense. Still, however that may be, I believe that the distinction between something which we call body and something which we call soul – a distinction which is made and assumed as a matter of course in the Church's doctrinal statements – is quite legitimate. So the Council of Vienne, for example, could define the substantial unity of body and soul and say that the *anima* (soul) was the *forma corporis* (the form of the body). And so the Fifth Lateran Council could define the immortality of the soul as a truth of faith which is binding on us, the body of course not being immortal in this sense.[18]

This being so, there is no need for me to justify the statement any further when I say that to make a distinction between body and soul is not merely possible but is also theologically correct, is required by

[17] Cf. here 'The Unity of Spirit and Matter in the Christian Understanding of Faith', *Theological Investigations* VI (London 1969), pp. 153–77; also, as summing up, J. Splett, 'Leib-Seele-Verhältnis', *Sacramentum Mundi* III (Freiburg 1969), 213–19 (with bibliography); also 'Body', *Encyclopaedia of Theology. A Concise Sacramentum Mundi* (London 1975), pp. 157–61.

[18] Cf. references to the conciliar statements in nn. 13 and 14.

the teachings of the Church, and is completely justifiable. But this distinction does not mean that it is possible to make a cleavage in the real or existential sense between what we call body and what we call soul; and in our context this is the important thing. In other words, this distinction is a metaphysical one – one might even say a meta-existential one. Not that it does not have great importance for man's existence, for the actual conduct of his life. Of course it does. But it is a metaphysical and meta-existential distinction in the sense that in actual fact man never encounters mere body and never encounters pure soul. What we call 'inwardness', our innermost heart, is the inwardness of an actual, bodily spirit, an incarnate spirit. And what we call man's externals are the external form of this very same incarnate spirit.[19] Wherever we encounter ourselves, wherever we are within our own grasp, as it were, inwardly or outwardly, we have to do with an actual, concrete person. And we can never so to speak materially separate these two from each other. The loftiest spiritual thought, the most sublime moral decision, the most radical act of a responsible liberty is still a bodily perception or a bodily decision. It is still incarnate perception and incarnate liberty – and hence, even by virtue of its own nature, it is still in interplay with everything that is not free, not spiritual, and so on. And conversely, even the most external thing about man is still something that really belongs to the realm of his spirituality; it is still something that is not just mere body.

b) Indivisible Unity

According to the doctrine of the Church, we have to go further than what we have just said. We must even maintain that an existential cleavage between the body and the soul is actually *impossible*.

Catholic doctrine is convinced that the Logos as its very self not only took up his dwelling in the summit of the human soul, as it were, but really became flesh. When we remember what we said about our having been redeemed through the death of Jesus Christ and through his passion, then we are bound to conclude that it is impossible to draw a smooth existentially pure line of demarcation,

[19] For the author's basic ideas here cf. K. Rahner, *Geist in Welt: Zur Metaphysik der endlichen Erkenntnis bei Thomas von Aquin*, 3rd edn (Munich 1964).

so to speak, between the bodily nature of the Logos and his human spirituality. For if that became possible, I should of course have to say that whatever actually lies beyond that demarcation line – the line drawn between Christ's human spirituality and his bodily nature – can no longer be of any significance for redemption. But it is! We have been redeemed through Christ's death and his blood. This must of course include his obedience and his love. But the converse applies equally. In this obedience and love of Christ the whole concrete and specific character of his passion is embodied in such a way that the two are not actually divisible. In other words, the unity of man has been originally so designed by God the Creator that although man knows that he is a unity of different elements, in the existential implementation of his existence he can never, as it were, get behind this unity, so as to take sides purely with the spirit or purely with the body.

As a result there is, for example, no Catholic ethic which could leave the concrete fact of bodily existence and what happens in it on one side as being irrelevant. And consequently there is no consummation of salvation through the sacraments which could detach itself from this sphere as being a matter of indifference. It is the impossibility of any existential cleavage of this kind which really emerges from the theological facts which we talked about earlier.

But we must now look at these facts again in somewhat more detail. And that brings us to the theological and metaphysical essence of the bodily condition, which emerges, in my view, as a theological conclusion from these theological facts.

c) Man as Spirit

In order to make my meaning clear, I should like to begin again with another point. I have already stressed that it is permissible for us to say – and indeed that we must say – that man is made up of body and soul. This is of course frequently stated in the catechism. All the same I believe that every Thomist theologian and philosopher will be bound to agree with me when I say that this mode of expression is really an empirically inexact one. It only conveys man's essential being in a highly primitive way, because man is not really built up out of body and soul, but out of spirit and *materia prima*, or 'first matter' – what one might translate as empty otherness. To say this is to make a statement in terms of Thomist philosophy or metaphysics; but this seems to bring out and integrate the facts of theology which I have been talking about, better than other possible Catholic philosophies. But what does this Thomist statement tell us?

When I say that man is made up of body and soul, I am assuming (even if this is not what the Church's teaching as such intends to say) that another true, concrete human bodiliness is being encountered which in its specific form has not as yet anything to do with man's spirit; the spirit is then added, and the whole is then man. But when I look at the matter thomistically, then I have to say that what I experience as man's bodily nature is itself the reality of the spirit, yielded up into that mysteriousness which is only accessible to metaphysics and which scholastic, Thomist philosophy calls 'first matter'. The body is already spirit, viewed in that aspect of self-consummation in which personal spirituality yields itself up in order to encounter directly and palpably what is different from itself. Bodily existence is not, therefore, something which is added to spirituality; it is the concrete existence of the spirit itself in space and time. Physical nature or the nature of the human body is not something already existing in itself. It is the self-expression of the spirit reaching out into space and time.

If we want to be sure whether we have understood the point at issue here, we only have to ask whether we find it self-evident to say that the body can be seen, but not the soul. If the answer is, 'Yes – of course that is so,' then we have not understood exactly what the point at issue is. I am naturally assuming that the answer to our question is, 'No – that is not the case.' If we wanted to give a Thomist answer, we should have to say, 'Yes, the soul can be seen, but only in part' (though 'part' does not here mean a quantitative section); in an ambiguous sense, I can see man's spirit. What I see the spirit of man in space and time to be is, in an ambiguous sense, precisely what I call body.

And if we say that, all the same, the body is still what I can see with my eyes; and that what I experience when I shut my eyes and think about God or my mother – i.e., what is 'within' me – belongs to the soul, then we ought, more correctly, to say, 'No, that is a different part of my reality, but it is just as much body-and-soul as what I can look at from the outside.' The intensity of the spirit's presentation as body can of course differ considerably. If I put someone like Kant on the scales and see that he weighs ten stone, then of course I have seen less of Kant than I would have done if I had talked to him. The intensity of the spirit's bodily existence can be great or small, inwardly or outwardly. But what I call the body is the outgoing of the spirit itself into the emptiness of space and time, which we call 'first matter', in which this spirituality now itself appears; so that outgoing into its bodily form is the condition which makes spiritual and personal self-discovery possible, not an obstacle in its way. There is no coming to oneself except by way of exit into the bodily reality into which the spirit first reaches out and finds itself, forming itself and going out of itself. And it is only this which makes personal, spiritual freedom possible. Of course this bodily nature, as the spatial and temporal existence of the spirit itself, is always an entering into the truly Other.

d) Christian Dualism?

It would be wrong to interpret what we have just said as being an absolute and radical metaphysical expressionism. The bringing-one-self-to-manifestation means bringing oneself truly to view in a truly other. And consequently this bringing-of-oneself-to-manifestation in another is really the bringing-of-oneself-to-manifestation in another through a subjection of oneself to an alien law. And if we now object that this really comes down to the same thing – that here we have the same dualism between body or spirit and first matter which we challenged when we met it earlier in the form of dualism between body and soul – then the following must be said. Of course in a Christian anthropology we have a dualism which is never ultimately abolished in man himself but only in the transcendent divine unity of the Creator of heaven and earth, of spirit and matter. But even in a dualism of this kind we do not fall back into the Greek or neo-platonic dualism of body and soul, which we objected to earlier; because in *our* dualistic conception – if we want to call it dualism at all – we are clear that what we actually encounter is always what has already been unified.

This has tremendous consequences. Everything that I experience as effect from outside in the sphere of my bodily existence, I experience from the very outset as the reality formed by me, which comes to me from outside. There is no suffering which I do not already experience as action, and there is no action which is not already suffering. There is no impression from without which is not already expression from within. What can actually be encountered is always the already completed synthesis of what is alien and what is already given from within. This metaphysical doctrine about a true difference between *materia prima* and spirit can maintain this without, therefore, having to fall back into a primitive empiristic dualism between a directly encounterable so-called body and a directly encounterable so-called soul – a dualism which, as it were, risks an existential cleavage.

But this means two important things. Firstly, since man, out of the substantial roots of his spiritual personality, utters himself into matter (this utterance being bodily identity itself) this utterance necessarily becomes ambiguous for man. Why? Whatever can actually be encountered by psychology, physiognomy, and so on is really the spirit. But it is the spirit which has uttered itself inwards into the otherness, the other form of being of *materia prima*, of space and time, of determination from without inwards. Whatever can be encountered is always merely the synthesis of the two. This one, already united synthesis between personal *actio* and *passio* cannot be completely abolished by man; for otherwise, as self-investigating spirit, he would have to be able to take up a position in which he would not always have to carry out the synthesis. In other words, he cannot existentially say exactly that one aspect of a particular concrete thing comes from within and another aspect of it comes from without. The bodily nature of man is man's utterance about himself which has become ambiguous. For man it is necessary and remains necessary for ever, for himself and even more, of course, for others. That is one of the points that emerges from what we have said.

The second point picks up a number of things which we mentioned before, in the first part of our discussion, and is this: this utterance in which man presents himself and completes his own spiritual and substantial foundation is an utterance into the common sphere of space and time. In other words, man utters himself and constitutes himself in his concrete nature and thereby opens himself by that very fact to the break-through from outside. In his bodily nature he enters into a sphere which does not belong to him alone. Now of course we might say that this is merely an abstruse way of stating the most obvious truism one can imagine. For whoever doubted that since I have a cheek, someone else can smack my face? And that since I have a head, a brick can fall on it? Or that since I have a body, I must have a mother? Of course this is a truism. But we now have to understand this truism in such a way that we really grasp the fact that these truths belong so radically to man's nature that they cannot be overridden in any way at all, and indeed ought not to be overridden either. Consequently it is precisely man's task to be true to this nature of his and not to try to escape from it. There is no area in which what we have just said is not true. There is no 'inwardness' which does not also stand open, as it were, to what is without. The ultimate, most personal freedom, which is to be found where man is inevitably himself, without any substitute or any excuse, at the heart of his being (or however we like to express it) – the place, that is to say, where he is virtually the absolute and irreplaceable subject – is where he still has something to do with Christ, and with all other men and women too. For there are no spheres which can be cleanly separated from one another in an existential cleavage.[20]

Although this seems so obvious, it has its tremendous consequences. It means, for example, that it is not a matter of indifference for me as spiritual person how the material sphere in which I live is constituted. I cannot and must not say, 'What is out there is a matter of indifference. That is not the important thing. I shall withdraw to the unconquerable fortress of my innermost spiritual personality.' That would be Stoicism or something else of the kind – perhaps something splendid in itself; but it would be completely un-Christian. Two thousand years ago someone died on the cross in all the darkness of his death out of love for the Father. And this took place from the very outset in a sphere which is my own reality. How I am now to react to it is another matter.

e) Our Reality as Open System

Through bodiliness the whole world belongs to me from the start, in everything that happens. Of course we must not get the impression in this connection that our body stops where our skin stops, as if we were a sack containing a number of different things, which clearly ceases to be what it is where its 'skin', the sacking, stops. No. Let us think in quite simple terms (without going into details) about modern physics. In some sense we are an open system. Of course I can say, 'This chair is not part of my body.' But when we ask in terms of physics what that actually means, then the matter becomes very

---

[20] Here personal 'intersubjectivity' (for the neglect of which the present writer has often been criticised) also has its place. This was admittedly not sufficiently prominent in the account; but all the same the criticism in its usual form is inaccurate and unjustified.

obscure. If there were no moon or no sun, our bodies would be different, too. In a certain sense – and I am exaggerating here, in order to make what I want to say clearer – we are all living in one and the same body – the world. And because that is so (and this is really the metaphysical, theological premise) something of the nature of original sin, and something of the nature of redemption can exist too. This one total physical existence as the common space which makes intercommunication between individual spiritual subjects possible from the start – this one concrete space can of course be accepted by the individual spiritual subject in various ways: it can be loved, put up with, or hated.

Let me draw attention to one small result of this, although it really takes us too far. The transfiguration of the End-time, therefore, means the resurrection of the individual, and a new earth and a new heaven. And let us just ask ourselves whether what we call blessedness, heaven and hell, might not be thought of as being distinguished for us in a matchless way by the manner in which a particular person accepts this common reality. Since everyone, as spiritual person, lives essentially in the space of existence that is common to all, into which he continually acts – and acts into the whole – and from which he continually receives, he is continually active and continually passive. What he specifically experiences as himself is always the unity of the act suffered, committed by everything towards him, and the self-fulfilment from within, which he actively expresses outwards. We can see in this way what the communion of saints really means. This one 'concrete' existence in which we consummate our own spiritual, final liberty, is itself involved in a dynamic history which sometime ends in transfiguration, in a reality not only of the spiritual person, but also of his common sphere of being.[21] The question then arises: how do I accept the final condition of the sphere in which I necessarily am? Do I accept it as the transfigured world, or as what the Bible calls hell fire?

The body is therefore nothing other than the self-consummation of the spirit in space and time. But this self-consummation of everything except God is of such a kind that it is essentially ambiguous and takes place in a sphere of existence in which all men and women communicate with one another from the very beginning.

---

[21] This one, all-embracing history is one of Christianity's essential features. To use a traditional term, it may be described as 'catholic'.

In the narrower sense of the word, the body is that through which I fulfil myself in the one world in which all spiritual persons exist. And it is from this starting point that we should have to think through anew the individual and more specific features of a Christian view of the body.

8

MYSTICAL EXPERIENCE AND MYSTICAL THEOLOGY

THE only purpose of the ideas I am about to develop is to peg out the ground for what is dealt with – and what can be dealt with – in a Catholic theology of mysticism; for there is really no generally accepted theology of mysticism, as a distinct part of Catholic theology.[1]

What we do have, however, are great mystics who testify to their own experience. Among these, and among the classic Spanish mystics particularly, there are some who have tried to some extent to reduce their experience and their mystic 'way' to a theological system. But reflections on mystic experience which attempt to reduce that experience to a system always run across the conceptions of faith and theology which a mystic inevitably brings with him. For it is these that he applies when he tries to describe or systematise his original experiences so as to be able to fit it into the co-ordinate system of his other philosophical and theological opinions and convictions.

That is why classic Spanish mysticism in particular displays an unusual variety of accounts and systematic summaries of mystical experiences, although this does not imply any doubt about the real experience that lies behind them. Apart from works of this kind, we must at least mention the spiritual literature, which cannot be overlooked, in which mystical experience continually finds expression and is clearly the ultimate source of its genuineness and vitality. But of course it is even less possible to talk about a generally accepted

[1] The original version of these ideas is to be found in the preface to C. Albrecht's book, *Das mystische Wort: Erleben und Sprechen in Versunkenheit*, ed. H. A. Fischer-Barnicol (Mainz 1974). The present writer knew the author personally and feels indebted to him in more than one respect.

theology of mysticism in the case of these occasional testimonies to mystical experience which only become influential now and again.

One of the most important presuppositions for a theology of mysticism is still lacking in spite of a few beginnings – an adequate study of the relationship between Christian and non-Christian mysticism. The same may be said about the relationship between mystical and parapsychological phenomena. Of course attempts at a systematic theology of mysticism have been made, even if they have not been expressly called that. We can find them from the period of Spanish mysticism at least down to our own time.[2] But unfortunately interest in a mystical theology of this kind seems largely to have died away today.

It must, however, be said that such attempts as we have, generally deal too briefly and in too simple-minded a way with the *ultimate* fundamental questions. Their various sections often more or less repeat descriptions of mystical experience and the mystic way which were already worked out in Spain in the classical period. Sometimes in the course of this repetition they smooth out or blur fundamental distinctions, or use somewhat superficial arguments to prolong the dispute over the question of whether 'infused contemplation' or other mystical graces belong to normal Christian strivings for perfection, or whether they are merely special gifts, relatively seldom conferred, which can even be lacking in 'the heroic virtues of the saints'. These representations of mystical theology are often somewhat too naïvely and unreflectively dominated by an 'extrinsic' conceptual scheme, according to which direct divine 'intervention' is thought of in the case of mystical phenomena. What contemporary theology has to say about the relation between 'nature' and grace, and about the unity of the two, is hardly brought to bear at all here.

THE MYSTIC AND HIS EXPERIENCE

The first basic problem which a theology of mysticism would have to elucidate is how the mystic stands in relation to what he experiences

[2] I am deliberately avoiding the problem involved today in the very term 'mysticism'. Here it is used in a wide and formal sense; but these remarks do suggest starting points for an understanding of the way the term is really interpreted, and what are the experiences supposed to be summed up and described by the term, cf. H. Fischer, 'Mysticism', *Sacramentum Mundi* III (New York and London 1969), 136–42 (with bibliography); also 'Mysticism', *Encyclopaedia of Theology: a Concise Sacramentum Mundi* (London 1975), pp. 1004–11.

as having been conferred on him in 'absolute proximity'.[3] For if, and to the extent in which, the 'mystical' subject is not, in mystical experience, merely thrown back on himself through objects belonging to the categories of everyday, but encounters the 'mystery' *per se*, or reality itself, or God (or whatever name we may give to this 'something' which is not *from the outset* identical with the mystical subject) then identity and difference in this experience become a problem. For there is simply no other way of talking about religious mysticism. Experience can basically present the experiencing person and what he experiences as being one; or it can at this precise point bring out and really actualise for the first time the difference which still exists between God and the creature, even in the highest degree of grace. Seen in the abstract, this remaining distinction in mystical experience could be overlooked for various reasons, although a true metaphysics and a true Christian theology must require it to be present. Perhaps a conceivable 'mystical' experience of the unity between subject and '*world*' is also too quickly equated with an experience of the unity between the mystical subject and *God*. Possibly, too, the elimination of egoistical, particularist individualisation in a mystically experienced radical love for the self-communicating God simply leads, in subsequent reflection, to a mistaken belief in an absolute cessation of the finite subject. All these reasons and possibilities would make it seem particularly interesting to hear what the mystic himself has to say. How does he feel and interpret his experience? For we should not depend solely on the views of the metaphysician on the human spirit and its absolute transcendental nature, nor merely on the theologian, with his account of the difference between God and created being. We must also hear the views of the person who himself experiences most clearly and with the least distortion the relationship which exists between the human subject and the reality which we call God.

GRACE AND FAITH

But mystical theology is immediately faced with a second problem. This arises when we come up against the relationship between grace

---

[3] Cf. for example the two essays about the doctrine of the spiritual senses in Origen and Bonaventure, 'The "Spiritual Senses" according to Origen' and 'The Doctrine of the "Spiritual Sense" in the Middle Ages', *Theological Investigations* XVI (London 1979), pp. 81–103 and 104–34 respectively.

and faith on the one hand and mystical experience on the other. Yet, traditional mystical theology continually finds itself in considerable difficulty when it calls mystical experience 'grace(s)', because behind mystical experience it would like to perceive a special intervention on God's part, confined to a particular point – a totally undeserved intervention, in which the inaccessible God communicates himself in a quite special way. But what is the relation between this grace and those other graces which Christianity proclaims as God's offer to *all* men? Even if mystical grace is basically viewed as the development of the supernatural capacities of justified man, the answer to this question remains unclear. This becomes most evident in the question about the difference and the similarity between mystical experience and that 'experience'★ which we term Christian faith and which is sustained by God's Spirit. According to the usual account, God is supposed to communicate himself so 'directly' in mystical illumina- tion and mystical unity that it is really no longer possible to see why faith is not superseded by this mystical light, at least at the moment of illumination itself. A true theology of grace, faith, possession of the Spirit, the indwelling of God etc., deals with realities which cannot be merely understood as objective gifts, existing beyond the consciousness, as a modern Molinist misinterpretation would suggest. It cannot possibly interpose between faith and the experience of grace on the one hand, and glory on the other, some intermediate state which differs essentially from both, theologically speaking.[4] That would have to transcend the gift of grace to the Christian, which is always associated with the *experience* of grace. It would have both to surpass it specifically, in the true sense, and in its significance for salvation. It would not be a temporary participation in the contem- plation of God which (contrary to certain views in some mystical theologies) is after all supposed to be reserved for those who through death have entered into the true finality itself. The deification of man and the possession of uncreated grace, which Christianity grants to all the justified, cannot in a real sense be surpassed by anything which is not glory and the direct contemplation of God. But these are reserved for man's final consummation. Mystical experience cannot

★ The German word for experience – *Erfahrung* – originally meant 'to travel through – a correct and significant indication here.
    [4] On 'the grace of faith' cf. especially 'Anonymous Christianity and the Missionary Task of the Church', *Theological Investigations* XII (London 1974), pp. 161–80.

leave behind it the sphere of 'faith' and the experience of God's spirit which faith confers, by means of a new experience which would no longer be faith at all. On the contrary, mysticism can be conceived of only within the normal framework of grace and faith.

This means that whenever mystical *theology* aims to be more than 'parapsychology' in the broadest sense of the word (which covers everything which average, everyday consciousness knows nothing of) it can only – according to its own principles – be part of genuine dogmatics. This proposition involves two things. On the one hand, it does not say that the dogmatic theologian as such can and must say something about mystical experiences to the extent in which these differ *psychologically* from the everyday experiences of Christian grace. If this were to be the case, even down to 'essential' differences *of a psychological kind*, then either the mystic himself or the empirical psychologist would be the competent authority; it would certainly not be the dogmatic theologian. The dogmatic theologian can only determine that on earth there cannot be any higher experience in the *theological* sense than the experience of faith in the spirit of God. But this means that every genuine mystical experience (as distinct from natural phenomena of interior absorption or suspension of the faculties etc.) can also be understood as merely one mode of the experience of grace in faith. Probably even the mystic himself and the psychologist would have to explain more precisely where this mode of Christian experience of grace in faith comes from.

Secondly, the proposition I have put forward does not assert either that a theology of mysticism can be worked out only with the usual methods and sources which traditional dogmatics work with, too – i.e. the Scriptures, the doctrines of the Church, its tradition etc. If mystical experience is distinguished strictly from conceivable natural (and hence basically learnable) phenomena of interior absorption or suspension of the faculties, as well as from parapsychological phenomena in the normal sense of the word; and if it is just one variety of the experience of the Spirit offered to everyone; and if therefore a theology of mysticism is part of dogmatics – then the specific object of that experience of the Spirit through grace which is given to people with faith, hope and love in God's communication of himself must belong to the mystic's domain. The unique *mode* of this experience of the Spirit may include elements of a 'natural' kind. But, described empirically, it will certainly belong to the theology of revelation, because this experience tells us about real, deifying grace and because even customary revelation in the Word only objectifies in words through a process of reflection what fundamentally happens and is experienced in God's self-communication through grace. This is also true because the pure and authentic objectification of God's self-communication has actually found expression in Jesus Christ, as its irreversible climax and zenith, and afterwards in Christian doctrine as statement of the truth.[5] The experience of grace is, therefore, possible in non-Christian mysticism as well, and a corresponding theology of mysticism could be a piece of revelation theology, even though it would always continue to take its direction from the theology which is related expressly to the crucified and risen Jesus. For in Jesus the mystical event of the surrender to God as he really is finally succeeded through his saving death, and has therefore become historically and victoriously manifest.

NATURE AND GRACE

The relationship between nature and grace inevitably brings us to a third basic problem of mystical theology.[6] Both terms are, of course, understood here in their strict theological sense. As we said above, mystical experience must not be interpreted as something which fundamentally transcends and supersedes the supernatural experience of the Spirit in faith. That is why the 'specific difference' of such experience, as distinct from the Christian's 'normal' experience of the Spirit, must belong to man's 'natural' sphere. It would consequently be the special mode of an experience of transcendence and 'return' to the self which is in itself natural. This does not contradict what we have just said about mysticism as the experience of grace. *Psychologically* mystical experiences differ from normal everyday processes in the mind, only in the natural sphere; and in so far as they are fundamentally learnable. Like every other act of man's – for example a

---

[5] This problem is more closely, if briefly, formulated in 'Grundlinien einer systematischen Christologie' in K. Rahner and W. Thüsing, *Christologie – systematisch und exegetisch* (Quaestiones Disputatae 55) (Freiburg 1972), pp. 15–78.

[6] The present writer has frequently, and in detail, expressed his views on the relationship between nature and grace. For his fundamental viewpoint, cf. 'Concerning the Relationship Between Nature and Grace', *Theological Investigations* I (London 1961), pp. 297–318; also later discussions about the concept of the 'supernatural existential'.

conscious act, a free act or an act of reflection – these really natural spiritual processes can also be 'elevated' through God's self-communication, habitually or at any given moment. That is to say, they can acquire radical form, in the direction of the immediacy of the self-communicating God. This normally takes place in the normal 'supernatural' acts of faith, hope and love, which constitute the Christian life as such.

The particular psychological, and really natural, character of such experiences can help to make them take deeper root existentially in the person's inmost being, so that as supernaturally exalted acts they can in a higher degree give their stamp to the whole subject, forming him through and through. This greater personal profundity of the mystical act also brings with it a greater reflectiveness in the experience of transcendence, which is really natural, though exalted by grace. A *theology* of mysticism by itself cannot decide whether this experience is achieved in some miraculous way (preternaturally), or whether it can also be attained by natural means, through practice, on the basis of certain pre-conditions; or whether both may be possible, according to the level at which the phenomenon occurs. Open though the question therefore is, the possibility of purely natural phenomena of interior absorption would of course also be conceivable – phenomena, that is to say, in which the mediation of the experience through categories was wholly or partly lacking. If we then want to talk about 'natural mysticism', no fundamental objection can be raised;[7] but it would undoubtedly be better to keep the term 'mysticism' for those psychologically unusual experiences which we referred to above, which are exalted by grace and really include supernatural experience of the Spirit.

In this case we should still have to answer the more precise question whether existentially central neutral phenomena such as interior absorption and so forth, are really *only* natural, or whether they are

---

[7] We have already indicated the problem involved in the use of the word mysticism today (cf. n. 2). Individual writers give the term their own particular emphasis, in accordance with their way of looking at things and their own approach. Cf. C. Clemen, *Die Mystik nach Wesen, Entwicklung und Bedeutung* (Bonn 1923), but also the work of C. Albrecht – *Psychologie des mystischen Bewußtseins.* (Bremen 1951); *Das Mystische Erkennen* (Bremen 1958), – where the concept of 'suspension of the faculties' is worked out. D. Baumgardt makes a distinction in the mysticism of inwardness, nature and history, according to the object or place; cf. his *Mystik und Wissenschaft* (Witten 1963).

simply apprehended as such in the process itself and in the reflection that follows, although they are actually always exalted supernaturally by what we call Christian grace. This is a question for *the theology of grace*. If we now see the supernatural elevation of the spiritually personal acts of man (acts of really unlimited transcendence) only as intermittent – as taking place in time and space, at a certain point only, and as happening under certain predetermined conditions – then the answer must be in the first sense, that there are natural phenomena of suspension of the faculties which are really *only* natural. But if another theology of grace assumes, legitimately enough, that man's transcendental nature was always and everywhere and from the very beginning finalised and given radical form by God's self-communication in grace, which streams from the midst of existence outwards in the direction of the divine immediacy, then we should have to answer in the second sense.[8] Here it is also a matter of indifference whether the supernatural gift of grace takes the form of a mere advance gift, or the form of acceptance or rejection, as one aspect of human liberty. Every natural act of suspension of the faculties and so forth, would in this case always and everywhere be elevated by grace, and hence be an act of real mysticism and an act of salvation, even if this unique character of the mystic event were not yet particularly clear, or were perhaps overlooked in subsequent reflection, or were misinterpreted subsequently, in line with pantheistic 'mysticism', as a manifestation of undifferentiated unity.

Our own reflections here make us decide in favour of the second answer to the question, even if the space at our disposal makes it impossible to present the presuppositions and viewpoints of the theology of grace which are behind this choice. For mystical theology it is essential to make clear at this point that mystic experiences sustained by the Spirit, which make God's spirit accessible, do not differ from normal Christian existence because they are of a higher nature simply by virtue of being *mystical* experiences of the Spirit.

[8] Contrary to B. van der Heijden's opinion in *Karl Rahner. Darstellung und Kritik seiner Grundpositionen* (Einsiedeln 1973), the present writer's theology of grace is not initially derived historically from a treatise of traditional theology. It is based on much earlier attempts at a theological consideration of the experience of grace, which Ignatian spirituality is particularly aware of, and which is also of special interest to people concerned with that spirituality. The experience of grace is continually shared by every Christian in the forgiving encounter with God in the act of repentance.

They are different because their natural substratum (for example an experience of suspension of the faculties) is as such different from the psychological circumstances of everyday life.

THE NORMAL WAY OF SALVATION AND MYSTICAL EXPERIENCE

After what we have just said, an approach might perhaps also be formulated which would make it possible to answer the question whether mystical 'experience' is a normal stage of development on the way to Christian perfection, or whether it is an extraordinary phenomenon which is not to be reckoned with, even in a highly intensively lived Christian life. Following what we have said, we must again stress here that mystical experience, where it touches on man's union with God through grace and on the believer's experience of the Spirit, does not represent a 'higher' stage of the Christian's life in grace. That could at most be claimed *indirectly*, in so far as the mystical phenomenon can, as cause and effect, be an indication that a Christian has accepted the offered grace of God's communication of himself to an existentially intensive degree. Apart from that, however, this question, too, would have to be left to empirical psychology. Always presupposing that psychology is capable of saying something about man as the singular and plural subject of an ultimate history of freedom before God (a history directed towards finality), it ought to try to make us understand how such radical self-discovery of the subject is possible in the unconditional surrender to the mystery which we call God – a surrender which comprehends the whole of existence – *without* these natural phenomena of suspension of the faculties. If this were possible, then our new question would have to be answered in the negative. Not every personal and Christian maturing process in the direction of an asymptotic – a continually approaching – perfection, which the Christian hopes to achieve in this life, also includes natural phenomena of suspension of the faculties, even though these may possibly be a useful auxiliary. That is why mysticism is not necessarily part of every Christian life.[9]

If, in reply to this conclusion, the appropriate psychology were to explain that these really natural phenomena – where the faculties are

[9] It will be clear from what has already been said that this conclusion is dependent on the content one associates with the word 'mysticism'. The choice arrived at here, however, is supported by general linguistic usage; cf. also I. Behn's well-known book, *Spanische Mystik* (Düsseldorf 1957).

suspended and so forth – are necessarily part of a personal maturing process, even if they are not always 'technically' cultivated and are perhaps frequently not subjected to reflective processes, then mysticism in the true sense would also be a normal manifestation. It would be part of the process of becoming a complete person and a complete Christian. At the same time, it would still be an open question whether, how far, and with what result, such mystical experience is a matter of conscious reflection, in the good or bad sense.

As we said at the beginning, what we are concerned with here is merely to find guidelines, or a framework, or certain premises for a theology of mysticism. This is necessary today if Christian life is not to be secularised and to end up as a flat, humanitarian affair, and if the 'charismatic' movements which are everywhere gaining a footing in the Churches in our time are to find the way to a genuine self-understanding, and come to terms with themselves in a self-critical way.[10] Finally, a mystical theology must also acquire new life in the West so that we can enter into a sympathetic and critical dialogue with the mystical theology and the mystical phenomena of the East.

[10] A number of other essays in this volume take as their starting point the modern phenomenon of 'charismatic' movements. These essays should also be taken into consideration as supplements to the question we have been dealing with here, and as deepening the viewpoint. On the presuppositions for possible dialogue with Christians in the Eastern churches on the basis of their experience, cf. V. Lossky, *Die Mystische Theologie der morgenländischen Kirche* (Graz 1961), ET *The Mystical Theology of the Eastern Church* (Cambridge 1957).

9

THE LIBERTY OF THE SICK, THEOLOGICALLY CONSIDERED

A N essay on the liberty of the sick, seen from a theological
standpoint, is not just the same thing as an account of the
Church's doctrinal statements on the subject. Of course this
essay is not intended to go beyond the limits of what the Church's
official doctrine says about the liberty of the sick, either directly and
expressly, or indirectly and implicitly. But in so far as the teaching
of the Church has actually been formulated, it does not come to grips
closely enough with what we mean by the phrase 'the liberty of the
sick'. Consequently, however carefully the theologian may take the
Church's doctrine into consideration, he is bound to try to say something about this subject on his own account and at his own risk, in
the light of the theological data and using theological methods.

Here we shall be limiting the subject to those illnesses in which the
sick person is confronted, objectively and subjectively, with death as
something that is threatening him and that is pressingly close.[1] A
cold, an upset stomach, or any illness which does not really force the
person affected out of the circle of the people who are actively able
to control their lives freely, does not present any theological problem
of its own.

In the first section we shall say something about the nature of
liberty as the theologian sees it. From the theological standpoint,

[1] The original text of this essay was published in *StdZ* 193 (1975), pp. 31–
40, but notes and cross-references have been supplied for the present volume.
Some points considered here have already been dealt with by the present
author in *Zur Theologie des Todes* (Quaestiones Disputatae 2), 4th edn (Freiburg 1963); ET *On the Theology of Death* (Edinburgh and London 1961). The
new angle from which the subject is treated here may, however, open up
some fresh aspects.

liberty is something other than a merely psychological freedom of choice in the individual act, and it differs, too, from a purely legal and civic responsibility for one's actions. Of course this first, theological section is bound to be no more than a fragment; and it stresses – and to some degree isolates – those elements of liberty, in its theological essence, which are of particular importance for our question.[2] In the second part we shall ask what the liberty of the sick as such consists of; and we shall finally inquire about the invalid's claim to liberty where this touches on his relationship to his doctor.

ON THE ESSENCE OF LIBERTY

First of all we must mention a number of features of human liberty which are specifically theological and which are of particular importance for our subject. When the word 'liberty' is used in the secular sphere, it is either understood sociologically, as the absence of social compulsions and estrangements; or it is meant psychologically, as the person's freedom of choice in any given act of decision – always provided that we do not adopt the determinist view, which denies the existence of psychological freedom of choice in general, and tries to interpret responsibility, social sanctions and so forth without the concept of free choice. The theological concept of liberty certainly implies the concept of psychological freedom of choice, but it is more comprehensive and more radical.

The theological concept of liberty is theological in the first place because it explicitly or implicitly includes the thesis that whenever there is a radically responsible, true freedom of choice, there is also a definite relation to God. This is so even though in certain circumstances – in fact very often – this relation is not conscious or considered, in any explicit sense. Real, personal freedom of choice is possible only when individual good and individual value are exceeded – even if unconsciously – in man's transcendental self, in anticipation of the Good in general and per se. But this means the existence of a theological dimension of liberty – relatedness to God – even if this is not the subject of conscious reflection. And this is inescapable, whether this relatedness is conscious and reduced to terms and ter-

[2] On the problem of liberty, cf. especially *Gnade als Freiheit*, Herder Bücherei 322 (Freiburg 1968), with the second group of essays: 'Ermächtigung zur wahren Freiheit', pp. 31–89.

minology or not. It is inescapable, whether liberty accepts this relatedness in true self-affirmation, or whether it rejects it in that ultimate denial of the self to which we theologically give the name of sin.[3]

Liberty in the theological sense, therefore, deeply and fundamentally, is not merely the ability to do one thing rather than another, let alone the possibility of always being able to do the opposite of what one has done before. It is rather the possibility open to the free subject or person of disposing totally and finally of himself and his life, as an individual and a whole. Liberty in the theological sense means, first and last, the one and total subject himself in so far as he is object for himself – in so far as the actor, the act, and what has been performed are one – in so far as the one and total life is set in irrevocable finality through this act of liberty; in so far, that is to say, as what we are accustomed to call the eternal being of man comes into existence. And by eternity we do not mean an endlessly continuing time that succeeds our earthly life. We mean the freely ordered finality of the person and his earthly life before God.

These indications of the theological nature of liberty show that there are two different groups of related problems which we must consider in a little more detail. The first is the problem of the relationship between liberty in the theological sense, and the individual, empirical, single object, which can be objectified and expressed in words. The second is the problem of the relationship between liberty and time.

As far as the first problem is concerned, we must here briefly say that the fulfilment of human liberty (by which we mean the self-determination of the total subject in the direction of finality) is, of course, inevitably mediated through some individual object of an *a posteriori* kind, existing in space, time and history. It is to this that liberty chooses to be related in its act of choice, though of course in order to establish its own real nature, which is the self-fulfilment of the person or subject. But this individual object, which is indispensable if liberty is to be consummated, in itself gives no final and certain information as to what the self-consummation of the subject really

---

[3] For additional material which may give added depth to our view of the subject, cf. what has been said about 'choice' in the following essays in *Theological Investigations* XVI (London 1979): 'Experience of the Spirit and Existential Commitment', pp. 24–34; 'Modern Piety and the Experience of Retreats', pp. 135–55; and 'Reflections on a New Task for Fundamental Theology', pp. 156–66.

is, and whether it is for good or evil. It is possible for a person to align himself with God for his salvation, at least unconsciously, because he lets himself fall into the incomprehensibility of his existence in serene hope; though it may well be that the object on which this saving disposal of the self is exercised is materially not only very unimportant and limited, but even ought not to exist, and ought not to be realised at all, if it is tested against the obligatory norms and circumstances of this world.[4]

It is therefore, fundamentally speaking, quite possible for personal liberty to be fulfilled even when the material for decision which is offered to the actual free subject *a posteriori* can no longer be fitted into the 'normal' contexts of human life and society, with its structures and norms, where the person who is 'served' by his experience only in this way is no longer 'responsible' in the civic and psychiatric sense. It is quite conceivable, basically speaking, for a free and personal self-ordering of the subject to get along with a much smaller amount of mediating material than we have to assume and demand in normal civic life if we are to concede responsibility to someone. It is conceivable that a particular objective material which is presented to a person from outside and is in itself conceptually understood, may not be eligible at all as material for the person's real self-fulfilment, because of the actual structure or make-up of the person himself.

The second problem is the obscure relationship between liberty and time. Theologically, liberty must be understood as the personal self-determination of the subject, through which he completes himself as a whole, together with his whole earthly life, in the direction of its final and ultimate form.[5] But then the conceptual scheme which Christian practice and pastoral care employ is insufficient. For there the assumption is that the final fate of men and women, in the sense of salvation or perdition, is simply determined by the final free act

---

[4] For the idea of decision as fundamental option, the author is indebted to Ignatius Loyola's *Spiritual Exercises*. His theological work has been continually influenced by the desire to work out the theological implications of the spiritual stimulus he has found there, and to make that stimulus fruitful theologically, cf. the essays quoted in n. 3.

[5] On the question of time, seen theologically, cf. the essays on the subject which have been gathered together from the different volumes of *Theological Investigations* and printed in paperback form in K. Rahner, *Zur Theologie der Zukunft* (dtv 4076) (Munich 1971).

in time, in the history of a given individual. It is decided by an act which stands at the end in temporal isolation, as it were, and this act by itself governs the whole of the person's previous life. On the other hand, the fundamental option of a person over the totality of himself as subject and over a life extending over a period of time, cannot be thought of as simply taking place outside time and history, and as revealing itself from this meta-historical point only in the many temporally distributed acts of the person. Even free acts, in which the person orders himself and his life in its totality, must take place in history, and must have a place in time and space within the history of the person himself. Otherwise history – and salvation-history above all – becomes a semblance without an essence, on to which a liberty which is above time is projected.

Because of the incongruence we have already indicated between the material through which liberty is mediated and the original act of liberty as the self-ordering of the personal subject himself, the place and time at which such an act of liberty takes place in a person's life can never be unequivocally stated. Nor should we maintain that a fundamental option of this kind is possible only once, and that it cannot be revised later by the same existentially radical act of decision in the form of a later choice. It is true that human liberty as self-ordering does not imply the arbitrary revisability of its decisions, as if these decisions could continually be remade indefinitely; it wants these decisions to take the form of final decisions. But as liberty that is finite and materially mediated, it always exposes itself to still current time; and so it arrives at the fulfilment of its own nature only through the fact that time stops, because of an event which is not simply within the power of liberty itself, although by virtue of its own nature it lays itself open to that event.

THE LIBERTY OF THE SICK PERSON

Here the liberty of the sick means quite specifically the liberty of the sick person in his confrontation with death. This relationship between liberty, in the theological sense, and death is of a quite particular kind. But it is easily understandable if we remember what we have just said about liberty in the theological sense; and if at the same time we take into account the Christian conviction that in death a person's free history assumes its final form. This means that the final 'Judgement' of the person takes place. It means that the person who in his liberty always has to do consciously or unconsciously with God, finally finds him or loses him.

The situation of approaching death is really an unusual situation for liberty. For death brings to an end the time and space in which a person orders himself in the direction of finality. At all events the free subject cannot be certain that a radical, fundamental choice has already been made in his lifetime in such a way that there is no longer any danger of its being upset again in sickness or dying. This means that the situation of approaching death is really a radical challenge to liberty to decide finally for God on the very basis of the 'material' offered by the process of dying, with its helplessness and loneliness. It should decide for God by accepting serenely and hopefully this 'hopeless' situation of radical helplessness and of being engulfed by the incomprehensibility of what we call God.[6]

This means that a person ought to die 'consciously' as far as possible. He ought not simply to *suffer* death but should also paradoxically *suffer it actively* as an act of liberty. He therefore has the right to know that he is going to die, and when. If and in so far as this knowledge can reach the dying person only by means of a communication made to him by the people round him, this communication must not be withheld. If the moment when this communication is made, and the way in which it is made, are chosen properly, it does not have to come as a frightening shock to the dying person. The very helplessness which the patient experiences inwardly can awake a gently composed awareness of death as the situation confronting him. For unless it is a completely sudden death, biologically speaking, the dying are aware of the situation they are in, even if they suppress their awareness for a while.

Because, and in so far as, death (or the act of dying) is a special situation for liberty in the theological sense, man has a right, and even something of a duty, to mould the situation in such a way that it offers as many opportunities for liberty as possible, even in an empirical sense. An alleviation of suffering which does not simply reduce the sick person to unconsciousness, but leaves him conscious and makes a greater serenity of spirit possible than would be the case if he were overwhelmed by pain in the physiological sense, is there-

---

[6] In view of the process of dying, the present author does not share the familiar 'hypothesis of a final decision' which is supported by L. Boros in *The Movement of Truth: Mysterium Mortis* (London 1965).

fore not merely a claim made by the vital self-assertion of the patient himself. It is also a demand of liberty in the theological sense, which rightly desires to win for itself as extensive a space as possible and, as far as possible, right up to the frontier of death. The alleviation of pain is not merely important for the patient's physiological and psychological well-being. It is also important in the struggle for the greatest possible area of liberty in the theological sense – an area where a history of salvation may be played out.

What we have just said, however, is not a final answer to the problem of an alleviation of pain which makes the sick person more or less unconscious and incapable of responsible decision. In our present context we need only say that there is no need to dispense with an alleviation of this sort, as long as it does not mean directly killing the patient, and as long as the nature and violence of the pain would in any case permit no more extensive area of liberty.[7]

'STYLES OF DYING'

In the course of Christian history, the awareness that death (i.e. the act of dying, as distinct from the state of having died) is a special situation for liberty in the theological sense has given rise to what Arthur Jores has called different 'styles of dying'.[8] It is not merely a question of administering the 'sacraments of the dying' (which is not simply and directly obvious). There is not merely a special sacrament for the sick who are near death.[9] Formerly there was also a social and religious ritual for dying, which has largely faded into disuse today. Dying was not merely seen as a biological happening. It was a personal, historical, free event, which quite actively brought life to its final state: eternity. The dying person gathered his family round him, gave them his final blessing, expressed his last wishes, affirmed his

---

[7] On the problem of illness and the sick person cf, especially 'The Saving Force and Healing Power of Faith', *Theological Investigations* V (London 1966), pp. 460–7; 'Proving Oneself in Time of Sickness', *Theological Investigations VII* (London 1971), pp. 275–84.

[8] cf. A. Jores, *Menschsein als Auftrag* (Bern 1964), especially pp. 114–17 and 121–34.

[9] On the sacrament of the anointing of the sick, cf. K. Rahner, *Kirche und Sakramente* (Quaestiones Disputatae 10) (Freiburg 1960), especially pp. 100–4; 'Bergend und heilend – Über das Sakrament der Kranken' in K. Rahner, *Die siebenfältige Gabe – Über die Sakramente der Kirche* (Munich 1974), pp. 115–37.

faith and hope in a gracious God, prayed the prayers for the dying with those round him and so on. All this can be significant as the completion and proclamation of the task of dying as part of a person's own history of freedom. The sober courage befitting the Christian in the hour of death, and indeed a great deal else in this traditional style of dying, may seem to be the reflection of a genuine kind of liberty in the face of death. All the same, this particular 'style of dying' is, when all is said and done, historically conditioned in many ways, and need not in itself be permanently adopted. (We shall come back later to the sacraments of the dying, which are distinct from the other 'stylistic' elements of dying in its traditional form.)

That is one side of the matter. But it is impossible to maintain that the total and final consummation of liberty on the part of the human subject in the direction of finality – i.e. death as total act of liberty – always takes place in immediate proximity to death in the medical sense. In most cases the doctors will have before them a dying person whose condition in any case makes it difficult to conceive (without arbitrary hypotheses) how he could be capable of any radical personal act in this situation – by which I mean an act through which he freely disposes of himself and the ultimate meaning of his life in a thoroughly radical way. Moreover, there is no cogent theological reason for postulating the opposite of what the medical situation would lead us to suppose. The act in which a person freely orders himself in the direction of finality can, even in the case of a 'responsible' person, take place much earlier and can, for internal or external reasons, be the final act of this kind even though it takes place a considerable time before death in the medical sense. Dying in the medical sense and dying as an act of liberty need not coincide chronologically. What took place and could take place in life as an act of free and final disposal of the self, on the basis of a relatively modest and not at all explicit 'material' for the exercise of liberty, is not necessarily also possible in the case of dying in the medical sense, not even if the 'material' there is more explicitly religious and the situation of the dying person is a 'devout' one.

HUMAN AND RELIGIOUS HELP IN DYING

There are people who under certain circumstances are called to help the sick person to arrive at a clearly religious death and an explicitly religious act of liberty in dying. (This help does not always have to be an official pastoral duty. It may also be a humane and Christian duty of love on the part of nurses and doctors.) For these people what we have just said has particular consequences. These helpers should draw on the gift of 'testing the spirits', so as to try to help the dying person to the attitude which is open to this particular individual in the light of his life history and his religious knowledge and capabilities. A helper of this kind should not therefore exploit the sick person's weakness in order to clothe his death with the hastily donned garment of a religious act which he is not actually able to perform existentially, and which, therefore, contributes nothing to his eternal salvation. If a dying person rejects the visit of a priest or pastor, or any other religious help, his wish should be respected. There should be no attempt to enlist the indiscreet help of relatives or nurses, in order to influence him to the contrary. These people may perhaps be more concerned about social 'respectability' than about the religious meaning of the anointing of the sick and the viaticum, or the eternal salvation of the sick person. (But this is not intended to lay down rules for a person who is charismatically endowed and who can trust himself to achieve a deeper and more genuine conversion or repentance in the spirit of the sick person.) When a dying person is no longer able to arrive at an obviously religiously articulated acceptance of death, or a free and saving act, the question of his salvation is completely open for the person who is at his side. It is a question he cannot decide. For the dying person the personally decisive hour of salvation may have taken place much earlier, while he was still in the midst of life, and the material for his free act may not have been expressly and verbally religious at all.

When it is possible to help the dying person to find an expressly religious significance in his death, and when this is accepted by the sick person, the most important thing, even for Catholics, is that the dying person should arrive at a religiously existential attitude towards death. Receiving the 'Last Sacraments' is only secondary to this. In the case of a Catholic who has practised his religion with normal zeal, these things normally coincide. But this is not true of people who have hitherto been used to little or no expressly religious observance. With these people it may be possible under certain circumstances – and it is also theologically legitimate – to help them to acquire a right inner attitude to the possibility of death (hopeful resignation to their fate etc.). There is no need to expect them immediately to accept a sacramental act. That would only overtax and shock them. Of course in a situation of this kind an earlier sacramental practice, which the dying person was accustomed to a long time previously, can be revived without any great difficulty, so that the sacramental event, in its tangibility and clarity, may facilitate and confirm the act of hopeful resignation to death as God's decree. But this is not always the case, and where there is any doubt the decision should be in favour of help in the existential acts of the dying person. Nobody should force a sacramental event on him which, quite innocently perhaps, he cannot really endorse, and which for that reason he quite rightly refuses.

Of course a position of this kind also means that the people surrounding the sick person are not simply released from the outset from the duty of giving any kind of religious help, just because the invalid is incapable of receiving the sacraments or rejects them. Explicit contrition for the sins of one's past life is really an essential part of a free and living act at the hour of death – if, and in so far as, this sense of sin is alive in the person or can be awakened out of its suppression. But the hoping act of acceptance of one's own situation can be implicit contrition. A person may sometimes succeed in achieving that more easily than in finding an express relationship to past events, to which he no longer feels related. This must also be remembered in connection with religious help for the sick – for example, with regard to the content of prayers said in the presence of the sick person.

THE FREE CHOICE OF DOCTOR

When we come to the claim which the liberty of the sick makes on the physician, we must first of all say something about the free choice of doctor. This is an essential sphere for the liberty of the sick person. If illness were a purely biological event which took place in some realm detached from the actual free person himself, it might be judged an open question whether the sick person must basically have the right to choose his doctor freely, or whether the State could prescribe a health-service functionary, in the same way that it prescribes other functionaries without asking our permission first.

But for the free person as such, a severe illness means a particular and unique situation. In order for him to fulfil his inner liberty, a person must in principle be conceded as wide a sphere of liberty as possible. Consequently the free choice of doctor is one of the essentials for liberty. Institutions and procedures such as the licensing of medical personnel, the appointment of official doctors for particular groups of people, the compulsory medical examinations required by the State – all these things should continually lead us to ask whether they are not reducing the free choice of doctor more than is absolutely necessary. And 'absolutely necessary' means more than is legitimately required by circumstances and by the legitimate pursuit of other benefits for society as a whole.

It is undoubtedly true that the free choice of doctor is often a mere faded ideal, which for social and economic reasons is largely becoming an illusion. Where this is the case, these social and economic conditions must be altered, in order to facilitate, in real terms, as free a choice of doctor as possible. Of course the right to a free choice of doctor must continually be a matter of fresh compromise with other human values and rights. We must not see it in isolation. But we might also ask whether the possibility of choosing one's doctor freely is not restricted by the unjustifiably high fees which doctors themselves charge. We might well ask whether it is right for doctors' fees to be thrown open to free competition, like the prices of other commodities, and whether to do so is not a contradiction of the sick person's right to choose his doctor freely.

THE RIGHT TO DIE

Part of the sick person's liberty with regard to his doctor is the right to die. We need not inquire here whether under certain circumstances the sick person may even have a duty to claim this right. At all events, the patient, as a free person, is not simply the object of the doctor who allows himself to be guided solely by his aim to prolong the biological life of the sick person for as long as possible, without any reference to other points of view held by the patient himself or by society. There are other values and aims which may make the sick person (or, it may be, someone close to him who represents his interests and is also called to defend his other rights too) freely express the wish not to be prevented from dying.

It is true that, according to the general Christian and Catholic view, it is not objectively and morally legitimate to will an action which is aimed directly at causing the death of the sick person. That is to say, no direct control over a person's biological life as a whole can be morally justified. But according to the view of Catholic moral theology, this does not mean that the patient or the doctor has the positive duty to apply every conceivable and actually possible means to prolong biological life. It is the generally accepted view of Catholic moral theology that the application of measures for a positively useful purpose – for example the relief of pain – is permissible even when these measures involve a certain curtailment of the patient's life, if this is an unintentional though known and accepted side-effect. For this is no different from what happens at other times in human life, when a person puts up with something which is harmful from a purely biological point of view if he can thereby arrive at a higher quality of living.

There are theoretical obscurities about these specific rules, which try to distinguish between the legitimate permitting of a person to die, and direct killing. These need further clarification. This clarification might perhaps bring about a considerable re-structuring of the answer to the problems we have touched on here. There are also practical difficulties about the actual application of these rules. But since it is impossible simply to get rid of the problems themselves, we may and must meanwhile work with rules and distinctions of this kind, in order to find a 'middle of the road' between euthanasia on the one hand (by which we mean the direct killing of a sick person at his request) and an absolute, unconditional will to preserve bio-logical life, without taking any other points of view into account. If we reject euthanasia in the sense in which we have defined it, and if we hold the preservation of biological life at all costs (even at the cost of inhumanity) to be wrong, then we shall have to accept the validity of the rule-of-thumb view we have indicated. We must simply see it *as* a pure rule of thumb, and hope that the moral theologians will clarify the problem further in the future.[10]

A more specialised question arises in this context too. Does the sick person's right to be allowed to die merely *permit* the doctor to accept his wishes, or does it actually lay on him the *duty* of allowing the patient to die? In a conflict between the patient's wish for a speedy end, and the doctor's will to preserve life for as long as possible, the doctor will in practice generally have his way and will override the patient's wishes. This will be the case especially if he has the impres-sion that the patient's desire is the expression of his illness and his

---

[10] For moral theology's view of euthanasia, cf. the articles by W. Schöllgen in *LThK* III, 2nd edn (Freiburg 1959), 1207–8, and H. Vorgrimler in *LThK* IX, 2nd edn (Freiburg 1964), 1053–4; also the bibliographies.

pain, rather than a genuine, personal decision; and if he is understand-
ably reluctant to do anything except fulfil his primary task as doctor
– to defend and preserve life. But this is not a solution to the problem.
Does the genuine, personal, carefully considered decision and will of
the sick person to accept death, even if it could be postponed for a
certain time, correspond on the doctor's side to a real moral duty to
carry out his patient's wish? For as doctor he has not merely entered
into the service of a physiological defence of life. When he accepts a
sick person as patient he accepts the duty to serve a person and his
total and entire life history (even if under a particular aspect).

It might be said that a problem of this kind is highly academic and
arises only in rare cases, because it can only be a question of the will
of a sick person during his illness, not while he is still in good health.
A decision of this kind made in health cannot simply be accepted as
being valid in the situation of illness. In illness itself a truly personal
will of this kind seldom exists, and the doctor is seldom able to
discern unequivocally that it exists. But we cannot view such cases
as impossible, and that means that the problem exists. In addition
there is the problem of whether the relatives of an unconscious and
dying person can on his behalf express the will to allow him to die,
and can express it in such a way that the doctor has the duty to carry
out their wish.

The question seems an obscure one. For in general a person's wish,
even though it may be morally legitimate, does not imply another's
duty to enable him to carry out his intention. Also – unless there is
an express agreement between patient and doctor – it is impossible
to prove that the acceptance of medical duties towards a particular
patient necessarily implies the readiness to carry out the patient's
wishes in this particular respect. Admittedly the opposite cannot be
proved either, in view of the doctor's role towards the patient as a
total person. We must also consider whether a doctor can opt out of
a doctor-patient relationship which was freely entered into on both
sides, if he is clearly confronted with the sick person's will to be
allowed to die. This question is hard to answer too; for on the one
hand a relationship that has been freely entered into can equally freely
be terminated; on the other hand, a sick person in the cases we are
assuming here will find it hard to find another doctor.

Basically speaking, I incline to the view that the doctor does have
the duty we have been discussing. This is the only way in which an
inhumane and undignified prolongation of life can be prevented. And

a doctor who recognises this duty will more easily get over his understandable reluctance to let a person die, even though he could have preserved his life for a while longer. But in these questions even Christian ethics no longer succeed in formulating rules which are factually   unambiguous,   directly   applicable   and   generally comprehensible.

Liberty is a mystery. In its fundamental character, it is the necessity imposed on man to decide freely for or against the Incomprehensibility which we call God. It is the possibility of letting oneself fall in hope and in unconditional trust into this Incomprehensibility as goal, bliss and human fulfilment. The highest power which liberty has is consummated in the helplessness of death. The doctor, too, is drawn into this individual history of liberty and death. He can really fulfil his very own, specific task (as distinct from other human acts) only if he is more than a physician – if, in the fulfilment of his medical task, he is truly man and even (anonymously[11] or expressly) a Christian. For that reason the liberty of the sick person, which arrives at its final frontier and its completion in the process of dying, cannot be a matter of indifference to him. He, too, is fighting for the space for, and the right to, this same ultimate liberty. He – as well as the sick person – should resign himself in silent and serene hope to the mystery of death, after he has fought for this earthly life to the last possible moment. The doctor is a servant of liberty.

[11] For 'anonymous' in this sense, cf. 'Anonymous and Explicit Faith', *Theological Investigations* XVI (London 1979), pp. 52–9.

10

'THE INTERMEDIATE STATE'

HOW dogmatically binding is the concept of what we call 'the intermediate state'? I should like to offer a few ideas on this subject here. What is meant by the doctrine of the intermediate state is that between the death of any individual person, if it takes place before the general eschatological perfecting of all men, and the final consummation of all history (which we generally call 'the resurrection of the flesh' and 'the Last Judgement') there is an intermediate temporal state. Initially, we need not go into what the word 'temporality' could mean here, or how precisely we ought to conceive of it. What we are interested in is that, according to the definition of Benedict XII,[1] the glorification of the body does not take place 'simultaneously' with the personal state of the beatific vision, or purgatory or damnation, which ensue immediately after death.

My intention here is not to deny the doctrine of the intermediate state. I should only like to point out that it is not a dogma, and can therefore remain open to the free discussion of theologians. We shall leave the question open, whether in our time the doctrine of the intermediate state does not perhaps enjoy a certain merit on kerygmatic or didactical grounds, or for reasons connected with religious instruction, or with the history of thought. Where this intellectual framework is still alive and undisputed, and where it can without difficulty make clear to people what is really meant – the blessedness

[1] Benedict XII, pope 1334–42. Cf. his constitution *Benedictus Deus* of 1336 (Denz. 1000–2). According to the preliminary remark in DS this is a *definitio ex cathedra*, cf. A. Ahlbrecht, 'Zwischenzustand', *LThK* X, 2nd edn (Freiburg 1965), 1441–2 (with bibliography).

of their souls and the glorification of their bodies – no objection can be levied against it, even today. There is no reason against the proclamation of the real truths involved in the form of this particular notion. But again we need not go into that here.

Basically, I should like to postulate only the following: it is by no means certain that the doctrine about the intermediate state is *anything more* than an intellectual framework, or way of thinking. So whatever it has to tell us (apart from statements about the commencement through death of the final form of man's history of freedom, and about the inclusion of the body in this final form) does not necessarily have to be part of Christian eschatology itself. We might put the matter differently and say: no one is in danger of defending a heresy if he maintains the view that the single and total perfecting of man in 'body' and 'soul' takes place immediately after death; that the resurrection of the flesh and the general judgement take place 'parallel' to the temporal history of the world; and that both coincide with the sum of the particular judgements of individual men and women. As long as he can produce good reasons for his view he can go on maintaining his opinion, always provided that he does not mean that the time scheme of world history itself can also be eliminated from his theological statement.

If we are properly to appreciate the arguments for the latter thesis, in the form to which we have narrowed it down, we must not overlook the fact that it is essentially a negative one. That is to say, it explicitly does not aim to offer any stringent proof which would lead to a direct denial of the intermediate state. However, we can here only briefly indicate the line of argument; for my aim is merely to encourage a further investigation of the question.

The doctrinal statements of the Church as we have them, in the dogmatically binding form in which Benedict XII and others put them forward, were not really concerned thematically and directly with the question which we have defined above. They are concerned to make other assertions, even though they do rest on the assumption that there is such a thing as an intermediate state (a presupposition which they do not really consider as if it were a separate question of its own). For this is what seems to follow from the fact that the glorification of the body has not yet taken place, although the person has already passed through death. It is this unconsidered assumption, therefore, which lies behind the doctrinal statements we have referred to. The statements themselves talk about the things which they want to say clearly and unequivocally, in the light of this assumption; but they do not teach the assumption itself as a truth that is binding for faith. There is no doubt that what the defined statements want to do is to stress the perfecting of the soul and the glorification of the body as Christian truths. Anyone who thinks that he can maintain this doctrine in all its fullness without continuing to presuppose an inter-mediate state in the sense in which we have defined it, is not com-pelled to go along with the underlying assumption behind the doctrinal assertion. We might illustrate this by taking just one specific example from the recent history of theology: monogenism – the idea that mankind stems biologically from a single pair of ancestors.. Any-one who can make it plain today that we can adhere to the doctrine of original sin even without the notion of monogenism, is not bound to acknowledge monogenism for the sake of original sin; even though traditionally and hitherto the two tenets have always been formulated together.[2]

WHAT DO THE SCRIPTURES SAY?

But is not the tradition we have mentioned in connection with our question really derived from holy Scripture? In other words, ought we not to judge the presupposition too as belonging to revelation? In order to understand and interpret the statements of Scripture correctly here, we must remember that in the Scriptures 'the resurrection of the flesh' is not understood as being the final destiny of the body as such. On the contrary, the statement always means the destiny of the one and total person who as such *is* 'flesh'.[3] It is true that Scripture is also familiar with the phrase 'to be with Christ', which belongs to the Christian's death – that is to say, entry into paradise 'today', at the moment of death.[4] But the two assertions belong to two quite different series of statements or statement complexes, and they are not harmonised in the Scriptures by means of the notion of the intermediate state.

[2] For details see the recent account by the present author in the digression 'Erbsünde und Monogenismus' in K.-H. Weger, *Theologie der Erbsünde* (Quaestiones Disputatae 44) (Freiburg 1970), pp. 176–223. Here the author also considers his own earlier remarks on the subject.

[3] Cf. also the essay 'The Body in the Order of Salvation', pp. 71–89 in this volume.

[4] Cf. Luke 23:43; John 5:24.

If we are to see this clearly, we must notice the origin and history of the two statement complexes in the New Testament. The relatively late doctrine about the future resurrection of the righteous, and then of all men (which was still disputed at the time of Jesus), was based on the conviction that God demonstrates his mighty will to salvation for his people of the covenant.[5] This divine will salvation is subsequently applied to the individual as such, because this individual is to participate in the final salvation of God's people, even if he dies before that people is finally redeemed by God. He must be saved, he must 'rise again'. But this salvation means the one and total person, not merely his body; for even the 'Sheol' of the Old Testament[6] is anything but the *salvation* of the 'soul'. Consequently we can in no way appeal to 'Sheol' for the idea of a (happy) intermediate state. So when we read in the New Testament that at the moment of death a person is already 'in paradise', or 'with Christ', this only means that death, too, belongs to the powers and forces which ultimately cannot harm the man or woman who lives through his faith in Jesus Christ. The actual way in which this idea is to be realised (and above all the way in which it can perhaps be harmonised with the doctrine about the eschatological raising of the dead) is not considered in any detail in the Scriptures. Can the two statement complexes be made to coincide, partially or wholly? That is the very question which must remain open. Traditionally, people have tried to reconcile the two ideas theologically by means of the notion of the intermediate state. But the success of the attempt is just what we are calling in question here. At all events, this idea must be laid to the account of this late theology; and it is that theology which risked this formulation. It is not in itself New Testament doctrine. In this connection it is interesting to note that, in interpreting the liberation from Sheol of the people who died before Christ by the dead and risen Christ himself, the great majority of the Fathers understood it in the light of Jewish teaching about the resurrection. They saw it as a *physical* resurrection, not as the freeing of the soul alone for the contemplation of God. The attempt to harmonise the statements of an individual and a collective eschatology is accordingly a problem of theological history in the first place. At

[5] Cf. Paul's behaviour before the Sanhedrin, Acts 23:6–8; also Luke 20:27; Acts 24:15, 21.

[6] For an explanation DB points to '*enfer*' (hell) and Hades; cf. *DBS* II (Paris 1934), 1063–76. Haag, *Bibel-Lexikon*, 2nd edn (Zürich 1968), 1537, refers the reader to '*Hölle*' (ibid., 758–9) and '*Totenreich*' (ibid., 1773–4).

the period of Benedict XII it received an answer to some degree, and at least temporarily, through Benedict's decision, according to which the soul was assigned a perfection of its own, which is completely independent of the future fate of the body. But even this decision does not forbid anyone to teach that the soul may possibly enjoy *greater* blessedness *after* the resurrection of the body.

IMPLICATIONS FOR THE HISTORY OF THEOLOGY

After all that we have said, we must come to the conclusion that the genesis of the idea of an intermediate state in the Middle Ages was a stage in the history of theology, but no more than that. It is the attempt to reconcile the collective and the individual view of eschatological perfection. But the word 'intermediate' is not really covered by what is meant. It has to be understood as the 'intermediate' point between two other points in a movement of thought which, though it starts from two different statement complexes, is supposed to come together today in complete identification, by way of the partial identification of the statements with the help of the notion of the intermediate state. But to see and formulate the matter in this way by no means involves asserting that in our own time we no longer need to think about the nature of collective, cosmic perfection, simply because we want to bring together the collective aspect of eschatology, in the resurrection of the dead, and the individual eschatological blessedness of the individual soul, without any such intermediate state – that is to say, without an intermediate period of time. For we ought at least to read what we have said about the individual into the concept of the final consummation, as one element of a progressive transformation of world history and the cosmos in general.

But the idea of the intermediate state also comes up against considerable intellectual difficulties, even if we ignore for a moment the problems which could not even be entirely suppressed in classical theology. These difficulties are above all those which are related to the question of 'time' 'after' death. The assumption of an intermediate state raises new, difficult problems here, which do not crop up at all if the one and total person is removed from empirical time through his death. How are we to think of time and the temporality of a departed soul, if on the one hand the soul is already with God in its perfected state, but on the other hand has 'to wait' for the reassumption of its function towards its own body? Does not a word such as *aevum*, or the like (which designates the duration of a finite but completed substance, no longer possessing a free history of its own), simply cover up the problem, instead of illuminating it? Do not words of this kind smack somewhat of mythology? Do they not blur what is really a radical difference – the radical difference between, on the one hand, a temporal state which is not merely our experience of time in the sense of physics, but which has freedom as its very essence; and, on the other hand, the final consummation of the history of freedom which can then no longer be thought of in terms of time at all? For otherwise we should be immediately faced once more with the question, why in such an *aevum* (or whatever we like to call this 'time') free history is no longer possible. Here, however, as we said above, we shall leave these problems about time on one side, although people were highly conscious of them earlier as well, in connection with the notion of the intermediate state. But there are still other difficulties today.

The classical doctrine of the intermediate state must reckon speculatively with an *anima separata*. But this idea leads to a number of dilemmas, which seem insoluble if we take as our premise the doctrine of the soul which defines it as being the *forma corporis*, and which asserts the real, substantial unity of body and soul.[7] For if we really take seriously this doctrine of the *anima* as being the *forma corporis* through its own substantial reality, the act whereby the body is 'informed' by the soul is not an additional and (in the scholastic sense) 'accidental' determination of that soul. The informing is identical with the soul itself. A denial of this statement would mean the abolition of a real substantial unity of man, whether this be admitted or not.

But then, how can there afterwards still be an *anima separata*? Can the soul lose something with which it is identical, without itself ceasing to exist? Earlier, I myself tried to avoid this dilemma by postulating a cosmic relation between the finite human spirit and matter, that is to say, the *one* matter of *the world*. This relation would then still remain and would be preserved even when the precise way in which, during its earthly life, the body is formed through this relation between matter and spirit ceased to exist. But it must be admitted that the whole problem becomes much easier if this enduring relation between spirit and matter is expressed scholastically as the

[7] Council of Vienne, 1312: Constitution *Fidei catholicae*, cf. Denz. 902.

enduring 'informedness' of the glorified body by the perfected spiritual soul. Indeed, probably no metaphysically thinking theologian would continue to maintain today (for either philosophical or theological reasons) that the identity of the glorified body and the earthly body is only ensured if some material fragment of the earthly body is found again in the glorified body. For this kind of identity cannot even be found in the earthly body, because of its radical metabolic processes. And this kind of thinking is completely inconceivable with a modern conception of matter, since for modern natural philosophy it is extremely problematical, if not impossible, to split up mere matter into so many 'substantial' and clearly divisible particles, as pre-scientific experience believed could be done. How would it in any way serve the identity between the earthly and the glorified body if we were to think into the resurrection body a material particle of this kind, which had earlier been the 'property' of the earthly body? Anything of this kind is today simply no longer tenable or conceivable. For us, identity consists, now and in the future, of the identity of the free, spiritual subject, which we call 'the soul'. That is why even empirical experience of the corpse in the grave can no longer provide an argument for there having been no 'resurrection'. So why should we not put the resurrection at that particular moment when the person's history of freedom is finally consummated, which is to say at his death?'

PHILOSOPHICAL BACKGROUND

A modern philosophy may be able to affirm and go along with the doctrine of the real distinction between body and soul, since this also makes it comprehensible that the person as subject of what is transcendent without limit, and therefore as the subject of freedom, cannot simply be matter in the normal sense of the material objects with which we are otherwise familiar.

But this means that for such a philosophy man counts empirically and ontologically, first and last, as being *one*. A pluralism of substance in him can only be viewed as the multiplicity of metaphysical elements, that is to say, ontological *principia entis*. It cannot be seen as the fundamental multiplicity of substantial realities, thought of as existing in themselves. At all events, contemporary philosophy only recognises man's spiritual life in so far as it is also and at the same time material in any given case. It simply does not exist in any other way and cannot be understood by philosophy in any other way either. Even the most spiritual act of man always has in reality a material element. An act of this kind may perhaps be thought of in abstract terms as being purely spiritual, but this is simply a process of intellectual conceptualisation.

On these presuppositions, the evidence for man's 'immortality' offered by a metaphysical anthropology cannot mean that the 'soul's' immortality has been established. On the contrary, the aim must be to show here that man, as a being of transcendence and freedom and of absolute responsibility in hope, must not think of himself in any way other than as a being who, through his own history of freedom, acquires finality before God. I believe that it is quite possible to show that this is so. In other words, in modern philosophy generally, what we traditionally distinguish (talking about the immortality of the soul on the one hand, and the resurrection of the body on the other) can only be grasped as *being one*.

But this means that the notion of the intermediate state recedes from the outset behind the questions which a philosophical anthropology is faced with today. It must be noted here, however, that the dogma of the resurrection of the body – as long as it is not misinterpreted in a mythological sense – can by no means be known only by way of revelation. Consequently it may be said that, in view of its understanding of the unity of man, modern metaphysical anthropology can never (or only with the greatest reservations) consider that an intermediate state, or an absolutely non-material mode of existence on the part of the spiritual subject, is possible.

The traditional scholastic doctrine about the *anima* as *forma in se subsistens*, which can then also exist as *separata*, is, in its own sense, not directly affected by this. That is to say, it can remain correct and meaningful, provided that it is no longer intended to mean more than that through his death man is not destroyed, but arrives at perfection. If, on the other hand, the doctrine is linked also with the notion that a soul can go on existing just by itself (since it no longer has its body), then *this* proof (which is really the only one which scholasticism puts forward) rests on an assumption for which there is no evidence. Indeed it can quite well be disputed, as is clear from what we said above. For it means quite simply the soul's absolute liberation from the body after death.

But quite apart from this assumption, a *forma in se subsistens*, which can be free of the body, has no sound reason in itself. For – once one has penetrated the determining conditions – why should a doctrine of the intermediate state still be forced on to a contemporary anthropology? For it is not at all certain that in theology this notion was ever more than a conceptual aid, designed to make clear (in the light of existing secular philosophical or vulgarly empirical views) that the Christian may be responsible before God for the final nature of his own free history. At the same time he would understand from this standpoint, too, that he cannot on his side exclude from this promised finality, *a priori* and platonically, what we know as his specific historical character, which is to say his body.

THEOLOGICAL OBJECTIONS

But the theologian might still have something more to say here. Against the view we have expounded, he might put forward the idea that the doctrine of the Assumption of the Blessed Virgin into eternal glory 'in body and soul'[8] proves after all the very fact that apart from Jesus other men and women are not granted such a destiny immediately after their death. But the definition of the Blessed Virgin's assumption does not tell us that this was a privilege which was reserved for her alone. Whether, when this dogmatic declaration was drawn up, those involved may privately have thought something like this is unimportant today. The patristic tradition (which there was certainly no intention to disavow through the dogma) often talks about such finally glorified persons. We may think, for example, of those whom the risen Lord liberated from Sheol. At the same time, there is a factual difference in the case of the Virgin Mary which also lent the express assertion its special cogency, for – other than the rest of the saved – she enjoys a position in Christian salvation history which is hers alone. For this reason it was quite justifiable to state the truth explicitly, even if it really applies to everyone who achieves blessedness. At all events we cannot view it as illegitimate to make this statement. After all, the degree of theological certainty differs according as to whether one and the same statement is made about Mary, the Mother of the Lord, or about the redeemed in general. However that may be: if we want to defend Pope Pius XII's dogma convincingly and effectively (especially to Protestant theology) the task is made considerably easier (and has considerably more chance

[8] Const. Ap. *Munificentissimus Deus*, of 1 Nov. 1950; cf. Denz. 3900–4.

of success) if we assume that it is superfluous to posit an intermediate state in considering the eternal salvation for which all men and women are destined.

Of course numerous other objections can be raised against this proposition, with the help of Scripture and tradition. There seem to be texts enough in which the matter is described in such a way that there would seem to be an intermediate state of this kind – texts which in no way reckon with the possibility that the human body, too, could already be glorified at death. But, as we have already said, do these texts really intend to expound an intermediate state as a truth binding on faith? Or do they merely presuppose it because at the time when they were formulated, in the aftermath of Platonism and under the influence of a naively empirical view of the corpse in the grave, nothing else could be said with regard to what they had to expound clearly as being a genuine part of actual Christian faith? That is the hermeneutical problem with which we are presented here.

After what we have said, however, we may now venture an answer to this. If earlier these questions were not distinguished, and if they could not be distinguished at the time (for reasons which although by no means genuinely theological, were connected with the history of thought), this does not mean that today, too, we are obliged to neglect the distinction between the binding content of a statement and temporally conditioned modes of expression based on an intellectual framework belonging to a particular period. Anyone who wanted to call this hermeneutical principle in question today would have to cling to other intellectual frameworks or ways of thinking as well, as if they, too, were statements of fact, even though they have meanwhile been abandoned, with the tacit or express approval of the Church's doctrinal authority. This would mean that we should have to believe that the earth is the centre of the universe, and that animal species are constant. We should have to adhere to monogenism, a 'materialist' view of the resurrection body, hell-fire in the physical sense, and the idea of a unified 'substance' in the eucharistic bread. We should have to believe that angels are located between the earth and the moon; that the longevity of the human race is strictly limited; that hell is to be found in the centre of the earth, and so forth.

In my view, the idea of the intermediate state contains a little harmless mythology, which is not dangerous as long as we do not take the idea too seriously and do not view it as binding on faith. Seen in that light, the strenuous efforts we have made here have perhaps used rather too heavy an artillery. On the other hand, it is impossible to overlook the difficulties many people find in this idea today. For these people it may be a help to say that the idea is not really strictly binding from a theological point of view, and that consequently it is open to the individual believer to follow the theological arguments which he finds convincing. And, as we said at the beginning, that is all we intended to establish here.

PART THREE

The Ministry and the Spirit

11

OPPOSITION IN THE CHURCH

THE POSSIBILITIES AND THE LIMITS

CRITICISM and opposition are part of human life in all its dimensions. But as a general rule they have a point only when the subjects and aspects concerned have a positive significance, fundamentally speaking, and therefore demand the courage for affirmation and inner open-mindedness. Anyone who can only criticise and oppose out of irritation repudiates himself, not the reality he is criticising. An allergic reaction, aggression, criticism and opposition can certainly be justified when someone is faced with any of the real facts of experience. But these are not a person's ultimate and sustaining basic attitudes.

When we talk here about opposition in the Church, we are not talking about criticism from outside, or about opposition in which someone says 'No' to the Church because he is outside it and – for whatever reasons – rejects it fundamentally and wholesale. What we are considering here is opposition within the Church. And this presupposes that the opponent still has a basically positive relationship to the Church. But we must realise at the very beginning that a positive relationship of this kind to the Church (and hence the position from which opposition within the Church operates) can be very varied and very intricate, both theoretically and practically. Accordingly the opposition itself will vary too; and the possibilities and limits of that opposition will not be the same for everyone.[1]

[1] The term 'opposition' generally means 'contrast' or 'resistance'. It is used mainly in politics and sociology (cf. *Brockhaus Enzyklopädie* XIII, 17th edn 1971, 762) for groups who want to destroy the influence of another group. The term is not used in that sense here (cf. below). On the contrary, here it means the attitude of independent criticism, or an independent opinion.

A person may be baptised as a baby; as he grows up he may have some connection with the Church's doctrine and life; he may support the Church financially; may draw on what the Church has to offer religiously, to some extent or other; and may not think of leaving the Church, for individual psychological and social reasons of the most varied kind – reasons which may perhaps be judged in a thoroughly positive way. Yet that person will not necessarily have that relationship to the Church which it fundamentally requires of its adult members, in the light of what it understands itself to be. For this relationship to the Church exists only when faith in its true Christian sense exists, too, and when, together with this faith, the Church is affirmed as well, as an integral part of its reality. That is to say, there is a proper relationship to the Church only when, in an absolute commitment of one's own existence, the God is apprehended who promises himself once and for all in Jesus, the crucified and risen One; and where, in this ultimate commitment to God in Jesus, the community of faith sustained by his Spirit is also accepted, as the irrevocable place of this faith; and is accepted in its fundamental institutional character as well.

But many Catholics who belong to the Church as a social institution do not have this real, believing relationship to the Church, or do not possess it clearly enough. They are members of the Church, perhaps because of family or social background, or the way they were brought up, or because they have a respect for it – all of which are reasons that precede faith. Because of the permanent temptation even to genuine faith, it is impossible to say with well-considered certainty in any specific, individual case, whether a Catholic has that relationship to the Church which is founded on faith, or only has faith's more limited, preliminary forms.

The nature of this relationship to the Church will also mean that opposition within it will take essentially different forms too. And individual Catholics will define the limits of their opposition in very different ways. If a person's relationship to the Church is merely a provisional one and is in no way based on faith's ultimate decision for God in Jesus Christ, that person will probably also consider that in certain circumstances opposition in the Church can be accentuated to the point of leaving it altogether. On the other hand, the person who takes the absolute character of his believing commitment to God in Jesus Christ with radical seriousness will not view a withdrawal of this commitment as being for him a real, inner possibility. In so far as he then makes this 'yes' to the Church part of his absolute commitment, he can and will quite unequivocally understand opposition and criticism in it only within the context of the Church itself. These varying forms of criticism and opposition ought not to be ignored. But here the important thing is above all the critical attitude which a believing – that is to say absolute – relationship to the Church presupposes.

THE POSSIBILITY AND NECESSITY OF CRITICISM WITHIN THE CHURCH

The first thing that must be said about our subject is that, fundamentally speaking, there can and must be opposition and criticism in the Church, as one of its inner elements. Of course this critical opposition, which is part of belonging to the Church, must immediately be differentiated according to the actual facts which are the subject of criticism in any given case. A critical question about the sense of a defined dogma in the faith of the Church is quite different in kind from opposition to the Church's legal, pastoral or liturgical practices; for the Church itself declares that these things are historically conditioned and can be changed. A basic calling in question of the Church's authority in general and as a whole is something different from a protest against a concrete measure which, for example, a bishop may enforce, appealing thereby to the authority of his office.

But for the moment we will leave all these necessary and indeed highly essential differentiations on one side. They must not be allowed to obscure the basic thesis: the thesis that the Church's self-understanding and its own faith do not merely permit the Catholic to have an oppositional relationship to the Church (at least in the sense we have described), or make this unavoidable. An attitude of this kind is actually required of us.[2]

Even as a Christian, the Christian is a human being first of all. As human being he is unavoidably and rightly a critical being; and the scope of his 'criticism' is fundamentally identical with the scope of

---

[2] The attitude meant here is anchored in a basic attitude of mind which is essential for the Christian: repentance, or readiness for a new beginning. It is not only absolutely necessary for the individual Christian, but is also essential for the Church as community. On these related ideas in the thinking and work of the present author, cf. K. H. Neufeld, 'Fortschritt durch Umkehr – Zu Karl Rahners bußgeschichtlichen Arbeiten', *SdZ* 192 (1974), pp. 274–81.

his existence. It is true that he must always be aware that critical reflection never adequately catches up with the assumptions on which he lives; and that consequently the human person, with a certain quite legitimate naivety and originality, still has the right to live according to principles which he has not adequately reflected about in a critical way. But in spite of that, man – and therefore the Christian too – is a critical being. And this also applies to the faith to which he is totally committed. Absolute commitment in faith can certainly coexist with critical enquiry about that faith in any specific individual, and the two do not have to be mutually exclusive – even though considerable theoretical and practical difficulties are inherent in a co-existence of this kind.

From its own point of view, the Church undoubtedly desires to be a power which is open to critical questioning. Its faith and the basic character which derives from that faith can be grasped only in free assent. And a free assent of this kind is possible only when the actual, specific existence of the assenting person is involved also.

The faith of the Church and the specific existence of the human person therefore exist in a permanent correspondence. On the one hand the Church is invoked by faith and, on the other, that faith is critically questioned by the believer. It is only in this way that the believer can grasp faith existentially – and because of man's historical character this is a continually new task. In the case of the true believer this critical undertaking will be continuously underpinned by an absolute assent of faith. It is borne up by a continuously renewed hope that in the future, too, this critical process will never destroy the ultimate commitment of faith.

Other realities in the Church are even more open to question, because of what they themselves understand themselves to be; for they view the Church itself as historically conditioned, as resting on human decisions, and therefore as alterable. Every member of it is empowered and obliged to help to shape this historical process of the Church, in proportion to his function and the possibilities open to him. In its fundamental nature the Church is a community of faith, faith in Jesus as the crucified and risen Lord, and in the eschatologically abiding historical presence of this faith (of course also in a basically institutional form). Apart from this fundamental character, the Church's constitution is alterable and hence open to criticism. The same applies to its liturgy and sacraments to a large extent. It applies even more to its concrete relationship to the historical, cultural and social situation in which it lives. And it applies also, naturally, to the specific and individual decisions of its office-holders.[3]

In short, from the point of view of the Church's self-understanding, a critical attitude on the part of the Catholic Christian to it is an essential characteristic of its nature. It does not mean any weakening of its character as Church, let alone a calling in question of that character itself. This applies both to the individual and to groups in the Church, who have no need to be empowered 'from above' before they can be set up. Of course in all this we must not overlook the fact that criticism cannot be the first and the last thing, either in human life or in the Church; and that criticism, if it is to be criticism of the Church from within, must rest on the basis of an ultimate assent to the Church's message and its self-understanding.

THE POSSIBLE DIRECTIONS WHICH CRITICISM OF THE CHURCH FROM WITHIN MAY TAKE

When we enquire in what direction criticism within the Church should be directed, we must remember that criticism does not necessarily have to be of an explicit and formal kind. Nor does it always have to be sustained by groups which have been formally constituted. It can also crop up under quite different names, and diffusely, so to speak.

Criticism can first of all take the form of a demand that the official proclamation of the faith make a more adequate attempt to bridge the gap between our contemporary awareness of things and the concrete way in which faith is proclaimed. This is, therefore, a criticism of theology, and of the proclamation of faith which is dependent on theology. This criticism is, of course, useful only when its demands respect the faith of the Church, its permanent identity and its historical continuity. But the boundary between permanent faith and an obsolete statement of that faith cannot always be drawn immediately and unequivocally. In this sector, too, petrified conservatism is just as possible as fashionable progressivism. This means that criticism and counter-criticism are often long-drawn-out processes which produce a sense of bitterness on both sides. We have to see them through with mutual tolerance, patience and hope; and all parties must clearly ac-

[3] Cf. some fundamental observations on the subject in 'Basic Observations on the Subject of Changeable and Unchangeable Factors in the Church', *Theological Investigations* XIV (London 1976), pp. 3–23.

knowledge Christianity's one and abiding faith in God in Jesus Christ.

Legitimate opposition and criticism may also be levelled at the Church's lack of commitment in its task towards 'the world' (that is to say, modern society, with all its individual structures and tendencies), or at the insufficiency of that commitment or its wrong orientation. This is fundamentally important but it is often fashionably distorted. Such criticism is justifiable and necessary if the Church is to fulfil its critical function towards the world and society truly and decisively. In this sector no one in the Church – neither authority nor critics – is safe from mistaken attitudes and false decisions which can have unforseeable historical consequences. Discretionary judgements and decisions must continually be made. The Church cannot be exempted from this task, and is even so continually exposed to the danger of blunders and errors. That explains the necessity, and the difficulty, of all criticism.[4]

These two somewhat arbitrarily chosen examples of the direction opposition and criticism may take, show that the objects of the criticism vary considerably. When we talk about criticism and opposition, we tend to think – perhaps too much as a matter of course – of authorities: priest, bishop, episcopal conferences, the pope. Of course the authorities and office-holders are at the receiving end of opposition and criticism. But we must not overlook the fact that criticism can and must be directed towards other people as well. The Church as a whole, in its different formal and informal groups, can be the recipient of criticism. For it is not as if only the office-holders cherish attitudes and make decisions which are open to criticism. The narrow-minded mentality of individual parishes, the traditionalist theology which is animated by academic historicism rather than by the problems of human existence today, the institutions supported by the laity, which only defend the *status quo* – in short, every kind of false and anachronistic attitude shown by individuals or groups in the Church – are at least just as important targets for opposition and criticism, especially since it is not as if reactionary authorities, with all their limitations, were confronted by an enlightened laity filled with positive aspirations for the future. It happens just as often that the office-holders, together with their outlook and the decisions

---

[4] The present author's short book *Strukturwandel der Kirche als Aufgabe und Chance'*, Herder Bücherei 446, 3rd edn (Freiburg 1973); ET *The Shape of the Church to Come* (London 1974), was written with the aim of concrete criticism and stimulus of this kind.

which emerge from it, merely reflect the mentality and attitudes of a large proportion of the rank and file of the Church. And it is by no means always certain from the outset that the critics are always right. So criticism always necessarily evokes counter-criticism.[5]

FORMS OF CRITICISM WITH THE CHURCH

What possible forms of criticism can there be within the Church, and what forms ought we to reject? What must be rejected in the first place is the attempt to undermine the Church, and to give it a completely new function. We may leave on one side here whether there have already been attempts of this kind in Church history, if perhaps under a different name. Today, at all events, one can notice here and there (and not only in Western Europe, but also in Latin America, for example) that people do not leave the Church, even though they reject what it understands itself to be and the substance of its faith, as this has been passed down to us; instead they want to remain within it in order to undermine it and reshape it completely. The underlying conviction here is that the Church, with its considerable membership and with its extremely powerful and differentiated institutions, still represents an immense power potential, even in today's secular societies. The idea is that, instead of patiently letting the Church die, in a long-drawn-out process, it should be altered in such a way that both it and its social power potential are placed unequivocally and solely at the service of those secular social aims and purposes which are viewed as being the right ones, with the greatest promise for the future. In other words, the aim is to reshape the previous dynamic of a vertical eschatological hope into an exclusively horizontally directed utopian power for worldly and secular changes in society; and here it makes no difference whether these goals are to be realised in an evolutionary or a revolutionary way.[6]

---

[5] On the 'uncontemporary Church' cf. *Strukturwandel der Kirche als Aufgabe und Chance*, Herder Bücherei 446, 3rd edn (Freiburg 1973), pp. 38–41, ET *The Shape of the Church to Come* (London 1974), pp. 35–7; and for the ideas arising from a particular case, 'Die Pflicht zur Diskussion' in *Chancen des Glaubens*, Herder Bücherei 389, 2nd edn (Freiburg 1971), pp. 227–37; ET 'The Duty of Discussion', in *Opportunities for Faith* (London 1974), pp. 40–5, 214–22.

[6] On the problem of 'horizontalism' and 'verticalism', cf. 'The Church's Commission to Bring Salvation and the Humanization of the World', *Theological Investigations* XIV (London 1976), pp. 295–313.

We do not find these tendencies only – or even primarily – where totalitarian States put the Church (in so far as it is not already dead) at the service of their own political goals, and at most allow her a provisional right to existence in that light, preferring to make a pact with an official Church which inclines to too rash and too short-sighted a compromise, rather than to co-operate with the living and critical forces in the Church. There are tendencies towards undermining and remodelling among ourselves, in the 'critical Catholicism' of the West as well. It goes without saying that the true Christian believer will reject these tendencies, and must do so; for Christian faith is faith in God and in an eschatological salvation for all. It is not merely a hope for a future, emancipated humanity which is to be realised in some transcending but untranscendental utopia.

An attempt of this kind is doomed before it starts, in the sense that it has no true chance of becoming an ultimate Christian decision of faith. A Church which, according to this view, would merely be the old-fashioned precursor of a secularised, emancipated society, is too uninteresting. It would be dead historically before it had even been modified along these new lines. And it would only be the executive officer of a secular society which has no need of a Church of this kind at all. People who stay in the Church – really only because of their individual background and upbringing – and want to remodel it into a secular association for humane purposes, or to make it a buffer against the upholders of an established social power, would be better able to pursue their intentions usefully and effectively outside it. The Church is not a suitable medium for these aims. One can perhaps undermine parties, and try to change their self-understanding; but the Church is not a suitable object for an undertaking of this kind, even from a worldly point of view.

If we ask about the possible forms of internal criticism and opposition in the Church, then we must not overlook the fact that there can be, and are, informal, non-institutionalised forms of opposition and criticism in the Church as well. These are ultimately perhaps more decisive than criticism and opposition, which see themselves as such and therefore institutionalise themselves. Ways of thinking and movements which – without being expressly 'against' something – develop new living energies directed towards positive ends, can in actual fact, through their persuasive character, exert a highly critical function, because the better and more living thing they are aiming at constitutes a silent but effective criticism of what is merely traditional.

We could give examples from the history of theology and thought, down to most recent times. Ways of thinking and conceptions have almost silently made their way, in a kind of meta-historical process, and have been absorbed into the total consciousness of the Church, without having been preceded by the fierce questionings and controversies which might have been thought appropriate to the significance and profundity of these changes themselves. We may cite the absorption of Greek metaphysics into theology from Origen onwards; or the victory of Aristotelianism in Western theology in the thirteenth century; or we may call to mind the contemporary attitude to universal salvation, compared with Augustinian pessimism. Of course these changes were accompanied by struggles and crises. But compared with the extent and profundity of the process itself, these struggles and crises were trivial.

Informal criticism and opposition of great influence do therefore exist in the Church itself, and not merely in the theological sphere. We find it even more in questions of attitude, in Christian life, in liturgy, in the relationship of believers to the world, and so forth. We can always have the hope that living forces in the Church will bring about changes, even when they do not expressly declare themselves as criticism and opposition.[7]

Of course there can and must be formal criticism in the Church as well. In most cases (though not necessarily and exclusively) it will be directed against the Church authorities, and will call in question alterable structures or specific decisions and actions on the part of those authorities. To have real prospect of success, such criticism will generally be sustained by groups and not by individuals.

GROUPS AND PARTIES

The actual, specific form of critical groups of this kind can, of course, vary greatly. There can be groups which exert a considerable critical function, even though their real and primary intention is directed towards positive purposes, and not criticism at all. We may think, for example, of the different religious orders which (at least in their early years) exerted a critical function of this kind. Today we may

[7] The great spiritual uprisings which led to the foundation of the great religious orders, of course, belong to this context (cf. below). It must be stressed in general that all the energies of a living Christianity can be implemented only in a process which must inevitably have a critical component.

think of the various 'charismatic' or 'pentecostal' movements, which have become quite widespread in the United States.[8] They do not see themselves as critical groups. All the same, they probably have a not unimportant critical significance for the Church. We may think of groups of worker priests in France, or of similar groups in Spain and Latin América, for whom social criticism plays a greater part. These groups pursue directly positive goals in secular society; but they none the less have a critical task to perform in the Church's particular situation.

It is, further, quite conceivable that critical groups should grow up within ecclesiastical institutions themselves: in parish councils, pastoral councils, diocesan clerical councils, synods etc. The critical intention of groups of this kind, within a particular institution, will normally play a prominent part. For it is this that gives them their specific function, especially since it must be presupposed that they fundamentally endorse these institutional bodies themselves, with their advisory functions or powers of decision.

Should we (or must we) talk about parties or about groups in this context? It is largely a question of terminology. But it depends on the facts as well. We may associate the term 'party' with a political grouping in a parliamentary democracy. In that case we understand by the word 'party' a group striving for political power, which aims to fulfil goals which are not shared by all members of the country, or citizens of the State, and which has a permanent organisation. In that case we ought not to talk about parties in the Church. Nor should we aim to have critical groups which incline towards acquiring a monopoly of power, in the way that political parties do.[9]

For various reasons, which do not need to be developed here, parties of this kind are hardly adapted to the nature of the Church, even though we might say that the formation of parties within it is

[8] On the 'pentecostal' movement in the Catholic church, cf. K. and D. Ranaghan, *Catholic Pentecostals* (New York 1969); E. D. O'Connor, *The Pentecostal Movement in the Catholic Church* (Notre Dame, Indiana, 1971); D. L. Gelpi, *Pentecostalism. A theological Viewpoint* (New York 1971); and *Pentecostal Piety* (New York 1972).

[9] For a detailed consideration of the problem of 'democratisation' in the church, cf. 'The Teaching Office of the Church in the Present Day Crisis of Authority', *Theological Investigations* XII (London 1974), pp. 3–30; 'On the Theology of a 'Pastoral Synod', *Theological Investigations* XIV (London 1976), pp. 116–34.

primarily a political question, not a dogmatic one. Organised parties in the Church would lend an institutional, absolute, permanent and fixed form to religious differences. People and groups would remain permanently at enmity with one another. Ecclesiastical parties would be mixed up with political parties and different political systems. The result would be nothing less than the danger of a schism in the real sense. Consequently there were no parties at the Second Vatican Council, however distinct the various trends may have been. In all the decisions that were taken, great weight was laid on achieving a bigger majority than any individual group could produce by itself, even if that group alone was actually in a position to provide a majority as such.

A warning like this against the formation of parties in the Church is not of course intended to recommend or legitimate a state of affairs in which individuals or individual groups have no influence at all on the people who are in positions of power in it. That would really be precisely the same thing as the establishment of a particular party with absolute power, even though it rejected the name as such and wanted to give the impression that it alone was the representative of the whole, true Church.

There is, therefore, no objection to be made if groups are formed within the Church's institutions with distinct ways of thinking and aims. On the contrary, there is much to recommend it. These are party groups in a certain sense, and can provide a greater and more comprehensive flow of information among their members, can offer a better opportunity for intensive discussion, and guarantee a more regular, intelligible solution of conflicts within the institution in question. But there must be no party discipline in these groups, and no 'party whips'; that would be contrary to the nature of the Church. They should have ever-open doors, should be self-critical, and should not view their opponents as enemies. Moreover, they should not, out of group fanaticism, reject the compromises which are always necessary, in view of differences of mentality in the Church. They should not be worshippers of a mere formal democracy. They should also be able to leave controversial questions open. And they should prefer to elect persons, not the representatives of a particular 'party line'. Otherwise groups of this kind could damage the very character of the Church. For it ought to be the very place in which social antagonisms are overcome and absorbed, not multiplied by ecclesiastical antagonisms as well.

Even in the institutional sphere the Church must present itself as the community of faith, love and prayer in spiritual unity, in free consent and concord, and with mutual open-mindedness. The Church confesses Jesus as the One who was victorious in defeat; and one of its fundamental convictions is that the goals we have described cannot be seized by force, or by means of institutions and their power. We can arrive at them only through the bold powerlessness of the Spirit and of hope. Neither should groups within the Church view its authorities arrogantly as mere 'adversaries' of the Spirit, whom they reserve for themselves. They should rather try to activate the potential of hope (if we may so describe it) and to draw on that; and today this is often much greater among office-holders than resentful critics of the Church in its existing form believe. The attempt must be made. If the groups we have talked about were expressly or tacitly to be transformed into real, organised parties, then it must be feared that elements of essential importance would simply wither away, namely the living enthusiasm which is so necessary in the Church especially; the creative imagination that reaches out towards an unknown future; and the courage to think or do the unusual.[10]

[10] Cf. here 'Angst vor dem Geist' and 'Über das Experiment in christlich-kirchlichen Bereich', both in *Chancen des Glaubens*, Herder Bücherei 389, 2nd edn (Freiburg 1971), pp. 52–7 and 238–47; ET 'Fear of the Spirit' and 'Experiment in the Field of Christianity and the Church' in *Opportunties for Faith* (London 1974), pp. 40–5, 214–22.

12

'MYSTERIUM ECCLESIAE'

ON THE DECLARATION MADE BY THE CONGREGATION FOR THE DOCTRINE
OF THE FAITH ON THE DOCTRINE OF THE CHURCH

ON 24 June 1973, the Congregation for Doctrine published a 'Declaration (*Declaratio*) in defence of the Catholic doctrine on the Church against certain errors of the present day'. The Declaration was accompanied by the observation that Pope Paul VI had confirmed the declaration on 11 May 1973, and had ordered its publication.[1] In spite of its papal *imprimatur*, the *Declaratio* is of course the work of the Congregation for the Doctrine of the Faith, and has not the same authority as an act issuing from the pope himself. As a declaration of this kind, it cannot contain anything to

[1] ET *What We Believe: Declaration in Defence of the Catholic Doctrine on the Church against Certain Errors of the Present Day* (London 1973). For the official text of the Declaration, cf. *AAS 65* (1973), 396–408; Cf. also 'Irrtümer über die Kirche? Eine Dokumentation zur Erklärung der Glaubenskongregation vom 5. Juli' in *Herder Korrespondenz* 27, pp. 416–21 (German text) and 421–2 (comment by the secretariat of the German episcopal conference); 'Die Erklärung der römischen Glaubenskongregation "Mysterium Ecclesiae"' in *Herder Korrespondenz* 27 (1973), p. 487. It is generally accepted that the immediate occasion for the Declaration was the debate on infallibility started by Hans Küng. The original text of the present essay had to take express account of this topical question, which, however, may count today as superseded, at least from this point of view. Consequently the sections of the essay which had a particular bearing on that point have been omitted here, particularly since the present author's views on this particular case are sufficiently well known; cf. *Zum Problem Unfehlbarkeit: Antworten auf die Anfrage von Hans Küng* (Quaestiones Disputatae 54), 2nd edn (Freiburg 1971), and 'Schlußwort unter eine Debatte: Rahner-Küng' in *Publik-Forum* No. 11, pp. 12–15 (1 June 1973).

which a Catholic Christian has to give the absolute assent of faith; it is not, and does not claim to be, an 'infallible definition' of the magisterium. Of course this does not mean that many statements which represent the dogmas of the ordinary and extraordinary magisterium may in fact require this absolute assent of faith, because of their content and their binding character; but in this case the binding character is not lent by the document itself. Of course this general statement leaves many specific questions open, especially since the Second Vatican Council (which is frequently quoted in the Declaration) was not prepared to issue any new statements of faith. This means that, in spite of the appeal to definitions laid down by the First Vatican Council, the exact 'theological note' remains an open question in many other cases.

The Declaration is therefore an 'authentic' expression of the Roman magisterium. What this means in more precise terms does not have to be explained again here. The reader should turn to the letter on the magisterium issued by the German episcopal conference on 22 September 1967.[2] On the basis of that it must be said that, however much we may recognise the positively binding character of the document, the possibility that it may contain errors cannot *a priori* be excluded. Consequently a question of this kind may be investigated without reserve by Catholic theology, even though in the case of official definitions or dogmas of the ordinary magisterium (where these really are such, and are properly interpreted) no errors in the real sense may be detected. The interpretative possibilities which the document expressly concedes as regards magisterial declarations (and even dogmas) of course apply to the document itself as well.

The document has six sections, as well as an introduction. These sections are sometimes only loosely linked with one another. They deal with the following subjects: (1) The oneness of Christ's Church; (2) the infallibility of the universal Church; (3) the infallibility of the

[2] The 'Schreiben der deutschen Bischöfe an alle, die von der Kirche mit der Glaubensverkündigung beauftragt sind' ('Letter from the German bishops to all who have been entrusted by the Church with the proclamation of the faith') was distributed as an offprint by the secretariat of the German episcopal conference (2nd edn, Trier 1968). Cf. 'On the Encyclical "Humanae vitae"', *Theological Investigations* XI (London and New York 1974), pp. 263–87, and 'Heresies in the Church Today?', *Theological Investigations* XII (London 1974), pp. 116–41. The above letter is considered in detail in 'The Dispute Concerning the Church's Teaching Office', *Theological Investigations* XIV (London 1976), pp. 86–97.

Church's magisterium; (4) the Church's gift of infallibility not to be diminished; (5) the notion of the Church's infallibility not to be falsified; and (6) the Church associated with the priesthood of Christ (the general priesthood, and the official priesthood of its ministers). In the following pages we shall try to give a brief account of what is said in these different sections, and to add a critical appraisal. And here we shall allow ourselves the right to discuss the different points at greater length or more briefly, as the case may be.

The One Church of Christ

We shall pass over the introduction and turn directly to the first section, on the Roman Catholic Church as the 'one Church' of Christ. In view of the importance of its subject, this section is extremely brief. Broadly speaking, it merely repeats statements made by the Second Vatican Council.[3] Of course, one of the convictions of a Roman Catholic Christian is that he cannot quite plainly and simply concede the character of being the Church of Christ to the various other Christian Churches or ecclesiastical communities to an equal degree. An ecclesiological indifference of this kind is not practised, and cannot be practised, by the other Christian Churches towards one another either. All the same, we might have expected – and perhaps had the right to expect – that the document would show more of an ecumenical will towards real progress in the direction of Church unity here.

The fact that the Roman Catholic Church traces its origin to Jesus and his declaration to Peter is undeniable; but here it is stated too simply, from a historical point of view. We read that the Roman Catholic Church contains 'the fullness of the means of salvation', 'all divinely revealed truth', and 'the original Apostolic tradition, living and intact, which is the permanent heritage of doctrine and holiness of that same Church'; but it would not have been out of place to add at least a word to the effect that in the Catholic Church as it actually exists, the whole 'fullness' of what the Church contains is actually realised in its different parts and aspects to a very varying degree, and that much exists only potentially – especially if we compare merely

[3] Especially the dogmatic constitution on the Church 'Lumen gentium' (text in *The Documents of Vatican II*, ed. W. M. Abbott (London 1966), pp. 14–101.

potentially given elements of this kind with the degree in which they are realised in other Churches.

Why does this text avoid the issue by means of the statement that the Church is a Church containing many sinners, which is of no relevance in this particular context? Why does it not talk about the fact that in the course of history this sinfulness (if we see it properly) has also produced a frightful number of errors and distortions of the Christian spirit 'in the head and the members'? And that the Church is not merely a sinful Church, but an erring one as well, even though it cannot fall away from the truth of Christ when it teaches and believes with the absolute assent of faith?[4]

Why was the dividing line between the Roman Catholic Church and the other Churches not also seen in the light of the fact that the actual relationship between the Churches has changed considerably since our divisions began? At least we can find no trace of this idea. When the document says that a Catholic must not imagine that the Churches, though 'divided, still possess a certain unity', that is simply not correct. The Churches today do 'still possess a certain unity', and it is this very fact which enables and obliges us to strive for full unification.

Apart from this point, everything which is said in the first section may be binding on a Catholic. But many things are not said at all which ought to have been said, if we want really to reach the spirit and heart of the 'divided' brethren. In the spirit if not in the letter, this text lags behind the Second Vatican Council, although in the Council's spirit it might have taken us further by means of its theological reflections on the unity and division of the Churches, and on the self-understanding of the Catholic Church. For according to this very self-understanding, the Catholic Church is only what it ought to be, according to the will of Christ, when it has come to terms with the things in its own history which, whether culpably or not, have contributed to the division of Christendom (and even an orthodox Christian may doubt whether enough has been done here), and when all the Churches have once more become one. The first section would not have had to be much longer in order to say something clearer in this direction, and something with more promise for the future.

---

[4] Cf. here the present author's more recent reflections: 'Schism in the Catholic Church?', and 'Heresies in the Church Today?', *Theological Investigations* XII (London 1974), pp. 98–115 and 116–41 respectively.

The Infallibility of the Church

The second section of the document is divided into two parts. The first deals with 'the infallibility of the universal Church'. The second stresses the special function of the bishops' magisterium for the faith of the whole Church. This leads on to the following three sections. As far as the first part is concerned, we must first of all stress with satisfaction that the treatment of the Church's magisterium, which is infallible in certain circumstances, is subordinate to the statement that it is the Church as a whole which abides in the truth of Christ (though of course this truth is also articulated in the form of particular tenets). This is an advance which should be appreciated, and it is expressly and gratefully acknowledged.

Admittedly, when we read that the new people of God is itself infallible in faith, through 'a certain shared infallibility', bestowed by God, 'and restricted to matters of faith and morals, which is present when the whole People of God unhesitatingly holds a point of doctrine pertaining to these matters', then we might have wished for a more precise and careful formulation. For one thing, the limitations indicated by the word 'shared' must not be overlooked and ought to be considered by theologians much more carefully. For another, have there not also been convictions 'unhesitatingly' shared by 'the whole people of God' (in so far as this is an empirically comprehensible entity, and consequently at all relevant for the determination of faith) that this or that was part of faith, even though this firm conviction was mistaken? Instead of 'unhesitatingly holds' the document should have talked about 'an absolute assent of faith'.

Of course in this case another question would have become even more inescapable: how can we empirically determine this absolute 'assent of faith' as distinct from other firm convictions and opinions? For even 'generally shared' and 'firm' convictions can be erroneous. The difficulty we are faced with here is, therefore, very considerable, because in the case of particular dogmatic statements dating from earlier times we have to distinguish between the assent of faith and other 'general' and 'firm' convictions; and yet today we cannot clearly decide by historical means alone whether this distinction was consciously made. (When we are considering the period of the Council of Trent, for example, how are we to distinguish historically between the assent of faith to original sin – which was correctly understood – and the firm conviction of monogenism?) But again, we are grateful to the document for deciding, with Paul VI, that the official doctrine of the Church 'is nourished by the ecclesial life of the whole People of God'. That is to say, there is no one-way relationship between the two; it is a mutually conditioning relationship.

The second part of the second sanction is concerned with the special function of the Church's magisterium as represented by the pope and the bishops, compared with the total faith of the Church. Of course the pope and the bishops are not merely 'experts in Catholic doctrine'. Of course the pope cannot merely represent an already existing, silent consensus in the Church. Of course, in certain situations and according to certain norms (which no one will expect this section of the document to discuss), he can make a decision about a disputed question which is really a question of faith – a decision which can even be ultimately binding.

But must these axioms be formulated by saying that the hierarchy *'alone'* has the 'exclusive' task of teaching the Gospel 'authentically'? G. Philips warned about 'exclusive' formulas of this kind at the Council, on an occasion when the 'highest authority' intervened. Of course, the specific task of the hierarchical magisterium can be defined in such a way that this authority belongs to that hierarchy 'exclusively'. But even in the Church there is an authority of 'the thing itself', an authority of theological scholarship, an authority of the person who is charismatically endowed, and so forth. And without these the one authentic doctrine of the magisterium and the authority of the hierarchical magisterium cannot exist. Even less can it be efficacious; because all the elements in the Church always condition one another. The 'considerable assistance' which the fifth section says the theologians offer to the magisterium is in fact an indispensable aid, seen historically and theologically, which in no way detracts from the magisterium's dignity and specific function. The actual carrying out of the functions of the hierarchical doctrinal office is never 'exclusive', and it is not a one-way process. It is never merely 'from above', because it presupposes the life of the whole people of God, and presupposes, too, that this people 'abides in the truth'.[5]

A more fundamental desideratum must be understood in this light. The function of the magisterium is not linked clearly enough or with sufficient inner cogency with the infallible faith of the whole Church.

---

[5] Cf. the essays on ecclesiology in *Theological Investigations* XIV (London 1976), pp. 3–134.

It would have been more in keeping with contemporary theology and with vital and active acknowledgement of the authority of the hierarchical magisterium, if the magisterium's authority had not simply been based on the formal, 'legal' authorisation of Peter and the other apostles, and therefore of bishops and pope. We might wish that its existence and unique character had been made comprehensible in the light of the Church's character as the eschatologically definitive community of faith.

The Church is governed by a mutually conditioning relationship, as must be the case in a unity consisting of pluralistic elements: the community of faith would not exist at all if it did not have institutional form; in that way the faith of the whole Church is essentially co-conditioned by the specific function of its authentic teachers. On the other hand, their function is conceivable only as one aspect of the eschatologically indestructible community of faith. It does not supervene from outside, by means of an authorisation which is simply conceived of in juridical terms. A true understanding of the Church's infallibility is possible only if we heed this relationship between the authority of the magisterium and the whole Church's invincible grace of faith, from which even the office-bearers, with their specific function, live.

The Infallibility of the Magisterium

The third section repeats in the briefest possible terms the traditional doctrine about the 'charism of infallibility' which makes it possible to utter statements which are 'necessarily immune from error'. There is no attempt to give a reason for the First Vatican Council's definition of this infallibility.[6] It may of course be said, pointing to the first paragraph of the document's final declaration, that nothing of this kind was intended, and could not be attempted in view of the brevity required. But if what is in question is not an individual doctrine of faith (which can be safeguarded by an appeal to the general formal authority of a council or a papal definition), but is the formal authority of councils and the pope in general, then it is not enough to counter opponents, doubters and interpreters of this doctrine simply by quoting the statements this authority has made about itself. And this is

---

[6] Cf. 'Constitutio dogmatica I "Pastor aeternus" de Ecclesia Christi' of the First Vatican Council, Denz. 3074–5.

especially the case because today not only the infallible authority of the pope (which Vatican I taught in its capacity as council) but also even the authority of councils themselves is being called in question or narrowed down. A section of this kind does very little to substantiate the teaching of the two Vatican Councils, especially since it issues from an authority which is itself subordinate to the authority of pope and councils.

This brings us to a question of which the Church's authorities have up to now shown insufficient awareness and to which they have provided no adequately clear answer. To put it honestly and soberly: the Roman authorities apparently proceed from the assumption that they have to state correct doctrine and issue the correct edicts, appealing to their formal authority; and that when they have done this they have performed their task adequately. They still presuppose as a matter of course that what they have in front of them is an obedient flock. But today, more than in earlier times, they must see to it, not only that they are right, but also that they are seen to be right. They ought to present their authority in a more living and primal way, deriving it from the centre of the Christian faith. They ought to interpret their authority to contemporary believers persuasively. And they must not simply assume that the faithful are convinced of the authority of the papal office and the bishops, simply because they want to live in the Catholic Church.

A Roman theologian once said to me, when I pointed this out, that these things were the function of theologians and preachers, not the function of the magisterium itself. Of course theologians have tasks of which the magisterium should not and cannot relieve them. But this does not free the teaching authority from its duty, which is not simply to repeat the old formulations but as far as possible to present them in a modern and persuasive way. Otherwise progress in the official doctrine of the Church would be superfluous. All progress could lie only in the realm of theology. But this would contradict the document itself and would make a clear-cut distinction between statements of faith and statements of theology which does not and cannot exist.

Let me draw attention to one other statement in this section: the Church's doctrinal authorities must apply 'appropriate means' in order to ensure that its teaching really does represent divine revelation in any given case. For in this task it does not receive any 'new revelations' – nor, consequently, is it revealed that a particular, already existing doctrine is actually part of revelation. It is good that this should be said, although it has already been expressed in the proceedings of the First Vatican Council and in the text of the Second. But could not the magisterium say more clearly what these 'appropriate means' are? And what kind of procedure must it adopt, or does it intend to adopt, in the intellectual and social climate of today, in order to make a judgement?

As long as he is left in the dark about the nature of these necessary processes in arriving at a judgement, before decisions are made about doctrine, the average Christian and theologian has all too easily the impression that, without admitting it, Rome is convinced that it can operate with new revelations (at least where what is at issue is whether a particular statement is included' in revelation). It is not then surprising when some people mulishly kick against the magisterium. In order to make its authority effective, the magisterium ought today to make clearer and more transparent what the document calls the necessary processes by which it arrives at a decision. To take one specific example, something like this was attempted by commissions of bishops and theologians at the order of the pope in connection with '*Humanae Vitae*'. Unfortunately the final decision bypassed these commissions entirely. A doctor of the Church, Cardinal Bellarmine, gave an urgent warning against proceedings of this kind a long time ago.[7]

Warnings

The fourth section is a warning against any diminution of the Church's infallibility. We are told that 'the faithful are in no way permitted to see in the Church merely a fundamental permanence in truth, which, as some assert, could be reconciled with errors contained here and there in the propositions that the Church's Magisterium teaches to be held irrevocably, as also in the unhesitating assent of the people of God concerning matters of faith and morals'. The doctrine put forward here about the nature of truth and the freedom from error of the Church's dogmas is complex and subtle. Its ex-

---

[7] Cf. 'Epistola ad Clementem VIII circa controversiam de Auxiliis' (1602). The Italian original is printed in I. von Döllinger, *Beiträge zur politischen, kirchlichen und Cultur-Geschichte . . .* , vol. iii (Regensburg 1882), pp. 83–7; German translation in I. von Döllinger and Fr Reusch, *Die Selbstbiographie des Cardinals Bellarmin* (Bonn 1887), pp. 260–4.

pressly formulated statements give rise to a whole number of further problems, so that the theologian feels confirmed in his ultimate uncertainty. For this document does not say clearly what an erroneous theological proposition is, or how such a proposition is really to be distinguished from propositions whose historical character and imperfection this document admits, even in the case of dogmas. In fact, to put it briefly, the sentence we have quoted from the beginning of the fourth section of our document is correct. Apart from that little more can be said about this section.

The teaching of the Second Vatican Council about 'the hierarchy of the Church's dogmas' is reiterated. But when the document goes on to say that 'all dogmas must be believed with the same divine faith', this is too easy a way out; and the existential and ecclesiastical significance of the hierarchy of truths becomes illusory. Of course a Catholic Christian cannot absolutely deny any of the dogmas. But does every Catholic have to affirm every single dogma as such with a positive, absolute assent? If we presuppose this, then the doctrine about *'fides implicita'*, the theological question about the extent of what has to be explicitly believed as necessary for salvation, and really the teaching about the hierarchy of truths as well, would in fact no longer have any practical significance. We cannot go on to show here the great ecumenical import of this question. Of course, I do not mean to maintain that our text intends to say that every dogma has to be explicitly 'believed' in the sense we have rejected as inadmissible here. But would it not have been possible more clearly to avoid misunderstandings of this kind which harm the cause of ecumenism?

The Historical Character of Dogmatic Formulations

The fifth section seems to be the best in the whole document. The first part deals with the historically conditioned character of all statements of faith. Here the theologian can read statements which were largely foreign to the magisterial statements about the development of dogma. Up to now – really until Paul VI – it was conceded to a certain degree that dogmatic formulations have a history of their own. But, broadly speaking, it always seemed as if the magisterium admitted only to an *earlier* history, which had now reached a culmination never to be surpassed, (and which could not really proceed any further). Moreover, the terms used in the present dogmatic formulations were insistently claimed to be unambiguous and easily understood by everyone.[8]

What we hear in the first part of the fifth section is more courageous and more in accordance with historical reality. From the point of view of the stage reached by theology, what is said here could and should really have been said in Pius XII's encyclical '*Humani generis*' (1950). But let us be glad that this teaching has been formulated now, even if very late.[9]

The document establishes first of all that the transmission of divine revelation is impeded by historical situations. Even dogmatic formulations are conditioned by terms which are dependent on the language and total situation of a particular era of thought. In this section it is assumed as if it were self-evident (and hence all the more significantly) that the Church's magisterium cannot simply on its own, in complete self-sufficiency as it were, form and determine the terms which it wants for its statements. The document stresses that a dogmatic truth may be imperfectly defined first of all, and that later, in the wider context of other truths of faith and other naturally communicated knowledge, it may be stated more fully and completely, so as to answer new questions, or in order to distinguish the truth of faith from newly arisen errors. The declaration says explicitly that the Church's magisterium can under certain circumstances enunciate dogmatic truths in terms which bear traces of 'the changeable conceptions of a given epoch'. We are told, however, rather curiously, that anything of this kind only happens 'sometimes' and that there are also truths of faith which could be expressed without historically conditioned terminology of this kind. Here the authors of the document are evidently still influenced by the earlier notion of 'natural' and general human terminology, which can always and everywhere be understood without further explanation, and which is independent of the wider context of the history of thought as a whole.

[8] We cannot discuss in detail here what is really an important presupposition of the document: that the history of dogma and theology is really progressive purely in the positive sense, with improved formulations etc. This tacit assumption is problematical (in general, but also in view of the rank and dignity of the New Testament etc.). Basically speaking, we ought probably to reckon with the contrary development as well; or at least the history of dogma ought if possible to be conceived of without any 'progressive' pattern of this kind.

[9] Cf. 'Humani generis' in *AAS* 42 (1950), 561–78 (of 12 Aug. 1950).

But ultimately that is a matter of indifference for a theology of dogmatic development. If there can ever be dogmatic formulations using terminology which is historically conditioned, then it is not difficult theologically to concede this to all theological statements. Whether this happens sometimes, or is really always so, is a question of dogmatic and theological history that has no essential theological relevance. We are also told that certain dogmatic formulas remain living and fruitful (always providing that they are newly explained), but that others can be, and have been, replaced by new formulations which give clearer and fuller expression to what is meant by the old ones. Dogmatic formulations do not always communicate their real meaning to the understanding of faith 'to the same extent'.

All these statements in the text are made in somewhat too 'retrospective' terms. There is no very explicit look at the future (even though we are told that not all the ancient formulas will have permanence to the same degree). But even so it is clear that the document is aware that, even today, the history of dogma and theology has not come to an end. It will and must continue. Old dogmas will have a continuing history which we cannot foresee.

Of course other things are stressed too. Firstly, that changes of this kind in dogmatic statements have to take place under the control of the magisterium; secondly, that in the historical succession of the formulations, what is really meant remains the same; thirdly, that the old formulations are still quite suited to define revealed truth if they are understood correctly – and that John XXIII taught nothing else at the opening of the Second Vatican Council, even if he and Paul VI stressed that the ancient dogmas must be so expressed that they truly reach the minds and hearts of the people of our time.[10] If it is denied in this context that dogmatic formulations are merely *commutabiles approximationes* (alterable conceptions, which only represent what is meant approximately), we must distinguish more precisely than the text does in its attempt to ward off 'dogmatic relativism'. If, as the text expressly says, statements of this kind can be replaced by new ones, which are better and more in accordance with the particular intellectual and spiritual situation, then this presupposes a certain,

[10] Cf. *The Documents of Vatican II*, ed. W. M. Abbott (London 1966), pp. 710–19 (Pope John XXIII's opening address), and 'Das Zweite Vatikanische Ökumenische Konzil' in *Herder Korrespondenz* 18 (1963/4), pp. 76–83 (Pope Paul VI's opening address).

perhaps necessary, change. Dogmatic formulations are therefore not simply '*incommutabiles*'. And if one dogmatic statement can express the same content in a better, more living, more fruitful, more complete and more perfect way than another (as the document says), then the term *approximatio* does not necessarily have the heretical sense of a dogmatic relativism. It can also mean exactly what this document intends. If a dogmatic formula were to be totally identical with the reality meant – if, that is, it was not an *approximatio* in any way at all – how could there ever be a history of dogma, which the document itself says exists? How could we then talk about better or less adequate dogmatic formulations, let alone about formulations that have to be superseded?

What the document teaches about the historical character of dogmatic formulations is certainly still abstract and formal. Nor has it completely resisted the temptation to make things easy for itself by making a simple distinction between modes of expression and content (though there can never be content without a certain mode of expression). But all the same it contains important implications which are no longer avoidable if this doctrine is to be reconciled with other undeniable facts and perceptions. Like the document, we may start from the conviction that an incomplete or imperfect statement does not necessarily have to be wrong; and that a more complete and more perfect statement does not falsify the one it supersedes. But what does this common conviction mean exactly, when it is applied to particular dogmatic statements, if we read these statements in their earlier historical context (which the document actually requires of us, so that we may determine their true, permanent meaning), remembering thereby that the Church's magisterium can err, and has often erred, in non-defined statements? And that such errors (since they affect the total intellectual consciousness) also influence the actual, apperceived sense of the dogmas? What is the meaning of the statement that there are more imperfect and more incomplete dogmatic statements, if we assume (as we must) that the incompleteness of a statement cannot be taken to mean that, while part of the subject considered is absolutely clearly, perfectly and completely formulated, another, different part of what is meant is left unstated – if, that is, one is unable to escape from this difficulty by quantifying the statement's content?

What is the position when a new statement has to be added to an old formula so that it may be perceived in living and fruitful form, and in its original sense (a proceeding which the document also views as necessary); but when this new statement is not in fact provided, or not yet provided, by the magisterium or by the majority of theologians? This possibility cannot be excluded *a priori*, if there is such a thing as a history of dogma, which has to lead to newer, better reformulations necessary for a particular period, but if (as many examples show) this history proceeds too slowly. What is the position with regard to ancient formulas which can no longer perform their proper service in a later period? If we say with the document that they have only to be explained in the proper way by the magisterium (with the valuable help of the theologians) for them to remain living and fruitful, that is all well and good. But it helps only if we assume that these explanations are actually made (and are in some way or other permitted by the magisterium) when the new need arises because the ancient formulations have proved inadequate. But this is very often not the case. What happens when ancient formulas, which remain, or which have to be replaced by new ones meaning the same thing, actually incorporate errors? What happens when this incorporation is not consciously recognised, or when it is not immediately admitted that the connection between true and false can be dissolved once this connection begins to cause difficulties?

Let me give one example of what I mean. For a long time the inspiration of Scripture was understood in such a way that inspiration was held to exclude pseudonymity, in cases where today we quite calmly admit it. Indeed this was an interpretation which took a long time to crumble away. To take another example – we are still labouring today over the question of whether the tridentine dogma of original sin can be reconciled with polygenism; that is to say, whether the monogenism which was associated with this doctrine can be detached from it, even though ancient theology never thought of such a possibility, or could do, when it formulated this dogma.

Finally, there is one more thing that must be considered. The fifth section of the document somehow starts from the assumption that it is possible to distinguish the real meaning of a dogma from its changing formulation. It assumes that we can grasp the two things separately, compare the one with the other, and so determine the lesser or greater aptness of a dogmatic formulation. But if this is not the case (as a comparison between 'the thing in itself' and its interpretation in any given instance shows) – if, therefore, we can never determine and overcome the historical character of a formulation by means of a non-historically conditioned formulation – how are we to think of this historical development, which the document itself concedes? Is it possible to conceive of it in such a way that it covers the identity of faith, the continuity of the formulations of faith, and also the legitimacy of new formulations?

Of course it is impossible to expect the document to give a clear and unambiguous answer to all these questions, especially since the magisterium receives no new revelations, and theology, up till now, has failed to present the answer in an adequate and generally accepted way. But we can see from these reflections how difficult it is to determine where an 'incomplete', historically conditioned formulation (which must none the less count as being true for all time) stops, and what is really an error begins. With regard to the distinction between incomplete and erroneous statements, there is another point as well. Basically speaking, it is very hard to determine the background of understanding of a statement, and hence the point from which we have to determine its meaning, and, therefore, its quality as being true or erroneous. This is so, at least, in the case of 'metaphysical' and religious statements, where indeed reflection cannot determine these things adequately at all. This applies to earlier periods as well. That is why the meaning of a particular formula in the light of an earlier interpretative standpoint cannot be clearly determined by historical means alone. We can see this, too, from the difference in the interpretation of ancient and new formulations by the different theological schools.

In short, truth and error cannot be so easily and unequivocally distinguished without recourse to linguistic prescriptiveness in Church and society; or to the tenet that fundamentally the Church abides in the truth; or to the other constitutive elements of the Church's unity; or to the experience of a unity existing between experience of the Spirit and statements of faith.[11] We must not think that the question of this distinction between truth and error can be settled on the pattern of statements like $2 + 2 = 4$, which are directly verifiable or which we find self-evident. Nor is it enough to point out that a statement is true if it does not miss the mark of the reality that is meant. For we are still faced with the question of what the statement, which is supposed to correspond to a particular reality,

---

[11] This phrase may indicate how this essay can be fitted into the overall theme of the present volume, cf. also below.

really means. There is no other way of deciding the question of the truth, since, after all, the statement cannot be compared with, or checked against, the reality it represents. If we appeal (of course rightly) to the formal authority of the magisterium or of revelation, then we are only pushing the question out of theology into fundamental theology.

Now, I have certainly no intention of maintaining that there is no answer, and can be no answer, to questions of this kind; or that the problems they present justify dogmatic relativism or scepticism. But even if these problems cannot be worked out here, it will surely be permissible – with all respect for a document of this kind – to ask whether, in view of the implications of what it says, it was drawn up with the necessary awareness of the problem, and of the consequences (even disciplinary ones) which follow – or do not follow – from these declarations, once one becomes aware in this way of the problems involved.

The Priesthood of the Church

The sixth section deals with a completely new subject: the universal priesthood, and the particular, ministerial official priesthood. One may well have the impression that the document (deliberately or at least in fact) is also directed against the recently published memorandum of the German ecumenical university institutes, which is concerned with the possibility of a mutual recognition of the ministry of the different Churches.[12] It cannot be said that the document makes much progress, or introduces much ecumenical hope into this question. The doctrine about the sacramental character of priestly ordination is too rapidly adopted as the starting point and foundation for the doctrine of the priestly office; whereas that doctrine really seems rather to be a conclusion drawn from an interpretation of the official priesthood which can be apprehended even before the doctrine of its sacramental character. It may be pointed out to theologians and ecumenically concerned people who are disappointed by this section that

[12] Cf. *Reform und Anerkennung kirchlicher Ämter. Ein Memorandum der Arbeitsgemeinschaft ökumenischer Universitätsinstitute* (Munich, Mainz 1973). For the present author's views on this memorandum, cf. 'Vom Sinn und Auftrag des kirchlichen Amtes' in *Frankfurter Allgemeine Zeitung* (no. 38) of 14 Feb. 1973, p. 8 and *Vorfragen zu einem ökumenischen Amtsverständnis* (Quaestiones Disputatae 65) (Freiburg 1974).

the document itself declares that the essence of the sacramental character is explained in different ways by theologians, and that the celebration of the Eucharist without an ordained priest is declared to be invalid only if it is wilful and presumptuous ('*proprio ausu*'). The question of when 'wilfulness' of this kind exists, therefore, remains an open one. Equally open is the question of how the permanent character of priestly ordination has more precisely to be constituted and explained.

Why should a theologian not admit to a certain helpless perplexity at the end of reflections of this kind? Why should he not say that, even though he views the substance of the document as binding, he is still unclear what disciplinary measures are to be envisaged – or perhaps not to be envisaged – for the people against whom this document is directed? Why should not a theologian honestly say, on his own account and at his own risk, that the whole complex of questions which is dealt with here does not seem to have been clarified to such a degree that practical consequences ought now to be drawn? Why may he not hold the opinion that (as the first part of the fifth section says) there is much more to be discovered and formulated, in a further process of theological clarification, if the ancient formulations (which a theologian must not deny) are to be clarified and modulated in such a way that they can be understood and assimilated today to the degree we may expect, in view of our contemporary intellectual and spiritual situation, and in the light of the present state of dogma? Is it not permissible to think that it would not be particularly beneficial for the Church, its doctrine, and the authority of its magisterium, if a purely formal declaration of obedience were to be demanded or exacted of the faithful, if this were really to leave all the factual questions open?

It seems to me as if neither side has really said exactly what it means by 'error' in dogmatic statements. And there seems, therefore, no need to put an end to the controversy as yet. If on the one hand there is understanding for the difficulties of theology, and on the other a clearly perceptible respect for the Church's magisterium, a provisional continuation of the controversy does not seem to me to be damaging for the Church. Especially since – with the two provisos we have named – no tangible difference would have to be made in the practice of the Church's life, even in the dimension of faith.

13

THE AREA BISHOP: SOME THEOLOGICAL REFLECTIONS

IN the summer of 1968 Cardinal Döpfner divided up his diocese (Munich and Freising) into three pastoral areas, entrusting each of them to one of his three auxiliary bishops.[1] The one Vicar-General retained authority for the whole diocese, but each of the auxiliaries was to have an 'ordinary, representative authority' for the area entrusted to him. The idea was that the auxiliary, as episcopal vicar, should devote himself to constant contact with the parishes and parish priests; that he should make visitations; and that he should relieve the diocesan bishop in his episcopal functions. As auxiliaries, they are subject solely to the archbishop and are ordinary members of meetings of the ordinarial sessions.

What we are about to consider here are not questions of Canon Law, or pastoral care or theology. Nor are we concerned to evaluate as such the measure which provides the immediate occasion for these remarks. We shall only try to gather together a few ideas – most of them open to discussion – about the task of a regional bishop. These ideas belong to the framework of ecclesiology and sacramental theology. Whether they can throw any light at all on this particular task (which goes beyond the general theological problem presented by the 'suffragan' or 'auxiliary' bishop) must emerge from the reflections themselves.

---

[1] Cf. *Amtsblatt für das Erzbistum München und Freising*, 1968, no. 13, pp. 260–1; also Vatican II, *Christus Dominus* (bishops' responsibility for pastoral care), nos. 25–7, in *The Documents of Vatican* II, ed. W. M. Abbott (London 1966), pp. 414–17; and Pope Paul VI, Motuproprio 'Ecclesiae Sanctae' 6 Aug. 1966, nos. 13–14; in *AAS* 58 (1966) 757–87, especially 765–6.

PRESUPPOSITIONS

Here we can only indicate the background for what we want to say, in terms of our general thesis. We cannot give a proper theological justification. In the first place, even in the Church social realities can present themselves in various forms and interpretations, without being really different in essentials. This applies to the sacraments too (since they are public events in the community or society of the church) if, for example, these sacraments confer an office, or in some other way alter the circumstances of an individual in the Church as society. What happens in a proceeding of this kind, and what is intended, can be very different from what the minister or recipient of the sacrament explicitly 'thinks' at the time. An example might be a sacramental marriage between non-Catholic Christians who are convinced that the wedding ceremony has no sacramental character. Or a mediaeval bishop who administers the sacrament of episcopal ordination, even though he shares Thomas Aquinas's opinion that this ordination is not a sacrament at all. Or a bishop who, in earlier times, ordained an acolyte or sub-deacon, believing that in doing so he was administering a sacrament. We can recall the distinction, which may have existed objectively, but not subjectively, in the consciousness of a priest in pre-mediaeval times, when he anointed a healthy person on the one hand, and then again someone who was seriously ill. Here we need not explain the reasons for the difference we mean; nor do we have to describe how the difference can be bridged, so that one can talk in a humanly significant sense about the administration of a sacrament even though one actually believes that no sacrament exists. Here, initially, it is perhaps enough to show how the distinction can be applied: a sacrament can in fact be conferred even if the person who administers it does not think he is conferring one; and a sacrament is not necessarily present even though the minister believes that he is conferring one.[2]

The ministry of the Church is really indivisible. As such, as one and entire, it corresponds to the nature of the Church as the presence of God's irreversible, eschatological promise of salvation in Jesus Christ, the crucified and risen Lord; and as the community of faith,

---

[2] What is said here again rests on certain presuppositions. For example, not only has the consciousness of administering a sacrament changed in the course of time. The concept of 'sacrament' has altered, too. Here we are using the word 'sacrament' in the strict, contemporary sense.

which inevitably has an institutional form. This Church *as such* possesses a governing ministry whose fundamental authority lies in the proclamation of the public, manifesting Word of eschatologically victorious grace.[3] Since the eschatological community of faith rests on the Christ event, as God's final saving act in history, the ministry of this community also derives from Jesus Christ and is founded by him. This means that a derivation of ministry in the Church from the historical Jesus which can be expressed in historical terms cannot be denied, in so far as this can really be historically proved or shown to be probable. If we see the historical Jesus as 'founder' in this way, then it is really a matter of course that this ministry, or its authority, can be expressed, divided and subdivided in different ways, vertically and horizontally, according to the requirements of the Church in its particular, specific situation. Of course this does not call in question the one, comprehensive Petrine ministry in the Church – all the less because ministry in the Church, besides being generally derived from Jesus Christ (as we have just indicated), also has a direct and obvious foundation in Scripture. It should also be clear that the development of the Church's constitution in the form of this one ministry, and the way it has been divided up, implies irreversible decisions in particular cases, if not in all. (This at least applies to the apostolic period, which we may view as having continued for as long as it took for the New Testament writings to come into being.) And these irreversible decisions can therefore be seen as '*ius divinum*'. But – always presupposing these defining guidelines – the ministry of the Church is fundamentally much more flexible in configuration and specific form than people think. This normally applies both to the traditional division of the one ministry (as *potestas ordinis*) into its three grades of bishop – priest – deacon, and to the more precise content of this vertical division. But it also applies to the question whether the transmission of another, separate, important individual ministry in the Church can have a sacramental character; and whether a particular ministerial authority can be possessed, at least in essentials, by a collective holder as such.[4]

[3] Cf. 'What is a Sacrament?', *Theological Investigations* XIV (London 1976), pp. 135–48.

[4] This question cannot simply be answered in the negative from the outset; for the entire episcopal body is the collective holder of the Church's supreme jurisdiction and teaching authority; and it can be viewed historically as the collective holder of sacramental power in Eucharist, penance, the anointing

THE AREA BISHOP

What really 'happens' when a priest is consecrated as auxiliary bishop, and is entrusted with the tasks of an area bishop? In this question we shall be guided by the caution enjoined by our preliminary remarks; but it will probably be permissible to leave the problem of the correct Canon-Law terminology and its development on one side.[5] In the first place, a number of problems do not arise at all in the case of the institution of *area* bishops which otherwise exist at episcopal ordinations; for the area bishop has no territory of his own and/or (in the case of a 'personal bishopric') has no group of people actually assigned to him as his own 'flock'. Usefully and legitimately, even people who have no territorially defined area of their own can belong to the highest administrative body of the whole Church (the entire episcopate with, and under, the pope). This cannot be denied, above all, by the person who sees the essence of the episcopal office (even in the case of a 'local' or diocesan bishop) as lying precisely in his adherence to this highest administrative body, or at least as being most clearly tangible there. All other definitions of the essence of the episcopal office (as distinct from the priesthood) can in fact be maintained only with difficulty and inconclusively; because all the bishop's territorially limited powers of jurisdiction can also be held by someone who has not been ordained as bishop; and because it is at the very least uncertain whether a simple priest does not possess the sacramental power

---

of the sick and ordination. In this connection, therefore, it is possible only to ask whether, through a decision *iuris humani* in the Church, such a collective holder of sacramental power can be nominated as the *sole* legitimate one. Seen from both aspects (and taking into account the very close correlation of the power of jurisdiction and the power of order) the question remains open – at least partly – as to whether a 'synodal' governing body in the Catholic Church is not fundamentally conceivable even today, where we have a 'monarchical' holder of authority. This question has nothing to do with the assertion that a change of this kind is also desirable. Nor does it in any way deny that such a 'synodal' body would possess *those* powers that are described in traditional ecclesiology. The question is only whether, and to what degree, the holder of this authority has to be an individual, or can also be a group – as, for example, in the case of the Church's supreme governing body, in the episcopal college. For more detail, cf. 'Aspects of the Episcopal Office', *Theological Investigations* XIV (London 1976), pp. 185–201.

[5] Cf. here K. Mörsdorf in *Commentary on the Documents of Vatican II*, ed. H. Vorgrimler (New York and London 1968), vol. II, pp. 243–5.

to confirm and to ordain other priests.[6] But in the Roman Curia (and to some extent outside it as well) there are not a few titular bishops; and there seems to be no reason in their case why they should have been co-opted into the Church's supreme governing body through episcopal ordination, even though they really have a subordinate function, and certainly are not – with others – the collective holder of the Church's supreme leadership.

Compared with these, the area bishops have a clearer legitimation: they have a real, tangible flock; in the cases which give rise to our present discussion, this flock is bigger than many a diocese whose bishop counts as part of the episcopate as a whole, without there being any problem or question about it. In view of these facts, the consecration of an area bishop of this kind can certainly be understood as being 'relative' to a certain flock, irrespective of whether the official Canon Law interpretation holds an ordination of this kind to be absolute or relative. This may be said even if, according to *Christus Dominus* (nos 22–6), there can be no doubt that 'the primary aim is to divide up dioceses of excessive size. The appointment of auxiliary bishops is only a subsidiary measure – if, that is to say, a division of this kind, though really required, seems to be impracticable.'[7] But in actual practice the simple division of excessively large dioceses cannot be appropriate for today (cf. *Christus Dominus*, no. 22, which relates to dioceses consisting of large cities, which are to be made better adapted to their task by a new *internal* structure); and in these cases the appointment of an area bishop is quite legitimate, even though this is really a measure that is 'subsidiary' to the division of a diocese.

---

[6] In relation to the individual diocese the power of active episcopal ordination would really be superfluous if one really presupposed that every priest had the power of confirmation and priestly ordination, even if this power were restrained. *Here* the idea we have indicated is intended only to show that the distinction between bishop and priest is not as simple as people sometimes think; and that (though we cannot maintain his opinion today) Aquinas was not so wide of the mark when he held that the distinction between priest and bishop is only one of jurisdiction. But if for this reason membership of the Church's supreme governing body is not simply to be thought of as merely *following on* the episcopal office, but is essentially and primarily *co-constitutive* of it, then it is easier to understand why this membership does not necessarily and always presuppose a territorial diocese; for this characteristic of the 'normal' episcopal office cannot constitute the office *as such*.

[7] Cf. n. 1 and n. 5.

But the real theological problems which arise from the institution of an area bishop have hardly emerged from these practical and legal definitions. First of all we must consider the fact that, according to *Christus Dominus* and the Motuproprio of Pope Paul VI's, '*Ecclesiae sanctae*', it is even possible to conceive of '*vicarii episcopales*' who are not bishops at all.[8] We may, therefore, ask whether the pastoral situation of a large diocese really requires area *bishops*, if their function can also be carried out by simple priests. The fact that this is possible cannot be denied, as far as the power of jurisdiction and the powers to confirm are concerned. Quite apart from the fact that, dogmatically speaking, the valid ordination of a priest by another simple priest does not appear impossible (given the necessary conditions), the necessity of active ordination cannot be used as a legitimation of the institution of an area *bishop*, especially in view of our contemporary shortage of priests. Priestly orders can easily be conferred by the local or diocesan bishop himself. He needs no episcopal auxiliary for that. But it would be wise to avoid conferring any particular lustre on the exercise of the episcopal vicar's functions through episcopal consecration, and the latter should not be used in order to win particular status for this office. If the theology underlying the sacrament of order is taken to be genuine and true, only the content of the actually intended and actually existing power can provide the legitimate reason for the sacramental transmission of ministry. But this transmission should not aim through its sacramental character to give the ministry itself any higher significance or any special lustre. That is why the episcopal consecration of some Roman curials is felt to be unsuitable and nonsensical. But what is the position with regard to the episcopal consecration of the area bishop, if at first sight he is no more, and has no more extensive powers and functions, than a non-episcopal vicar would have who is not himself a bishop?

ORDINATION

We shall try to give a double answer to this by no means easy question about the significance of episcopal ordination. We shall assume that the office of an area *bishop*, since it actually exists, must to a certain degree have some theological significance.

We may presuppose that it is quite legitimate that very many

---

[8] Cf. n. 1. The Motuproprio is dated 6 Aug. 1966, cf. no. 13–14.

members of the entire episcopate, as the Church's highest governing body, should be the representatives of numerically small groups of believers, since there are about 2300 *ordinarii loci* in the whole Catholic Church and – since the Church as a whole numbers 560 million members – under each of these local ordinaries there will be on an average about 240,000 Catholics. (For the purposes of our discussion we are, quite legitimately, including in the number of local or diocesan bishops the non-episcopal ones as well.) From this point of view it seems to be quite right that a diocese of several million believers should be represented in the total episcopate by *several* bishops. For legitimate reasons (which are actually connected with what a diocese is, namely the local church which represents, to a more or less adequate degree, the whole Church in all its contemporary complexity) such a diocese can and should, perhaps, not be divided. If we acknowledge the validity of this reasoning, then we must admittedly also, to be consistent, really concede to an area bishop the powers and rights which naturally emanate from his membership of the entire episcopal body. And it must honestly be said that this reason for the existence of an area bishop as episcopal vicar can be given validity only if these bishops also actually have something to do with the episcopate as a whole, as the Church's supreme governing body. This would hardly be the case if an area bishop could be active in this respect only at a General Council, and if the Roman episcopal synod were a barely tolerated institution where 'merely' regional bishops did not *a priori* count at all.

There is another answer to the question as well. In order to make it more comprehensible, let me start from a fictitious case. Given the necessary preconditions and legitimate reasons, a bishop nominates one of his priests to represent him in a certain area of his diocese, but without having any intention of consecrating this priest as bishop. Let us suppose, for the sake of simplicity, that the bishop makes this 'nomination' using the rite of the laying on of hands, and the prayer for grace to exercise the ministry properly. In this case, or so we would maintain, this transmission of ministry would be a sacrament, even if the bishop were not actually and consciously aware of it.[9] The ecclesiastical ministry is conferred *eo ipso* in a sacramental rite when an important and new part of this ministry is conferred and where

---

[9] Cf. n. 2. The meaning of 'sacrament' is differently defined in the present case.

there is that tangibility and legitimacy in the public eye of the Church which is necessary for a sacrament. The sacramental character of a transmission of ministry is not an arbitrary addition to that transmission (supposing it to take place under the necessary conditions); the one is given *ipso facto* with the other. For we must simply assume that the Word of the Church (which fundamentally has an exhibitive character, because of her eschatological nature) is *opus operatum* and a sacrament when it is uttered with the full commitment of the Church in a critical situation in the life of an individual, or as the highest realisation of the fulfilling commitment of the congregation (the Eucharist). If this is not the case, it is impossible to give a theologically convincing justification for the sacramental character of most sacramental happenings. For they are lacking in adequate biblical justification; and there is no explicit, sufficiently obvious evidence from tradition going back to apostolic times. But if we start from the assumptions of a sacramental theology such as we have merely indicated here, then we must say (in our fictitious case) that what we have here is a sacramental transmission of ministry. An important, new and highly central ministry now exists, one which cannot simply be seen as an unimportant or merely external modification of a ministerial authority that is already possessed. Something new and more important is conferred, as for example when a layman is consecrated as deacon. But the inner nature of the event when part of the one ministry of the Church is conferred on someone, makes that event a sacrament (always given the presuppositions which we do not have to consider in detail here). It is not that a sacramental event is arbitrarily added, for incomprehensible reasons, in some cases where the partial gift of ministry is concerned, while in other cases it is not – even though the cases are factually of equal importance. We must point back to the presuppositions we have named here.

It might be objected to this notion, that if this is correct, then every conferring of the ministry of episcopal vicar would be a sacrament; but that in fact, as has already been said, there are episcopal vicars who are not bishops. Many objections might be raised here. Without lapsing into heresy, it might well be maintained that even the episcopal vicars would be sacramentally appointed to their ministry through an episcopal consecration; for the considered interpretation of this event as it is generally understood by theologians and canonists does not necessarily have to be correct.[10] Can the appointment to this ministry not very well be sacramental without its having therefore to be understood as a real *episcopal* consecration? It is by no means absolutely certain that an important and new transmission of ministry which, by reason of its inner nature, is then also a sacrament, can actually be conferred *only* in the *three* ordinations of deacon, priest and bishop. But quite apart from all that (and if we go back more specifically to the fictitious case we started from), we can simply say that what is in question from the outset in the appointment of a mere episcopal vicar who is not a bishop is the temporary conferring of a ministry. But this ministry has no new sacramental authority (for confirmation and active ordination); and consequently the appointment of a mere episcopal vicar is essentially distinguished from the transmission of ministry which we are considering here and maintaining to be sacramental. For this reason the conferring of ministry on a mere episcopal vicar does not take place with that absolute involvement on the part of the Church (and the recipient) which is actually given in our case (irrespective of whether this is consciously perceived or not) and which is necessary – but is also a sufficient presupposition – for a sacramental event as such. One could finally point to the fact that, at least in fact, the Church does not recognise as a sacramental event (i.e. that total involvement on the Church's part which makes its word *opus operatum*) any transmission of ministry is not associated with, and illustrated by, the laying on of hands. Should not the Church recognise certain transmissions of ministry as sacramental (at least as part of the one *Ordo*) because these ministries – by reason of their importance – undoubtedly enjoy the divine promise of grace, and because this promise must consequently be manifested by the Church in its social and historical apprehensibility too through a sacramental act? But as far as our actual question is concerned, that may be passed over. The objective difference between

---

[10] If, according to Pius XII, the three stages of ordination which we also recognise intellectually are conferred only through the laying on of hands, then we might still ask whether such a positive ecclesiastical directive is also applicable to the conferring of ministries which are not envisaged in *Sacramentum ordinis*. This mode of the transmission of a ministry through the laying on of hands is certainly not divine Law. Really such a transmission of ministry can be thought of as taking place in any way, provided it is evident and clear. Cf. Vat. II, *De Ecclesia*, n. 29, and Pius XII, constitution *Sacramentum ordinis*, 30 Nov. 1947, Denz. 3857–61.

a mere episcopal vicar and the diocesan bishop which we had in mind in our fictitious case, seems to be considerable enough to warrant our interpreting the conferment of the former ministry as non-sacramental, and the conferment of the latter as sacramental.

But what significance does this fictitious case have for our actual subject? It shows that we cannot think of the ministry given to an area bishop (which is at least in some respects understood as being irrevocably conferred) as being non-sacramentally conferred. If we leave on one side (as we shall no doubt be permitted to do) the possibility we have suggested above – that is to say, a sacramental assignment of ministry which would be neither priestly ordination nor a real episcopal consecration – and assume that this office is passed on through the laying on of hands, then we can say that the appointment of the head of a large area within a diocese carried out in *this* way, together with the powers conferred with this appointment, and conferred to some extent irrevocably, *cannot* be understood in any other way than as a sacramental, episcopal consecration.

<h2 style="text-align:center">SUMMING UP</h2>

An area bishop is appointed through a sacramental transmission of ministry because, and in so far as, he is co-opted into the whole episcopate – appropriately so, since he is the legitimate co-representative of an unusually large and indivisible diocese; and because, and in so far as, the appointment to this ministry (which is conferred through the laying on of hands) is so new and important, compared with the merely priestly office, that it is *eo ipso* a sacrament – to be specific: an episcopal consecration.

In saying this we have of course not even glimpsed most of the theological questions raised by the appointment of area bishops, let alone the questions which arise for Canon Law and pastoral theology. One question, for example, might well be, how and why the *equal* position of an area bishop in the whole episcopate (where he is quite evidently not subordinate to his diocesan or local bishop) is reconcilable with his subordinate position vis-à-vis his local bishop in his particular diocese. We can certainly not escape from this difficulty simply by calling to our aid the distinction between the power of order (in which the two bishops are equal) and the power of jurisdiction (in which there is a distinction between the two); for it is the whole episcopate which is the supreme holder precisely of the power of teaching and the power of jurisdiction in the Church. We might again ask, even more earnestly, whether and why the character of a member of the Church's supreme governing body is reconcilable theologically with a simultaneously subordinate position in relation to another bishop. The Church's ancient patriarchal and metropolitan constitutions and structures do not provide a theologically adequate justification for this because on the one hand we can raise the same question in regard to these constitutions, and because, in the ultimate resort, it is still an open question whether some minor 'bishop' in early or later times, though certainly bearing a bishop's title and going under this legal designation, was not in actual fact merely a priest or 'itinerant' bishop, without perhaps really being a bishop at all. Even today, no truly definable border-line can be clearly and convincingly drawn between priest and bishop which is *absolute* as regards the power of order; and, as far as jurisdiction is concerned, many a simple bishop was in hardly a better position towards his patriarch or metropolitan than a dean or other head of part of a large diocese. But we cannot go on to talk about these questions and others like them here, even though they inevitably arise in connection with the institution of area bishops.

Let me, in closing, just say one thing. It is not in accordance with the spirit of the Second Vatican Council or with the character of an auxiliary bishop as a fully authorised member of the entire episcopate (and if he is not to be that, then he should not be consecrated as bishop at all) if bishops of this kind are to be viewed and treated in an episcopal conference more or less as semi-undesirable members of merely secondary rank.

14

TRANSFORMATIONS IN THE CHURCH AND SECULAR SOCIETY

D O transformations in the Church perhaps have some effect on secular society today? And if so, what kind of effect? I should like to try to answer this question here, at least in broad outline.[1] But before we can start to consider the subject we have defined in this way, we ought to agree about the sense in which we are talking about the changes and transformations of and in the Church. We may, however, take it to be a statement of fact when we say that, for a considerable time now, the Church has been involved in a process of change; and that in the coming decades this process will probably be more widespread and more evident all over the world. What is actually happening in this process, however, has been described in a multitude of bewildering interpretations; and the word 'transformation' or 'change' certainly suggests many things that are not meant here.

In the first place, it cannot be a question of a transformation which would affect the very nature of the Church – the Church which a definition that has come down to us from scholastic theology de-

---

[1] This essay is based on the revised manuscript of a lecture given at a symposium in Madrid in the spring of 1974, in which the present author took part, together with Professors Jürgen Moltmann and J. B. Metz. The subject was chosen by the organisers of the symposium and was based on the little book *Strukturwandel der Kirche als Aufgabe und Chance*, Herder Bücherei 446, 3rd edn (Freiburg 1973); ET *The Shape of the Church to Come* (London 1974). In the analysis of the various situations, the reader will discover much that has already been said; but the essay as a whole contains sufficient fresh material to justify its inclusion in the present volume.

scribes as *iuris divini*.[2] Of course this term itself is not as clear as people casually suppose; and that means that it is weighed down by particular problems of its own. Naturally there is nothing in the Church which is in itself plainly and simply, quite expressly and in the abstract, *iuris divini*, and which in actual, specific fact is not also historically conditioned and subject to change. So a transformation of the Church cannot mean that there can ever be a time when the living fellowship of believers ceases to confess, as the incomprehensible foundation and goal of all history, the living God who in Jesus Christ, the crucified and risen Lord, has irrevocably promised himself to the world as victorious grace and forgiveness. The transformation of the Church will not mean, either, that sometime or other the petrine and episcopal structure of the ecclesiastical society will cease to exist. And yet it is a matter of course that this Church will continually experience changes which it cannot estimate in advance, particularly in the dimension of its social character and its Law. And even the papal and episcopal function in its specific, ecclesiastical form is therefore not excluded from far-reaching changes.

WHAT TRANSFORMATION?

The following ideas are designed to centre on those lasting and, above all, institutional changes in the Church which have already been made or which we may expect in the foreseeable future, on the basis of the fact that, in all countries, and even in the so-called Christian parts of the world, the Church has become, or is beginning to become, the gnoseological minority. Of course it is true that the points of departure for this vary greatly, just as the development itself is coming about with varying swiftness and in ways which differ from case to case. But the living space of the Church today – which is to say the secular pluralistic or even authoritarian anti-Christian societies and

---

[2] Cf. 'Reflection on the Concept of "Ius Divinum" in Catholic Thought', *Theological Investigations* V (London 1966), pp. 219–43; also in *Theological Investigations* XIV (London, 1976), the following essays: 'On the Theology of a Pastoral Synod', pp. 116–34; 'Aspects of the Episcopal Office', pp. 185–201; and 'How the Priest Should View his Official Ministry', pp. 202–19. Recently, in connection with reflections on the Church's office and ministry, the present author has also proposed the creation of a 'law based on the nature of the Church', as the foundation for its hierarchical structure; cf. *Vorfragen zu einem Ökumenischen Amtsverständnis* (Quaestiones Disputatae 65) (Freiburg 1974), especially pp. 35–9.

States – brings with it a minority status which either already exists or can be foreseen for the near future. This minority status inevitably brings change with it, even if the changes are slow and meet with resistance in the Church. And these changes are to be found even in places where Christians who belong to the Church are still in the majority numerically, in that particular society as a whole. According to the principles of civic tolerance (which after all are religious and Christian principles as well[3]), Christians must in this case recognise the social legitimacy of large minorities of considerable cultural and political importance; and they must, therefore, submit to the Law of a pluralistic society.

What emerges for the Church in the way of change in this situation, where the Church is part of modern, secular society, or what suggests itself in that direction, particularly where the Church's institutional form is concerned, can – as we have already said – vary in nature, extent and urgency in the different countries and continents. But it is self-evident that, in view of the minority status of Christians and the Church, changes in ecclesiastical structures will come, even if they are opposed by the Church in its official character, and in spite of the dislike of traditionally attached groups of Christians. Moreover, since ultimately these changes rest on a common cause, they will generally crop up everywhere in similar form. But we should be better able to recognise and interpret them if we could investigate their cause more exactly – that is to say, the conditions that contribute to these changes in the history of thought, in social and political life, and no doubt in salvation-history, too. Of course, we cannot carry out this investigation here. In our present discussion we shall give only a few indications which may help to illustrate the transformation in and of, the Church, before going on to consider in more detail the possible influence of this process on secular society.

A first characteristic of these changes in the Church is the fact that its mind is no longer identical with the mind of the public as a whole. On the contrary, the two are related to each other in an inevitable process of mutual dependence and reciprocity. Seen empirically, the secular mind of society shows itself to be, if not the *all*-powerful part of this relationship, at least clearly the *more* powerful part. We cannot overlook the fact that now this secular social consciousness, which

[3] Cf. here especially Vatican II's 'Declaration on Religious Freedom'; text in *The Documents of Vatican* II, ed. W. M. Abbott (London 1965).

sees itself expressly as non-Christian, none the less includes, if anony-mously, much that is Christian; and it can be partly marked by what a Christian calls sin. Consequently it is not a question of Christianity and the Church on the one hand, and a neutrally secular and secular-ised consciousness on the other. The mutual relationship is much more complex than that; for again, the actual consciousness of people in the Church itself is also partly sustained by the contemporary secularised consciousness of the society around them – quite apart from the fact that even the Church's awareness can also be distorted by sin and error in particular cases.

This closely interrelated relationship between awareness in the Church, as a minority group, and the pluralistic mentality of secular society, determines a second characteristic of change for the Church. Its proclamation of its faith, and the theology required for this, present themselves today in a much more 'pluralistic' form than formerly. For by reason of its nature and of the task assigned to it, theology is a reflection about Christian faith in its actual relationship to reality and to the task man is entrusted with in life. This means that from the very beginning it is necessarily related to the whole of human existence. But, even before theological reflection, man is a pluralistic being who can never adequately synthesise the protean manifestations of his reality, his history and his experience – and today less than ever. The human situation cannot be abolished, but it is only today that people have become more clearly and more fully aware of what it is. Of course, this situation also has its effects on the theology of the Church, particularly because theology (as distinct from faith, which derives from the experience of Jesus and the incomprehensi-bility of God) contains in itself a number of different approaches and outlines for the future in this world. The influence of all these different secular, pluralistic backgrounds to understanding derives from man's free position in finite time. For that reason it can never be entirely compensated for, which is one reason among others for the pluralism in theology which people are very conscious of today but which is insurmountable. There will never be another scholastic theology, which could be understood by everyone in the same way and could be practised by everyone. It is impossible to show in detail here what this assertion means for the Church's magisterium and what conse-quences that magisterium ought to draw. But these consequences already exist, even if they have not yet been sufficiently recognised and taken into account in official quarters.

A third characteristic arising from the Church's minority status in our time is the new and growing importance of the rank and file, or the 'grass roots' of the Church's people.[4] For the real, specific impact of its office and ministry depends to an increasing degree on this rank and file. However, the theological legitimation of the Church's official ministry may be thought of in a Catholic ecclesiology as coming 'from the top'; today at least its real effectiveness, its 'power', is no longer simply presented as a given fact for the response of the rank and file, as it was in earlier times. Today it follows from their good will and is dependent on that. Whether one welcomes this phenomenon or not makes no difference to the facts. However long the process, which began with the Second Vatican Council, may continue before tangible and established results become crystallised, it may already be said now that, through the dependency of the Church's ministry and office on the grass roots which we have already mentioned, the mutual relationship between the two is going to assume a more democratic form.[5] The rank and file of the Church will also acquire a legally institutionalised and important influence on the 'official' Church in some form or other; and the latter will no longer exercise its function in a closed circle of officials, who make all the decisions themselves.

THE PRACTICAL CONSEQUENCES FOR SECULAR SOCIETY

Having said that, let us break off our brief discussion about the transformation of and in the Church. Can we now perhaps go on to talk about the effect of these changes on secular society? Before we consider this subject, it must be emphasised that we have no intention here of describing and elaborating all the real, essential services which the Church can perform in secular society, in the light of its nature, its mission and its life. In the future as in the past, it will continue to be of the greatest importance for secular society that the Church believes in the living Lord of all history, and in the blessed end of this history which he has promised; that, contrary to all the hopelessness which this history continually reiterates, the Church goes on

---

[4] On this term cf. K. H. Neufeld, 'Berufung auf die Basis?' in *Entschluß* 28 (1972/3), pp. 469–81.
[5] Cf. 'The Teaching Office of the Church in the Present-Day Crisis of Authority', *Theological Investigations* XII (London 1974); and in the present volume 'Opposition in the Church', pp. 127–38.

hoping; that it prays for, and feels responsible for, the poor and the oppressed, for people who have not had their fair share of things in this world, and for the dead; that the Church stands in the way when people want to turn history into a mere tale of victors and survivors;[6] and that in the world the Church continually upholds with vital force a position from which both proved tradition and the tempting future can be quite soberly and critically called in question, and in the face of which no tangible historical reality can claim to be God, either theoretically or practically. All this and much more besides is of vital importance for secular society too. And, of course, this is more important than anything which we can now mention as being the result for secular society of changes in the Church determined by a particular period.

But all the same, we must, because of our subject, address ourselves to just this possible influence. Now that we have narrowed things down, we shall think in more detail of two possible effects of structural alterations in the Church. Even so, not all the details can be described in our present framework, especially since it is fundamentally not at all clear whether the unique features of the transformation we have described can really have any effect on secular society – whether ecclesiastical changes of this kind can be translated at all into secular contexts and can encourage similar manifestations there. If we once presuppose that this is possible (i.e. that these alterations, which are wrung from the Church, so to speak, because of its minority status, could provoke analagous effects in secular society), then in spite of its actual situation the Church could perhaps play a part even in a pluralistic society, in which it would not simply run after the secular historical transformation, but actually set an example by running ahead of it. For its status as a minority no longer allows the Church to surrender its development to the law of inertia, as secular society still does. A swifter and more deliberate implementation of necessary changes can therefore give the Church the position of a pace-setter in the society around it. But we must quite certainly not make our Christian faith and our church membership dependent on a hope of this kind.[7] So ought we simply to deny that hope from the

---

[6] Cf. the lecture given by J. B. Metz on the occasion of the same symposium in Madrid, 'Kirche und Volk', printed in *StdZ* 192 (1974), pp. 797–811.

[7] This would seem to be the case, for example in G. Hasenhüttl, *Herrschaftsfreie Kirche* (Düsseldorf 1974).

very beginning, as if it were quite certain that the power of the Church to influence world history to any considerable degree has been exhausted once and for all? We do not share this opinion either.

a) Shared Basic Convictions

In my view, the initial contribution which transformations in the Church can make to secular society seems highly remote. But even a secular society with its institutions cannot – in spite of its liberal and pluralistic self-understanding – live and get along without a certain basic stock of common convictions which are respected by everyone in that society. This basic stock cannot simply be replaced either by particular maxims and institutionalisms which happen to be obviously useful, or by the pure brute force of the State, any more than it can consist of an inexhaustible heritage of tradition stemming from the past, or can automatically renew itself again purely and simply out of the depths of human nature itself, as it were. On the contrary, society itself has the task and the duty – and indeed is continually faced with the necessity – of quite deliberately preserving this basic stock of common convictions by its own methods; and where necessary it also has the task and duty of regenerating and changing these shared convictions.

The power and possibility of preserving this basic stock of convictions and altering it in accordance with the times, certainly belong to *everyone*, basically speaking, because of the dignity every individual enjoys. But in fact this power and possibility have principally to be implemented by the people who actually have the power to do so, and who bear special responsibility in this direction – that is to say, the representatives of the State. In saying this we are already presupposing that State and society are never quite identical as historical entities, and that an identity of this kind would not even be desirable. So when it is a question of breaking down structures of dominance and constraints and human self-alienation (to name in catchword form some of the generally familiar basic social and political demands), then the power to do this lies with particular individuals or groups. For it is they who define the sphere of freedom open to any individual, and they define it before the individual is consulted at all. For it is simply impossible for everyone adequately to think through all the processes of decision, irrespective of whether they affect them as individuals or whether they affect society. And this means that it is equally impossible to institutionalise these processes of decision in such a way that they are sufficiently clear to everyone. We must therefore start from the assumption that there will always be more powerful people and less powerful people in a State, and that the more powerful ones are given in a special way the task and responsibility of preserving the basic stock of convictions that we have been talking about.

The question that emerges can, therefore, only be *how* the power of the State can specifically attempt to achieve the necessary regeneration of this basic stock of common convictions and norms which is essential for society – a regeneration which must be tackled again and again; and how they can do this without infringing the individual's freedom of conviction and way of living, which must be safeguarded to the greatest possible degree. It is not an easy task, continually to try afresh to reconcile, on the one hand, freedom of conviction, and the opportunity to proclaim that conviction publicly and to realise that freedom in specific terms, and, on the other hand, the positive cultivation and maintenance of common social basic convictions. A glance at societies and States in the world today – whether they are predominantly democratic or authoritarian in form – shows clearly that this effort cannot be avoided simply by making a radical choice for one alternative or the other. But we have no need to enter into that in any more detail here.

If we take the historical character of all human truth seriously, then of course no ready-made principles can be put forward in this question either – principles which we should only have to apply for the problem in a specific society to be solved once and for all. Faced with this historical decision, no one can be spared the difficulty of searching, of experiencing, of struggling without the benefit of any tangible arbiter. On the other hand, this does not exclude the possibility of perhaps evolving patterns which are better adapted than the earlier ones to help us hold our ground in this ever-new and ever-necessary struggle between freedom of opinion and the need for a common social 'ideology' (to use the word in an entirely neutral sense); and for holding our ground without infringing the respect due to one another. The result will in any case be a precarious one and can never be any more than a temporary balance between the two co-existent entities. The need for these new patterns is becoming increasingly clear in all the secular societies of the world; but it will probably be legitimate to maintain, without any further proof, that they are still largely lacking.

b) The Formulation of Fundamental Convictions

In this sense transformations in the Church and the new structures arising out of them could provide a model for secular societies, too. It is true that the Church is still involved in the process we have indicated, but it ought to survive in such a way that the new equilibrium between authority and freedom in its own life may ultimately bring with it patterns which may be of use beyond the sphere of the Church itself. There is no doubt that in the past the Church has preferred authoritarian forms, and has cultivated them especially for the protection of the common convictions of its faith. In view of its present-day minority status, and since the 'secular arm' can no longer be counted on for support, these forms are no longer effective. This is true even where a person against whose views the protest of the Church and the magisterium is directed, basically recognises the Church's teaching authority. That is why today a relatively wide consensus in the Church's general sense of faith, and in theology, is a necessary precondition even for authentic declarations by the magisterium, so that it can act legitimately and can count on being really effective.

We have already said enough about today's pluralism; we have pointed to the lack of a common background of understanding, shared as a matter of course. This, and conscious historical examination of the historical influence and contingency of ideas which were up to now, largely speaking, unquestioningly shared, are now, to a previously unknown degree, hampering utterances on the part of the Church's magisterium which would be both generally binding and generally comprehensible. If the authorities concerned, therefore, wanted to fall back on authentic but non-defining declarations, they would renounce their binding character and could reckon only with a limited effect on the actual awareness of the church member. On the other hand, however, in our time, in contrast to earlier situations of mind and faith, new definitions presuppose a whole series of conditions which are difficult to fulfil. For that reason, in the future we shall probably only seldom, or never, have to reckon with definitions[8] which are more than an emphatic repetition of earlier statements.

In addition to all earlier difficulties, today the historically conditioned conscious or unconscious variety in backgrounds of understanding (which cannot really be synthesised at all in the actual consciousness of either the individual or even the representatives of the Church's magisterium) raises an alarming question: are the existing, officially valid formulations of faith really so alive in the consciousness of individual church members or church groups that they really cover and express the same convictions of faith? For example, the notion of a hierarchy of truths, which found expression at the Second Vatican Council,[9] also shows that agreement in the sense of faith (which used normally to be presupposed) is not so tangibly and susceptibility present as had probably been assumed. The ecumenical strivings towards unity in faith point in the same direction, since they reckon as a matter of course with differences in the histories of faith in the future too. In earlier times, when the Church's teaching authority was exercised, a uniformity of faith was usually assumed to be both the premise and the goal; at the very least, this goal cannot be so easily reached or determined as people once thought.

Moreover, in our period the magisterium also has to take account of a series of unique features in the human situation which used to be treated differently. For today the *bona fides* of the individual believer and theologian must be taken into consideration in a totally different way, if they seem to stray from the Church's sense of faith. It is impossible to do anything else in a society which in general proclaims freedom of conscience, if the Church does not want to lose all credibility with regard to its own message. One could say and add many things here. But in spite of everything, I will not pretend that we in the Church already know exactly *how today* (in contrast to earlier times) the authority of the ecclesial community of shared faith can be reconciled with the authority of freedom.

[8] Cf. 'Pluralism in Theology and the Unity of the Creed in the Church', *Theological Investigations* XI (London 1974), pp. 3–23; 'The Future of Theology', pp. 137–48; 'The Teaching Office of the Church in the Present-Day Crisis of Authority', *Theological Investigations* XII (London 1974), pp. 3–30; and above all 'On the Concept of Infallibility in Catholic Theology', *Theological Investigations* XIV (London 1976), pp. 66–85, esp. pp. 71–5.

[9] Vatican II: 'Unitatis redintegratio' (Decree on Ecumenism), no. 11, in *Documents of Vatican II*, ed. W. M. Abbott (London 1966), p. 354.

What institutionalisms would then have to exist in the Church today, for the abiding authority of the magisterium to co-exist in a positive way with freedom of conscience – even though the co-existence may perhaps always have to be one of agonised tension? For it is in the conscience that the Church's sense of faith continues to develop; and this process cannot simply be controlled by the official authority of the Church. What must be preserved, finally, is also the legitimate liberty of theology, and difference in the development of the sense of faith in individual Christians, whose living conviction also has the right to be openly expressed, even if it does not simply coincide with the Church's sense of faith.

Now, of course, secular society should not, and cannot, simply take over or imitate the methods whereby the Church has to master the difficulties which still have to be solved for the future. The consciousness of society and Church are too different in origin, content and goal for that. But the new problems which force themselves on the Church and on secular society have a common origin, generally speaking;[10] so if the former were to arrive at a decision more quickly, it could develop practicable solutions for its problems which would also be of significance for secular society. In order to do this, without falling back into a mediaeval state of mind, or without continuing to maintain an attitude of this kind, it would have to find a way to preserve freedom of thought on the one hand, and yet to preserve and develop a common basic conviction (without which every society collapses) on the other.

How we are to conceive of this in concrete terms – how there is, and can be, a free, anti-authoritarian and yet effective magisterium in the Church – ought to be developed here at more length than space allows. Only a few somewhat random ideas may supplement and clarify this suggestion.

When all is said and done, secular society, with its state organisation, is also distinguished from the Church in our pluralistic world by the fact that no one can opt out of secular society, whereas he certainly can from the Church. This gives rise to a highly complicated dialectic of a double kind as regards the rigour and flexibility which

[10] Tertullian, *Apologeticum* 39, 7 (CCL 1), 151. On the problem of the connection between the Church and secular society in general, cf. also 'The Function of the Church as a Critic of Society', *Theological Investigations* XII (London 1974), pp. 229–49; also *Freiheit und Manipulation in Gesellschaft und Kirche* (Munich 1970).

are called for with regard to membership of the one or the other society. For this question one ought to consider the possibility of an ecclesiological 'marginal group', since here traditional ecclesiology can offer only the sterile, inappropriate and insufficiently differentiated word 'catechumen'.

What ought to be developed, too, would be a theology of co-existence, starting from statements which are apparently simply contradictory, logically speaking, but which, because they belong to different levels, existentially and socially, are not truly 'irreconcilable' after all. What ought to be brought out here is ultimately only this: with an eye to the possible co-existence between liberty of faith and the mutually binding confession of faith of the ecclesial community, the Church ought to develop new modes of action and new institutionalisms. Here its opportunity would be that, because of its minority situation, it is under great pressure from outside to push forward with these developments much more rapidly than is possible elsewhere. In this way it could become something of a model for secular society, which is faced with similar problems. For secular society does seem to stand in some perplexity before the dilemma of a social and state ideology enforced by authoritarian means on the one hand, and the increasing disappearance of common basic convictions on the other. But basic convictions are necessary for society, too; otherwise it would degenerate into anarchy, for which the 'remedy' would then probably again be the tyranny of a coercive ideology.

c) The Role of the 'Grass Roots'

At the beginning we mentioned, among other things, that in a Church whose official authority is no longer supported by secular society, the 'grass roots', freely developing groups of believers, takes on an entirely new importance for the Church, and for the effectiveness of its office and ministry. What does this statement really mean? An assessment would require us to trace the beginnings of a free activity of this kind from 'below' – the beginnings, for example, which found expression in the Second Vatican Council. We should have to know what tendencies were (and are) of determining importance for the further development of these beginnings; why such attempts have undergone considerable setbacks since the Council; whether and under what conditions these personal 'grass roots' communities are conceivable as the fundamental cells of the Church which are required today; how they are related to traditional parishes; and what new conceptions about the priest and his function could emerge as a result.

Unfortunately we cannot do more here than merely mention these points. But their bearing for our subject as a whole can be summed up with considerable clarity. The Church, in its present minority situation, where it is no longer supported by the secular powers of society, can only *be* the Church – and can only continually *become* the Church – by deliberately being the Church from below. Sociologically, it can no longer be a Church which is *presented to* the rank and file and *confronts* it. But this means that the relationship between the basic community and the authorities must also take a very different form from the one we have hitherto been used to. Nor will this new form leave structures and institutions untouched.

The problem in secular societies seems to me to show entirely analogous features. For whether we look at the Western democracies with the different nuances they give to their 'concept of democracy', or at the Socialist countries, with their different party oligarchies – everywhere in the world the relationship between the masses, the basic community, the people and the élite – the leaders – seems to be disturbed. The gap between them, at all events, is a wide one. Parliamentary representation is increasingly losing its earlier standing, and not infrequently gives the impression of being a mere façade behind which other powers and forces exercise their influence without any control at all. In that way it becomes ultimately unimportant which small and largely anonymous groups obtain this dominating position.

In the Socialist countries, the people are claimed to be the active upholders of economy and State; but even so, here, too, the observer of the different attempts at finding practicable models sees the same problem: how huge masses of the people – now educated anyway to a point where they can no longer be treated as minors – can remain in sufficient contact with the indispensable apparatus of higher officialdom for decisions to be made by the people (always assuming that something of the kind is really wanted).

Where this problem is concerned, the situation, the task and the means are certainly very different in the Church and secular society. But there will probably be no argument about the fact that the problem of active participation by the rank and file in the decisions of the leadership in both does exist. On both sides people are searching for forms and structures for a participation of this kind. We too should not simply think that this problem has already really been solved, and that our task is just to remain true to the democratic constitution, and at most to purify it in its already existing form.

After all that we have said, it will probably now no longer appear far-fetched to seek for models for secular society in the Church. But really this is nothing new. We can read of Christianity's early period: 'See how those Christians love one another'; so might it not later also be said of us: 'See how they really live *together*, in liberty and without coercion?' This hope may sound highly utopian, especially since the insight and will for profound alterations still seems hardly to exist in the Church. Perhaps the inexorable results of its minority status will have to force themselves even more urgently and inescapably on its consciousness. All the same, we believe that the Christian's sense of responsibility for secular society, which was newly proclaimed by the Second Vatican Council, can certainly enable us to perceive our duty and strengthen our determination to see that the relation between the rank and file on the one hand, and the official ministry on the other, is embedded in the structure of the Church in such a way that it may even take on, to some degree, an exemplary significance for secular society; and that in this way out-of-date patterns of inter-human relationships will cease to be cultivated when they have been abandoned everywhere else.

PART FOUR

Signs of the Times
for
the Church

15

THE ONE CHURCH AND THE MANY CHURCHES

OUR subject is the one Church and the many Churches.[1] We might also say, the one Church of God and of his Christ, and the many Churches of men and women. When we talk about the many Churches, we are looking at the Church as a historical specific social entity, with a human word, in which the Word of God finds expression, with sacramental signs and tokens, with institutions, with an office and ministry, and with everything else that belongs to a human society. It is obvious to us that the Church and the Churches do not consist merely of what belongs to them in their character as historical, social entities. We know that their real theological essence means the Spirit and grace; and that for them the decisive things are the faith, hope and love which in them come to fruition – indeed that these realities are to be found beyond the Churches themselves, wherever a person overcomes his own nature and listens to the voice of conscience. And we know, too, that all the tangible social realities to the Church and the Churches have significance only to the extent in which they are the sign, the incarnation and the mediation of these realities of grace, which link man with man, and so with Jesus Christ, and hence draw men and women into the mystery which we call God. But when we talk about the one Church and the many Churches, we also have to remember their historical and social dimension. For it is in relation to that, that the question of unity, diversity and division is raised.

[1] The same question is considered by the present author in somewhat different form in 'Church, Churches and Religions', *Theological Investigations* X (London 1973), pp. 30–49; 'On the Theology of the Ecumenical Discussion', *Theological Investigations* XI (London 1974); 'Perspectives for the Future of the Church', *Theological Investigations* XII (London 1974), pp. 202–17; also 'Theologische Deutung der Gegenwartssituation als Situation der Kirche', *HPTh* II/1 (Freiburg 1966), pp. 233–56.

THE PRESENT SITUATION AS AN ECCLESIOLOGICAL PROBLEM

Interpreting the question in this way, we can approach it from various directions. For a Catholic dogmatic theologian it would seem most obvious to start from dogmatic ecclesiology – which means, in specific terms, the theological self-understanding of the Catholic Church; and *from that starting point* to ask how we have to understand the unity of the Church theologically. We would then enquire how, in principle, even in a Catholic ecclesiology, the one Church is the communion of many particular Churches, with their own history, their own form, and each with the unique character of its own life. We would ask what difference in the particular Churches is irreconcilable with the theological character of the one Church, and therefore ought not to exist; what relationship the latter has to these many Churches; what positive theological status this Church can none the less concede to these many Churches; and why, how, and with what reservations the Catholic Church in its specific existing form sees itself as *the* Church of Christ.[2]

But here – for reasons which will soon emerge – we shall first of all choose another starting point, and shall pick a different approach. We shall search for a starting point and approach that is empirical, and begins with the sociology of religion. In doing so we are of course well aware that with this method we shall reach only part of the questions raised by this subject. When we talk about the many Churches, we do this almost inevitably under the influence of an interpretation of them – a way of looking at them – which may be theologically justifiable and even necessary, but which does not correspond to reality where the sociology of religion is concerned, or which – better – leaves out this sociological aspect altogether. For we do not merely conceive of each of these Churches as what it undoubtedly is – a social institution, with its different sections, its officials, a particular law, a particular history, and so forth; we tacitly assume that in every religious organisation of this kind a certain, clear conviction or profession of faith is to be found, a creed which plays

---

[2] On this terminology, cf. *Vatican II; Decree on Ecumenism*, art. 3 and 19, as well as the 'Dogmatic Constitution on the Church', art. 15, in *The Documents of Vatican* II, ed. W. M. Abbott (London 1966), pp. 345–6, 361–2 and 33–4 respectively. Cf. the commentary in *Commentary on the Documents of Vatican* II, ed. H. Vorgrimler, vols I and II (New York and London 1967 and 1968).

a prominent part for the people united in this society, and is binding
on them, and which therefore, distinguishes it from other ecclesiastical societies; because it is these credal discrepancies which divide
these churches.[3]

From a historical and theological viewpoint, this way of looking
at the Churches and their divisions may be correct. Formerly it was
certainly the only way. For earlier it was this confession of faith that
held each Church together; and every confession of faith that distinguished one Church from the other Churches took the form of a clear
conviction – at least among the church leaders, who were also the
socially authorised representatives. These leaders also really did have
behind them the people in the Church whom they represented and
could certainly feel themselves to be their spokesmen and representatives. For on the one hand these people, in so far as they had a
theological opinion at all, did not (and could not, sociologically speaking) have any opinion other than that held by these representatives,
who were also authorised by society and by the State. And on the
other hand, these representatives succeeded to a certainly considerable
degree in mediating to their people the denominational creed which
divided one Church from another. This meant that in each Church
they succeeded, practically speaking, in producing a homogeneous
denominational consciousness with an individual impress of its own.
In this sense the Protestant Churches, too, were themselves, by way
of their theological representatives, clerical, in spite of the wide individual theological differences which existed between them down to
the end of the nineteenth century, in spite of their acknowledgement
of the universal priesthood of all believers, and in spite of the sects
and revival movements which continually sprang up from below.
That is to say, a sociologically demarcated and institutionally formal
group (of pastors, with the princes as supreme episcopate)[*] were, in
theory and practice, responsible for their particular people as a whole.
In this way (and this is also true from the point of view of the
sociology of religion) each Church, divided from the others, was able
to form a homogeneous denomination.

---

[3] Cf. 'Transformations in the Church and in Secular Society', pp. 167–80
of the present volume.
   [*] The author's analysis here is based on the historical character of the
Protestant Churches in Germany [translator].

THE SITUATION OF THE CHURCHES FROM THE VIEWPOINT OF THE
SOCIOLOGY OF RELIGION

But what is today the real situation sociologically, and what is the relationship of the many Churches to one another, seen in this context? If we want to describe this situation and this relationship by means of common sociological terms, without making any claim to expert knowledge of the sociology of religion, we can and must probably say something like the following. For historical reasons, a great many people – what we may call the rank and file of the Church – live under the cover of a particular religious organisation. Each of these separate religious organisations has a 'statute of association', which is known as a profession of faith, and this is regarded as more or less binding, even though the compass of this profession and its binding character may vary greatly in the individual Churches. But the specific character of this statute of association and its difference from that of other Christian religious organisations is, practically speaking, known only to the administrative officials and the professional theologians. For the rank and file in the Church in its widest sense it is unknown or of no interest. When the rank and file of the Church itself (assuming that they know and affirm the separate character of these religious organisations) find the other religious organisations alien and reject them, this is usually for historical, cultural, psychological and institutional reasons. Yet according to the unanimous judgement of the functionaries and theologians of the divided Churches, reasons of *this* kind are not necessarily bound to divide them at all. We may think here, for example, of external differences in forms of worship, or religious customs, or differences of a cultural kind, or a historically conditioned style of Christian living, and so forth. What the rank and file receives from its particular Church, practically speaking, is largely common to all Christians: belief in God as the guarantor and goal of the moral order; hope for the forgiveness of sins; recognition of Jesus Christ as the mediator of salvation in some form or other, even if it is a cloudy one; prayer; hope for eternal life. One might put it very crudely and say that the 'official' reasons for the division of the Churches are not known at all, or hardly at all, to the ordinary members of the different Churches; while the sociological reasons, which in actual fact cut off the Churches from one another, are theologically and officially for the most part irrelevant. To put it in a somewhat malicious and certainly exaggerated way: from the point of view of the sociology of religion, the divided Churches are like shops next door to one another, in which the customers buy the same things, because the same things are on sale in all of them; and where the thing which is to be had in only one of the shops is not bought at all.[4]

Today this is the case not only in the Protestant Churches (where philosophical or ideological pluralism and the mental and spiritual differentiations of society make a swift and clear impact, because of the fundamental understanding of the Church and faith). It is true of the Catholic Church, as well. There, too, there are enough people for whom the seven sacraments, papal infallibility, veneration of saints, and of Mary, indulgences and much more, play no part in their real religious lives. There will probably be even more of these people in the future; and they are to be found not only among the 'modern pagans'—the indifferent, the merely baptised, and the people who only pay their financial dues—but even among the people who practise the basic substance of Christianity in the Church. These people deny, doubt or ignore in practice all the tenets we have mentioned, without of their own initiative feeling that this is a reason for leaving the Catholic Church, and without the authorities of the Catholic Church having any easily applicable, practicable ways of excluding them 'officially'—at least unless these differences make themselves clearly evident in the Church's public life.

DANGERS AND NEW OPPORTUNITIES

We have done no more than mention this sociological situation, without being able to go into the reasons for it. But what does this situation mean for the question of the one Church and the many Churches?

Union without Regard for the Question of Truth?

First of all we might think—and many Christians really do think today—that the historical and sociological transformation of religion has long since overtaken the traditional differences between the Churches. To take an example: in the actual consciousness of the

---

[4] The situation analysed here has been of concern to the present author for a considerable time, and has given rise to a number of theological reflections. It is also the basis of the ideas in the essay, 'Third Church?', pp. 215–27 of the present volume.

Protestant Christian (as distinct from the professional theologian) the *articulus stantis et cadentis ecclesiae* about the merely imputative justification of man through fiducial faith alone no longer really plays an important part; and the position is no different, sociologically and psychologically, on the Catholic side. So we might well think that a union of the Church (even an organisational one) no longer presents insurmountable difficulties today (provided only that we really take this sociological and psychological attitude on the part of church members seriously), or that the difference in religious organisation between the individual Churches is unimportant when we come to the theological unity of the Church.[5] In terms of the very broad metaphor we used earlier, we might· think that the various shops could well amalgamate, because in fact they simply sell the same goods anyway, and the old white elephants (which will never be sold any more) could be taken out of stock right away. Or we might say that the actual number of these shops, even if they continue to exist, makes no difference to their similarity and hence fundamental unity; indeed it even offers the advantage of a certain useful competitiveness and avoids an undue organisational concentration.

There are many practical indications that a number of Christians in the various Churches do think like this—indications which we cannot consider in detail here. We need only consider the movement for complete intercommunion, ahead of the settlement of doctrinal differences between the denominations, or tendencies towards a fusion between Catholic and Protestant student congregations; or the movement towards common church congresses, and the participation of Protestant Christians and theologians in Catholic synods—even though things of this kind are still open to varying interpretations.

Actual Facts and Norms of Existence

But in reality the matter is not as simple as it seems if we look at it only on the basis of these facts, drawn from the sociology of religion.

First of all, attention must be drawn to one basic truth. It is in general a dubious matter simply and without closer inspection to proclaim existing facts as being the norms of existence without more ado, thus making a *de jure* out of a *de facto*. In our case we must ask

[5] This subject is developed further in the essay 'Is Church Union Dogmatically Possible?', pp. 197–214 of the present volume.

if to do this would not be like deriving sexual morality as it should
be from the facts of the Kinsey Report. But we shall not develop that
any further here.[6]

A Secularisation of the Church?

Before we draw conclusions for our subject from the facts we have
indicated, which are drawn from the sociology of religion, we must
seriously consider something else. A large number of people who
today still help to determine the sociological picture of the different
Churches and make the unique character of these Churches and their
difference from the others indistinct, are actually, if we look at them
more closely, no longer Christians at all. People like this are often
'enrolled' or 'registered' members of their respective Churches because of their social background, or their parents, or their earlier
education in a church school, or because of a social code of behaviour.
They are not members because of a real, fundamental Christian conviction. This can very often be the case even if the person in question
has not as yet noticed it. He may actually be intensively engaged in
working for a transformation of the Church's image, in terms of
church politics. If we look more closely we shall notice that people
like this are chiefly animated by what is of course a highly estimable
humanitarian involvement—perhaps especially in the direction of
social politics—and, it may be, by a very vague and diffuse religious
feeling, a kind of philosophical and ethical theism. They are not
impelled by convictions of faith which, according to the origin and
the common basic conviction of all Christian denominations, are
specifically Christian and indispensable for a true Christian Church.
That is to say, these people do not even vitally share, as a living and
absolute conviction of faith which has to be adhered to, what the
basic formula of the World Council of Churches describes as being
the common profession of faith of all the Christian Churches.[7]

[6] On this problem, cf. K. Rahner, 'Theoretische und reale Moral in ihrer
Differenz', *HPTh* (Freiburg 1966), pp. 152–63.

[7] For the text of this declaration, cf. *Die Einheit der Kirche. Material der
ökumenischen Bewegung*, Theol. Bücherei 30 (Munich 1965), pp. 82f. (also
pp. 83–93). For a critical discussion, cf. R. Bultmann, 'Das christologische
Bekenntnis des Ökumenischen Rates', *EvTheol* 11 (Munich, 1951/2), pp. 1–
13. For its history, cf. R. Rouse and S. C. Neill, *History of the Ecumenical
Movement 1517–1948* (London 1954).

Men and women like this are of course, as people, often of the first order; but theologically they are Christians only in a social sense, for some fortuitous historical reason, even if they have not noticed this consciously. And people of this kind will actually explicitly or implicitly try to undermine the Church, so to speak. That is to say, they will try to make their own mentality the legitimate, even officially recognised 'creed' of their Churches, beyond which nothing may be demanded in that Church in the way of creed and conviction of faith.

Purely empirically and sociologically we cannot, of course, even know with certainty *a priori* that such an attempt to elevate what is really an individual's secularised mentality into the character and creed of his own particular Church will not succeed. Nor can it be known in advance how far such an attempt (which does not have to be undertaken explicitly and purposefully) will succeed in any individual Church.

The success of such an attempt would transform the Church in question into at best a movement and institution for a kind of moral rearmament, furnished with a few traditional ornaments of a Christian folk lore. It would take from the Christian Churches the chance of being truly Christian and would ultimately dissolve them into a secularised society with their own ethical ideas. But apart from that, *the Catholic Christian, at least, will cling stubbornly to the hoping conviction of his faith* that this attempt to secularise his Church (even if it be not called that) will not in fact succeed, even if in overcoming this trend the Catholic Church in its abiding Christian sense were to become numerically very small.

It is quite conceivable that to maintain the basic Christian substance of faith as the indispensable creed and essence of the Church and the Churches will lead to a numerically considerable emigration of many people, if these people have hitherto belonged to them for historical and social reasons, and if this basic Christian substance of faith (which they no longer really share) does not really provide the true theological and existential foundation for their membership of the Church.

FROM THE ESTABLISHED CHURCH TO THE COMMUNITY CHURCH

If we once presuppose that this will be the situation in the future, then the problem of the Church and the Churches presents itself in a quite different light from today. For today the dogmatic problem of the relationship between the Churches is overlaid and obscured by the sociological situation of the still existing established ones. If the members of the future Churches (which will not be established, or at least not to the extent in which they have been hitherto[8]) want truly to live from the free personal assent of faith to the real fundamental substance of the Christian faith, i.e. the living God in the immediacy of grace, Jesus Christ as the absolute and eschatological bringer of salvation, and the eternal life which transcends the possibilities of this world—and if they want to form the Church in the light of all this, then two points presumably emerge for the relationship between the denominationally divided Churches.

Growing Consciousness of Denominational Differences[9]

First, the people belonging to these future Churches could find that the denominational differences which used to separate them had once again become alive and relevant, in a certain sense and to a certain extent. For although historical reasons have played a very considerable part in the story of the divisions between the Churches of the West, yet in earlier times Christians did, all the same, experience their denominational, 'dividing' conviction as the articulation and result of the ultimate decision of their Christian faith. They did not feel that denominational differences were simply controversies which were added on top of an absolutely clear, basic Christian conviction common to all; their differences seemed to them to emanate quite conclusively from their ultimate, fundamental understanding of Christianity. So they always asked themselves—in spite of the Apostles' Creed which they had in common, and in spite of their one, common baptism—whether they really had the same fundamental Christian substance in common, or whether the denominational differences, secondary though they might appear in certain sense, did not all the same betray an ultimate difference in the fundamental understanding of Christianity. If this ultimate, basic substance of

[8] On the concept of the 'established' Churches in the particular German sense of *Volkskirchen*, cf. K. Rahner and N. Greinacher, 'Religion und Kirche in der modernen Gesellschaft', *HPTh* II/1 (Freiburg 1966), pp. 231–3.

[9] These ideas seem at first sight to contradict what is said in the essays 'Is Church Union Dogmatically Possible?' and 'Third Church?', both in the present volume (pp. 197–214 and 215–27 respectively). But here it is a question of a deepening of the 'basic Christian substance'—which these other essays also presuppose as being necessary.

Christianity again becomes radically evident, and if it moves again into the centre of Christian existence, because the Churches are detaching themselves from a secularised (even if thereby humanised) world, the people who then still belong to them could really become conscious of these denominational differences in a much sharper and more challenging way. It is quite possible that someone will then say, out of the very personal involvement of his faith, 'Because I believe in Jesus Christ as the sole mediator of salvation, I can only (for example) reject the primacy of the pope, in a final primal, Christian protest.' And another will say, 'Because I believe in the permanent incarnational, and thus social, presence of Christ's eschatological grace in the Church, the primacy of the pope is really for me self-evident.' It is, therefore, on the one hand quite possible that through the sociological transformation from 'established' Churches (into which one is, in a sense, born), into Churches that are dependent on personal decisions of faith, the theological difference between them will again become clearer; and that in this way the question about the many Churches and the one Churches will again take on existential importance.

The Meaning of the Fundamental Substance of Christianity

But this, secondly, does not mean that our question returns us to the historical point at which it first became a question, in the sixteenth century. For there is a radical difference between the situation at that time, on the one hand, and the situation of faith now and in the future on the other. It may well be that the ultimate basic understanding of Christianity was not adequately considered or sufficiently differentiated, and expressed itself only indirectly in what were, after all, secondary differences of doctrine. But even though this has not been clearly enough recognised, that basic understanding was still taken for granted on all sides of the confessional dispute. It was the starting point of these controversies, but not really the question on which everything hinged. Faith in the living God, in his verbal revelation, in Jesus Christ, in eternal life, in the possibility of addressing God personally in prayer, were matters of course—unquestioned assumptions—in some sense static parameters of understanding. And within these parameters the denominational controversies centred on questions which were of relatively secondary importance.

Today things are radically different. The traditional points of controversy dividing the Churches can still be seen as genuine questions from the standpoint of these basic Christian convictions; but the real, fundamental question of the person of today, if he wants to be a Christian, is concerned with the basic substance of Christianity itself. In specific and existential terms, he will be a member of a Church tomorrow, not because he takes the basic substance of Christianity for granted, and chooses that particular Church to be his own because it corresponds to his own conviction in its articulation of the secondary questions of Christianity. He will be a member of a Church because he affirms this basic substance of Christianity in faith, and is therefore determined to become a member of the Church as such. The basic substance of Christianity will itself be formative of the Church, since it is this that is called in question and consequently affirmed in a personal decision of faith. And the traditional points of controversy will be clearly felt to be secondary.[10] In such a situation, which crystallises only slowly, the traditional points of controversy between the individual Churches will simply take on a quite different importance. They will still be genuine questions of faith—indeed they will become so again—but any particular question will be enveloped by a much more radical question of making a decision of faith which is intellectually honest and existentially realisable and which relates to this real, basic substance of Christianity. In this situation, we may expect and hope, the question about the traditional points of controversy between the different denominations can be raised in a much more relaxed manner, freed from a great many emotionally laden factors; for it will be raised by people who are searching together in a totally new way for the innermost centre of the Christian faith, which at heart is no longer the self-evident presupposition of all Christians but is common to them all as their real task, their burden and their salvation.[11]

[10] cf here the notion of the 'hierarchy of truth', which has its special significance precisely in questions of this kind; Vatican II, 'Decree on Ecumenism' No. 11 in *The Documents of Vatican II*, ed. W. M. Abbott (London 1966), p. 354; commentary by J. Feiner in *Commentary on the Documents of Vatican II*, ed. H. Vogrimler, vol II (New York and London 1968), pp. 118–20.

[11] cf. the present author's attempt in 'Mitte des Glaubens' in A. Exeler, J. B. Metz and K. Rahner, *Hilfe zum Glauben*, Theol. Meditation 27 (Zürich 1971), pp. 39–56.

Easier Conversation between the Churches

If in this way, the denominational points of controversy, despite taking on a quite new lease of life, move away from the real centre of the actual Christian decision of faith and really shift to its fringe, then there is much more hope that they can be cleared up, and that we may progress in the direction of a common Christian profession of faith, even in secondary, denominational points of controversy. We may at least hope for this, because the realities in the Churches, to which these theoretical differences of doctrine are related, will present themselves in a quite different historical and social form from the one they assumed in the Reformation period. We only have to realise how much the image of the Catholic Church empirically experienced in the sixteenth century differs from that of the twentieth—how differently the papacy, the Mass, the relationship of Catholic theology to Scripture, indulgences, and many other things, presented themselves then and present themselves today.

In short: in a future situation which has already begun, a situation in which what is radically at stake in all denominations is the question of faith in the ultimate essence of Christianity as a whole, there will be a more genuine opportunity to solve the denominational differences of the past.[12]

The sociological state of affairs within the individual Churches certainly cannot make the question of truth appear unimportant, but—if it still exists in the future, in spite of the departure of a not inconsiderable number of people from all the Churches—it will still be able to help to overcome *the immobility of the Churches' leaders* who almost unavoidably think and work more for the preservation of their own *status quo* than for a further development of the Churches towards a future of the one Church.

THE CATHOLIC CHURCH OF THE FUTURE AND THE UNITY OF THE CHURCH

Although it would have been quite legitimate to do so, we have not taken as our starting point the question of truth; though it is this which stands between the individual Churches, and it is the varying

---

[12] cf. the brief meditative essays by the present author collected under the title, 'Grundfragen', *Wagnis des Christen—Geistliche Texte* (Freiburg 1974), pp. 13–56.

answers to this which prevent the unity of the many Churches in the unity of the same confession of faith. We have rather, very empirically and *a posteriori*, started from a sociological situation in the Churches which, at first glance, could almost suggest the view that the differences in theological doctrine have long since become out of date and unreal. But through this very approach we have come to see that this sociological situation engenders the theological question about the truth in a new and notable way. This has to be so, ultimately, simply because a free society of a religious kind cannot come into being in any way other than through a common creed. Otherwise it inevitably sinks into an ultimately uninteresting affair of folk lore—into a social relic which can only be explained historically and awaits complete dissolution. Today, and tomorrow, too, the question of the one Church and the many Churches cannot be decided irrespective of the question of truth, even though it may be a separate question what truth means in this connection, and how truth is to be realised in a Church. But this very sociological starting point has also shown that the question of truth really does present itself in a different way nowadays, compared with 450 years ago, and that this new situation also offers new opportunities for a common answer to the real question of truth.

For the Catholic who is a real Catholic—theologically, not merely in a sociological sense—one element of his Catholic faith is the living conviction that, if at some time or other there is to be a single Christian Church in our present era, it will be in a theological sense Catholic. But of course it will be *the Catholic Church of the future*, which will certainly show a legitimate, historical continuity with the present one, but is all the same not just the Church in the specific form in which it now presents itself to historical and empirical observation.

This Church will very clearly be the *communio* of the Churches which, in the light of their own historical origins and presuppositions, will bring and incorporate into this one Church all that God has given them in the way of positive Christian truth.

Once it has become clearer that all positive concerns of the Reformation Churches can also find a natural home in the Catholic Church; and when it has become even clearer theologically than hitherto that the threefold *sola* of the Reformation is absolutely Catholic (as long as it is not understood heretically but in a Catholic sense, i.e. positively as 'yea' and not as 'nay')—*then the Reformation Churches can also be asked*, at least with hope, whether they cannot acknowledge that the legitimate and full historical continuity between the present-day Churches and the Church of our beginnings is not to be found most clearly in the Catholic Church. They can be asked whether they cannot also recognise this in concrete terms, in shaping and unifying the Church, without having to feel that they are merely returning to an existing unity. Even under these pre-conditions, they could see themselves as Churches forming a unity of Churches, which is the sole hope of the future.

Whether such a unity of all the Christian Churches will one day be achieved in actual fact within world history, or whether Christ will be the Shepherd of the one flock only when history has come to an end—that we cannot know. But as Christians we must continually remind ourselves of one thing: we have to do what we can so that out of the many Churches the one Church of Christ may develop, even as an historical concrete reality; but we must not permit this to mean the simple abolition of the diversity of the Churches as communion in the one Church.

16

IS CHURCH UNION DOGMATICALLY POSSIBLE?

THERE is a considerable difference in all the Christian Churches between 'official' teaching and what is really believed by most members of the Church in question. It is this fact, at first sight surprising, which has provoked the following reflections.[1] But first of all we must say more precisely what we mean, before we consider its theological significance. After that we can go on to indicate its possible consequences.

THE DIFFERENCE BETWEEN THE OFFICIAL DOCTRINE OF THE CHURCH AND ACTUAL BELIEF

What we mean here is something that can be found in all the Christian Churches. That may be said, even though the 'official' doctrine in the different Churches is not upheld by the same body and has a different value, in accordance with the self-understanding of the individual Churches; and even though the gap between what is actually believed and what is officially taught may vary in extent.

This difference has by no means to be merely – or even primarily – one which takes the form of a real, direct and, as such, observed contradiction between an official statement of the Church which is declared to be binding, and the conviction which an individual member or group of members in that particular Church holds and maintains; although contradictions of this kind can exist too. It is rather that the actual awareness of what faith involves differs in its whole

---

[1] The author admits that he has often thought about this. Cf. 'Ecumenical Theology in the Future', *Theological Investigations* XIV (London 1976), pp. 254–69, and elsewhere. But these essays do not cover exactly the same ground.

structure from official doctrine. It may perhaps have a less explicitly expressed content; it may stress things differently, where the significance and binding character of particular theological statements are concerned; or it may take a different view of the significance of a particular doctrine for the actual life of the Christian.[2]

As we have already said, this difference can be found in *all* the Christian Churches. It is true that the gap is most clearly evident and most easily discernible in the Roman Catholic Church, because there we have a directly tangible, active magisterium and a precisely tangible or definable official church doctrine whose binding quality can be exactly stated and graded. But in the other Churches, too, there is something like an official doctrine. All the Christian Churches have their confessions of faith; all recognise Holy Scriptures as binding (at least in principle, even if the theological interpretation of what the word 'binding' means can again vary considerably); all of them have something like ministers, who feel themselves to be the representatives and spokesmen of their Church's convictions of faith; and all have something like professional theologians, who in some way or other claim to speak in the name of the Churches, with at least some degree of binding authority. Yet if here, too, we may speak of an 'official' doctrine, that doctrine is by no means certainly and from the outset identical with what actually goes on in the heads and hearts of church members.

The fact that we are considering here is, of course, first of all a self-evident truism. Churchmen and theologians in all the Churches are well aware that a large proportion of church members who belong 'officially' and sociologically to that particular Church, and who are also more or less practising members, are not particularly interested, are poorly informed, and are influenced in their actual sense of faith (beyond the doctrine and proclamation of the Church itself) by a great number of secular factors, which may be sociological, or may belong to the history of ideas and the climate of thought, or to the psychology of the individual. This means that it is quite impossible for the actual faith of most church members to be simply a pure and

---

[2] This was already a much earlier finding of the present author's; cf. *Gefahren im heutigen Katholizismus* (Einsiedeln 1950), and the various remarks on the subject of heresy, e.g., 'Schism in the Catholic Church?', *Theological Investigations* XII (London 1974), pp. 98–115; and 'Heresies in the Church Today?' ibid., pp. 116–41.

uncloudcd mirror of the 'official' doctrine of faith or of the 'pure Gospel'.

Here and there people have also given theological consideration to this fact: for example in Catholic theology, when its fundamental theology considers how the *rudes* can arrive at an adequate judgment of credibility about the existence of a divine revelation; or when elsewhere theologians have considered the meaning of *fides implicita*; or when the question was raised about what a person must definitely and expressly believe for him to achieve salvation, or for him to count as a member of the Christian Church; or when closer consideration is given to the question, under what circumstances and conditions an erroneous opinion (if it is obstinately maintained in public, for example) excludes a person from the Church.[3] The same considerations lie behind the continually formulated, brief summaries of the Christian faith, which are based on the assumption that the average Christian does not explicitly know very much more than this about the substance of faith. Something similar will also be found in the doctrine and practice of other Churches. The possibility of disciplinary proceedings in doctrinal questions, for example, makes this clear.

But in spite of this (or so it seems to me, at least, in the light of my limited experience), this difference between official doctrine and the actually existing sense of faith hardly plays any part in ecumenical theology and ecumenical dialogue as it is actually carried on. Or if it does, it is only very recently, and then it is a point taken up at the 'grass roots', rather than by churchmen and theologians. Ecumenical dialogues pursue their ecumenical purpose by comparing the official doctrines of the various Churches. Controversial theology is a controversy between the various confessions of faith writings. This is how theologians talked to theologians until very recently. For them it was an obvious assumption (even if it is really not obvious at all) that they were able to speak in the name of the actual persuasions of the members of their particular Churches. This tacit assumption, which was acted on almost up to the present, is simply a relic from earlier times, in which an élite (whether it was 'the powers that be' in the Church or the State, or whether it was the professional theologians, who alone were competent for these questions) considered

---

[3] cf. C. Pesch, *Praelectiones Dogmaticae* VIII, 4th–5th edns (Freiburg 1922): 'De fide theologica', esp. n. 297ff., and 'De necessitate fidei', n. 426ff.

themselves to be the representatives of a particular conviction. They therefore felt they could expect the rest – 'the man in the street' – to hold the same opinion; or that this ordinary member of the Church would in actual fact be brought to hold that opinion, through the power of secular or ecclesiastical social institutions; or that at least he would not raise any sort of socially relevant opposition against this view. In the light of this mental and sociological situation, it is understandable that the only question asked in ecumenical conversations was about the compatibility of the official teachings of the various Churches. Indeed faith as it actually existed in the Churches was hardly the subject of theological discussion at all.

THE NORMATIVE SIGNIFICANCE OF ACTUAL FAITH

This means that theology ought to reflect more explicitly on the theological relevance of this actual faith, before considering what ecumenical significance *this* faith has. First of all one thing ought to be seen more clearly, and more explicitly stated. *This* faith is what is actually meant, or ought to be meant, when we are talking theologically about the faith of the Church – *this* faith, primarily, and not the official faith the Churches profess. For it is this faith, and not initially the faith of the official creeds, which exists in the minds and hearts of people who are Christians. This is the faith that is lived, which counts before God and brings salvation. That is really a matter of course. But we lose sight of it as a natural assumption if, at the moment when we inquire about the saving faith of Christians – the faith that finds salvation – we immediately think about the faith which is officially taught by the Church, and cease to ask ourselves at all how much of this faith really exists in the actual faith that is held and personally implemented by the individual Christian in the Church. Of course we can say that even a real faith of this kind has its implications and inherent powers and unreflected backgrounds and depth; and that these are more clearly objectified in the official doctrine of the Church. That is to say, we might claim that, when all is said and done, the actual faith of the Christian still implies, in an unreflective way, the official doctrine of the Church. Of course we can also, in a sublime theology, describe the most essential and ultimate facts of Christian faith (even in its official interpretation) so formally and existentially, trying thereby to discover its essential saving character, that not very much material content is required to constitute this faith, and on the other hand a faith of the loftiest theology, seen in this way, can also be regarded more or less convincingly as being shared by every Christian.

A Catholic theology of faith can appeal to *fides implicita*,[4] saying that the normal Christian always and from the outset relates his faith (as *fides quae* – faith as object) to the faith and creed of his Church. Though this faith may be highly fragmentary, this personal faith of his is therefore always more than it first seems to be; and because of its relationship to the Church's understanding of faith, the individual may still be considered to hold this 'official' faith of the Church. All that may be quite correct. But it does not do away with the gap between faith as it is actually lived and the official faith of the Church. For it is precisely this distinction that is presupposed in the attempt to bridge the gap we have described.

In addition, the following criticism must be made, especially where a Catholic theology of faith appeals to *fides implicita*. In earlier times the theologically uninstructed Christians belonging to the Church, with their rudimentary faith ('rudimentary' always in the sense of *fides quae*, not necessarily as *fides qua*, or personal faith) may have related this faith of theirs clearly and firmly to the teaching authority of the Church. This was partly due to their general attitudes of mind (with its willing acceptance of authority) and their sociological background. And in their case *fides implicta* may well – for highly understandable reasons – have fulfilled the function which the scholastic theological tradition ascribed to it. But nowadays, even in the Catholic Church, the authority of the Church's magisterium, generally speaking (even where its own definitions are concerned), no longer in fact provides that absolute fixed point and unquestioned presupposition which is necessary for a *fides implicita* in the Church and which throws open the individually conditioned subjectivity of a person's faith to the Church's sense of faith as a whole. This means that even a Catholic theology of faith can no longer so easily bridge the gap between actual belief and official belief by appealing to the *fides implicita* of the Catholic Christian.

The following must also be said about the theology of actual, existing faith. It is not merely – in distinction to official doctrine –

[4] On *fides implicita* cf. C. Pesch, *Praelectiones Dogmaticae* VIII, 4th–5th edn. (Freiburg 1922), n. 195. Cf. also 'Dogmatic Notes on "Ecclesiological Piety"', *Theological Investigations* V (London 1966), pp. 336–65.

the faith by which Christianity lives and which brings the Christian salvation. We have continually to ask anew – and not merely theologically – how and why this faith can exist and can be a saving faith, even in its most rudimentary and implicit form (for example, in a person who maintains in good faith that he feels forced to be an atheist). The official faith of the Church is by no means simply and in every respect the factor that hovers over faith in its actually existing form, as a reality still to be attained, and as the absolute norm which actual faith merely has to reach. Of course we can quite well view the official teaching of the Church as normative for actual faith. People do so in all the Churches, even if in different ways and with different theological justification. But we must not forget that this official *fides quae*, in the sense in which it really exists for us and in which we can really grasp it, is itself an objectification and a historically conditioned codification of an actually lived faith on the part of the Church. So much so that this is even true of that official doctrinal faith which is normatively given in Scripture itself. The faith of the Church's teaching authority cannot therefore ultimately have a normative power for the actual faith of the Church in so far as it is qualitatively quite different from the latter. It can have that normative power only because, and in so far as, it is the successful reflection of just this actual faith of the Church, which includes the faith of many men and women, many different experiences of faith, and the faith of many different periods.

Nor does a view of this kind have to come into conflict with Catholic ecclesiology and its doctrine about the authoritative magisterium of the Church. For this magisterium means precisely the concrete, socially institutionalised way in which the Church's actual faith (which always logically precedes the teaching of the magisterium) becomes more clearly aware of itself, and brings its binding significance to bear on the individual.[5] It is therefore always true that the Church's actual sense of faith *ultimately* has its normative power and its critical authority within itself. It does not derive these things from any magisterial teaching. This is also true for a Catholic fun-

[5] The present writer has frequently discussed the problems associated with the magisterium today. What is to some extent a summing up may be found in the following essays, all in *Theological Investigations* XIV (London 1976): 'Does the Church Offer Any Ultimate Certainties?', pp. 47–65; 'On the Concept of Infallibility in Catholic Theology', pp. 66–85; and 'The Dispute Concerning the Church's Teaching Office', pp. 86–97; etc.

damental theology and ecclesiology, contrary to what a first glance would suggest. It is true, if only because the Church's magisterium is not at all a primary datum of faith, sustaining all the rest, even in a Catholic understanding of the Church. It is itself sustained by a *fides quae* and a *fides qua* which are ultimately based, not on the conviction of the Church's teaching authority, but solely on the power of the Gospel of God and his Christ, which is given by the Spirit. If this means that actual faith has its own self critical energy, this does not exclude – but (at least according to Catholic interpretation) includes – the fact that where this actual faith of absolute commitment (which Catholics call *fides divina et catholica*), has taken objective form in a particular statement, this commitment remains fundamentally valid for all time. This means that a statement of this kind can, as expressing the Church's teaching authority, still be implicitly normative later on for actual faith, where this faith again falls to some extent behind its earlier objectification (and of course it must not deny this objectification altogether).[6] Consequently, always assuming that this actual faith is seen as having its own self-criticial mobility and indebtedness to its own history, we can quite well say that it is even a critical court of appeal against the official teaching existing at any given time, since this teaching itself in a sense a 'snapshot' of actual faith, deriving from an earlier period, even if it is successful and hence authoritative.

As I have already said, this correct and important statement, (which really reverses the usual interpretation of the relationship between actual and official faith) does not entitle us, in a purely empirical, demographic and statistical way, to elevate this *de facto* faith into the sovereign judge of the official faith in the Church pure and simple. What we have said, that is, does not mean permitting average Christians, out of a very superficial awareness, to vote on what is binding in the official doctrines of the Church today, and what is not. A view of this kind is not infrequently to be heard today. But it is not the conclusion to be drawn from the real priority of actual, existing faith compared with 'official' faith; indeed it springs from a misinterpretation of that actual faith.

But though we must presuppose and clearly maintain all this, it

---

[6] Attention may be called here to the collection of essays edited by the present author and also containing his own views, *Zum Problem Unfehlbarkeit – Antworten auf die Anfrage von Hans Küng* (Quaestiones Disputatae 54) 2nd edn (Freiburg 1972).

ought to be possible to bring out the correct priority and the normative significance of the actual faith of the Church for official teaching in the Christian Churches and in their theologies, and to bring it to bear more courageously and unreservedly. If this actual faith is in fact the real faith which creates salvation, why are we theologians generally so suspicious of it in its actual form, its actual structure, its 'dosage', its perspectives, and so forth? Why do we generally feel this actual, existing faith to be merely a regrettable dilution and fashionable distortion, simply because we are much more familiar with the earlier historical objectivation of the actual faith which we – basically correctly – call the official faith of the Church, which we see as normative for present-day *de facto* faith? As I have already stressed, it is not a question of simply denying the truth and obligatory claim of particular individual statements of faith laid down by the magisterium, just because these statements are not part of – or are no longer part of – the superficial and empirical findings of present-day, actual faith (though these findings must not simply be identified with the actual faith itself), or because they are not found to have the same clarity and binding force they had formerly. To this extent theologians certainly always remain the advocates of giving a binding significance to the historical experience of faith of earlier times, which has taken objective form in earlier definitions, confessions of faith, etc., and without which the Christian would fall victim to the blind fashion of his own limited point in time, and his own shrunken present. But this does not seem to alter the fact that in the theologies of the Church, in ecumenical dialogues, and in the actions of the Churches' teaching authorities, the normative significance of actual faith does not carry sufficient weight. What makes itself felt in this faith is not infrequently too hastily viewed merely as danger, impoverishment, one-sidedness, fashion, or superficial modernism. If there is a 'hierarchy of truths' in the Christian sense of facts, if there is not merely an objective hierarchy of truths but also an existential one, which necessarily changes, individually and collectively, why is theology such a poor reflection of this existential hierarchy of truths, which always exists historically at any given time?[7] Or why is the reflection so long delayed? These questions, though I have expressed

---

[7] Vat. II: *Unitatis redintegratio* (Ecumenism) n. 11; for comment cf. 'The Faith of the Christian and the Doctrine of the Church', *Theological Investigations* XIV (London 1976), pp. 24–46.

them very vaguely and generally, are probably of the greatest importance for ecumenical discussion, because this actual faith does not, or does not seem to, vary nearly so much in the different Churches – as might be thought when, in ecumenical discussions, it is more or less taken for granted that Christians of individual Churches will also embody in their actual faith just *those* controversial theological points of doctrine about which the theologians and churchman of the divided Churches are at variance, or at least were at variance earlier. If we were more clearly convinced in actual practice about the normative power of faith as it really exists, much of our ecumenical discussion would perhaps have to be different, to be better, and to move more quickly than it does today, in the stagnating work of the ecumenical movement.

But really something else ought to be said first about the theology of actually existing faith. We ought above all to investigate the different degress of assent with which the actual faith of the Christian is related to individual theological tenets; and we ought to interpret this theologically. This differentiation is not simply identical with that which Catholic theology makes with regard to the 'qualification' of theological statements.[8] For what is under consideration there is an objective difference in the binding character of individual theological statements. And we are not now discussing how far it is possible to establish this, or in what way it is ultimately connected with, and dependent on, what we mean *here*. For what we are discussing here are the degrees of subjective assent to theological statements in the actual faith held by Christians in the actually existing Church. What we are concerned about is only that in the Christian's actual sense of faith, in regard to individual theological statements, there are variations in firmness of assent – or rejection – and in personal involvement; and the extent to which the statements are taken seriously varies too. Moreover these variations are not simply and in every case identical with variations in the theological 'qualification' which the Church's official teaching and theology make for these statements for and through themselves. These to some extent 'subjective' qualifications – which are of the most varying kind and gradation – in the

---

[8] Cf. A. Kolping, 'Qualifikationen', in *LThK* VIII, 2nd edn (Freiburg 1963), pp. 914–19; 'What is Heresy?', *Theological Investigations* V (London and Baltimore 1966), pp. 468–512, where the term is applied in connection with the believer.

actual sense of faith of Christians (in all the Churches, ultimately) also depend largely on the extent to which these theological statements contradict the content of the *secular* scientific and pre-scientific consciousness, and also on the different degrees to which that content is taken seriously. Though it may be that in general this contradiction is not very explicitly thought about.

In this connection one point is probably important. The subject-matter of man's consciousness is gradually becoming unsurveyable, and it is increasingly difficult, or indeed impossible, for him to integrate that subject-matter into a controllable 'system'. This means that he has perhaps a greater feeling than he had earlier for the provisional and hypothetical character of his knowledge and convictions, their openness to doubt and revision. So he is inclined to judge them as provisional opinions rather than as convictions which he has to hold and defend in an absolute way. This does not merely apply to the theological assertions he consciously holds. It is also true of what he knows in the secular sphere. He is inclined to view all knowledge of this kind as provisional working hypotheses, which for the moment help him to come to terms with life, until he arrives at a better explanation, once new experience of life has shown him that the previous working hypothesis is not after all quite sufficient – though this does not mean that he would have to reject the hypothesis wholesale as totally erroneous, in the old absolute style.[9]

This open attitude towards the provisional nature of knowledge which dominates the theological and secular consciousness of the man or woman of today, ought probably to be more explicitly reckoned with, in ecumenical discussions as well, than has usually been the case hitherto. Up to now, people let controversial theological statements of a more or less absolute kind rebound against one another; and the only question was which statement would win. This earlier way of thinking was not basically surmounted even if under certain circumstances a certain theological statement might be declared as not objectively absolutely binding, and so could be eliminated from real controversial theology (for even that was a decision which was fundamentally supposed to count as binding); or by introducing into the field of controversial theology a more closely differentiated theolo-

[9] P. E. Hodgson clarifies the character and origin of this modern way of thinking from the scientist's point of view in 'Zweifel und Gewißheit in den Naturwissenschaften', *StdZ* 193 (1975), pp. 187–98.

gical statement which could supersede the previous polemical opinion. Even so, fundamentally speaking, both sides always presupposed that absolute decisions had to be made, of which only one could be correct and capable of commanding real commitment in a cogent and binding way. The logical irreconcilability of the statements was taken as a matter of course – as evidence that the ways of thinking which formulated them were equally exclusive. But working hypotheses, provisional opinions and statements of this kind, and the attitudes that are embodied in them, have not at all the character which were ascribed to statements as a matter of course in earlier theological controversy.

Now, in saying this I do not mean to maintain that in theology it is permissible to work simply with a modern mental attitude of this kind; for in the sphere of faith and – as an offshoot of that – in the sphere of theology, there are absolute decisions as well (dogma, acknowledgement of a statement as being *articulus stantis et cadentis ecclesiae*); nor should we ignore the danger of an ultimately cheap and comfortable relativism in a mentality of this kind. But this mentality is also to be found, and is actually at work, in the real, existing faith of Christians today and could, if it were applied at the proper point, very well have a positive function. All differentiations in the 'qualification' of theological statements, even in the actual sense of faith of Christians and the Churches, are ultimately the result and expression of the historical nature[10] which belongs to the faith of people and Churches, and which is today as such the subject of reflection. This reflection makes possible and permissible explicitly formulated and accepted ways of behaviour which only used to be matters of fact, without our reflecting about them *as such*, and without their being fully implemented. Perhaps the ecumenical significance of these notions will be clearer if we now try to draw a fundamental conclusion for our ecumenical task from what we have said.

THE CONSEQUENCES FOR AN INSTITUTIONAL UNION OF THE CHURCHES

What fundamental conclusions can be drawn from these reflections for our ecumenical task? We must allow for the possibility, basically,

[10] On the question of historical contingency, cf. also 'The Historicity of Theology', *Theological Investigations* IX (London 1972), pp. 64–82; cf. also 'On the Concept of Infallibility in Catholic Theology', *Theological Investigations* XIV (London 1976), pp. 66–85.

that other facts which we have not considered here may involve conclusions which could nullify what the ideas we have put forward would seem to suggest. But with that proviso, we should probably be correct if we maintained the following: actual, *de facto* faith as we find it in the Churches does not today stand in the way of church union on an institutional level.

In saying this we are not thinking primarily of the fact that, in my opinion, ecumenical conversations at the summit level of expert theology – even where the official doctrine of the Churches is concerned – are hardly aware any more of any really insurmountable points of controversy – points which one cannot see how to eliminate (at least apart from the question of the papal office, as this was defined by the First Vatican Council and as it is binding on the conscience of a Catholic Christian). The Reformation's three-fold *sola* no longer means any doctrine about which the theologians of the Christian denominations could not agree, as long as they really desire union, and do not use their theological acumen to discover and play up new denominational differences once the old ones have been overcome. But, as we have said, this is not what we are discussing here.

What we are thinking about is the actual, average sense of faith of Christians in the different Churches. We are thereby presupposing the normative character of this actual faith, which I have – I hope cautiously – defined, and which requires the official teaching of the various Churches and their theologians to take this *de facto* faith seriously. We are further presupposing that the variations in the sense of faith indicated above are quite legitimate in the context of the existential hierarchy of truths which belongs to faith, and in the context of the 'qualification' of the theological statements, etc., are part of faith. But given these presuppositions we would say: the average faith of contemporary Christians in the various Churches hardly shows any differences. And so we must ask: why, really, should the official doctrinal differences between the individual Churches forbid that institutional unity which is the expression of a factual identity in the actual faith held in the individual Churches?

First of all, it will surely be permissible to say that what we have said really represents the true state of affairs. We are not talking about the theologically highly nuanced sense of faith of churchmen and professional theologians. We are talking about normal Christians in the different Churches, and certainly include the people who participate keenly in the life of their Church. But of these people it can be said that their sense of faith (always presupposing the breadth of variation in that sense within every individual Church) is identical with that of Christians belonging to another denomination. They believe in God; they entrust their lives to this living God of grace and forgiveness; they pray; they are baptised and celebrate the Lord's Supper; they recognise Jesus Christ, the crucified and risen Lord, as the definitive guarantor of God's saving bestowal of himself on them; they live the gospel; they know, too, that to be a Christian in this sense obliges them to participate in a corresponding *community* of faith, the Church. The traditional points of controversy between the Churches (if we leave the papacy on one side for the moment) are unknown to them, or are unimportant, or are at most noted and accepted as part of that provisional and relative character which we indicated above (which is in itself not necessarily existentially unjustified), and which is accepted nowadays as belonging naturally to the historical contingency of the human situation. This description of the actual faith which is identical in the different Churches cannot of course be substantiated more precisely here. But can this assertion seriously be disputed? Of course there are very many differences in the various Churches with regard to actual church practice, devotional style, and so forth. But quite apart from the fact that there are at least just as many differences of *this* kind in one and the same Church, if we look at different countries and social groups, differences of this kind between the denominations cannot claim to legitimise the division of the Churches theologically (or if they do, the claim is an illegitimate one, even according to the official principles of the Church). Faith as it is actually experienced is today the same in the different Churches, among average Christians. Has this fact consequences for the possibility and legitimacy of an institutional unity?

Before we venture to answer this question with an outright affirmative, we must clear up a number of difficulties, some of which have already been indicated while others which will seem obvious, at least to a Catholic theologian and churchman.

1. First of all, under the *doctrinal* aspect, it will be said that in this one Church at which we are aiming (which must also be a Church with a creed and teaching), there must be safeguards for the conviction of faith of people who, for example, hold the Roman Catholic faith – people, that is, who view as irrevocable elements of their faith doctrinal statements which are not shared by other Christians. We can first of all counter this objection, however, by saying that Christ-

ians who view a certain doctrine as being co-constitutive of their
Christian faith must maintain this conviction in this united Church;
and the chance to do so must be given them in that Church, both
humanly and institutionally. But the objection can also be answered
by another question. Does this conviction of faith also involve the
doctrine that *everyone* who lives in the same Church as this believer
has to share the conviction in question *positively* and explicitly? Or is
it enough if this doctrine is not positively condemned by the teaching
authorities and is not so publicly and decidedly rejected by the individual members of the same Church that the rejection amounts to a
genuine commitment of faith. The objection we are considering (on
the part of the Catholic Christian, in this hypothetical case) could be
answered by asking whether the person who makes this objection can
deny that one can legitimately decide, theologically, for the second
alternative with which we countered the objection (i.e., tacit acceptance)? Can he deny this in view of the actual sense of faith within the
Catholic Church and the official reaction to it – which either does
not exist, or is quite content as long as a doctrine defined by the
magisterium is not explicitly and officially denied and declared in-
compatible with true Christianity? In other words: if in the Catholic
Church today, and in the actual sense of faith of its average members,
many dogmas outside the real core of the Christian faith – on the
'fringe', that is, of the hierarchy of truths – are either not known at
all or are at least not consciously, inwardly realised with a final
commitment of faith; and if the official Church tacitly accepts this
situation – not seriously protesting against it at least, as long as such
an officially absolute, binding doctrine is not expressly and publicly
rejected outright by a church member – one could, even from a
Catholic standpoint, well consider that a similar attitude on the part
of the Church's authority would be theologically possible in this
institutionally united Church of the future.

From the doctrinal standpoint, we should then only have to ask
whether most Protestant Christians, who would have to help to
implement an institutional union of this kind, would feel absolutely
bound in conscience, because of what they believe, decidedly to reject
a particular Catholic doctrine as undoubtedly contrary to the gospel?
In today's state of scholarly ecumenical dialogue, and in view of the
actual sense of faith within the Protestant Churches, we may be
permitted to answer this question in the negative. The Protestant
conscience, in its bearing on faith, does not perhaps in its existing

form positively assent, with a believing affirmation, to quite a number of specific Catholic doctrines; but, provided that these Catholic doctrines are themselves properly interpreted, the actual, average Protestant, in his sense of faith, will not meet these Catholic assertions with a positive anathema. Nor does the theology taught in these Churches oblige him to do so.

Of course, even if we agree with what has just been said, we cannot reckon on the fact that simply all the people who have been baptised and call themselves Christians could in conscience join such an institutionally united Church, or that they would do so. There are certainly many Christian denominations and sects who would not agree with the expressly confessed and taught basic substance of the Christian faith which would have to be the confession of faith of these united Churches (the substance that is stated, for example, in the confession of faith of the World Council of Churches, with its christological and trinitarian content). And the same would, of course, have to be said about many individual Christians.

But if in the case of the major Protestant and Orthodox Churches we may assume that the actual sense of faith of the average Christian (even in its empirically and directly tangible form) has a positive, open relationship to the offical teaching of these churches – even if the actual sense of faith is not simply identical with official teaching – then we could after all expect a great proportion of Christians in all these Churches, and in the Catholic Church too, to agree with such a differentiated unity of faith, which would in no small degree be left to further historical development. The 'sometime' Catholic Christian in a Church united in this way could hope that the further history of the faith of this united Church would lead to the point when the 'sometime' Protestant or Orthodox Christian could give an absolute assent of faith to doctrines which were hitherto specifically Catholic. (And this is the hope he must have even now in his present Church, with regard to many individuals and many groups, if he wants to come to terms theologically with their actual sense of faith). The 'sometime' Protestant or Orthodox Christian (particularly if he is a theologian) will hope that the further historical development of the (actual and official) sense of faith of this united Church will arrive at the point where – as far as the more precise theological interpretation of Catholic doctrines is concerned, as well as their more precise practice-determining value – these doctrines will become so 'Protestant' or so 'Orthodox' that they will seem to him, not merely acceptable, but the positive expression of his own fundamental conviction.

But given these presuppositions, and since it is this hope that already sustains all ecumenical work, why should it not be possible to live this hope today, letting it find living expression *within* a Church which is sufficiently united, but not to a unifying degree? For in actual (and as such normative) faith the Christians united in this Church would be one. 'Sometime' Catholics would of course, in appeal to the faith experienced in the history of the Church, cling in faith to those doctrines which they have hitherto believed and which they can and should maintain in this united Church. (In a similar way, even today a Protestant theologian may maintain a certain doctrine as 'in itself' belonging to the Protestant faith, although his view is not generally accepted in the Church to which he belongs.) A 'formerly Catholic' doctrine would be nowhere decidedly condemned as contrary to faith – at all events not by the teaching authority. Within the limits we have indicated, only that unity of faith would be institutionally ratified which already actually existed. And as far as actually existing faith is concerned, unity is no greater than this today even in a single individual Church.

2. A second difficulty must be explicitly named and answered – a difficulty of a directly *institutional* kind. When he is faced with the notion we have put forward of a possible unification of the Churches, the Catholic will ask: 'What about the *papacy*? Because for us Catholics the papal office is not merely a dogmatically binding doctrine; it is a concrete entity which is constitutive of the Church.' This Catholic will perhaps say that he could agree with the Church we are striving towards, if it were only the papal office as *doctrine* that we had to take into account. But it is an actual institution, with rights and claims, and he cannot conceive of any Church in which this institution was not existent and operative.

The answer to this is as follows. Of course a Catholic Christian and theologian, for whom – in so far as he is these things – the doctrine of the First and Second Vatican Councils is of course binding, cannot conceive that any Church could be acceptable in which the papacy, as papal office, did not exist. Of course the Catholic Christian and theologian will interpret this petrine ministry, inasmuch as it exists in the Church of today and tomorrow, in accordance with faith, in the sense of the two Vatican councils. But can the papal office as a concrete institution in a future Church only be thought of in such a way that the powers which it *actually* claims and realises would have to founder immediately on the absolute protest of faith made by 'sometime' Protestant or Orthodox Christians?

I think we can say 'no' to this question. But of course in saying no, we must make two assumptions, although we may take it that they are assumptions that could be fulfilled. On the one hand, the relative independence of the particular Churches (with their different historical origins and traditions) must be conceived so broadly, and must be so guarded institutionally and legally that there will be no danger (at least in practical terms) of Rome's appealing to the pre-rogative of the papal office and the self-concept of the Roman Church, and intervening in the life of these particular part-Churches. There must be no danger, at least, of its intervening in such a way that these Churches would inevitably be faced – in human or institutional terms, theologically, historically, and so forth (whether in the absolute or merely relative sense is irrelevant here) – with a contradiction which would lead to schism. According to Catholic dogmatics it is certainly possible for the full authority of the papal office to impose a legal self-limitation on itself (*iure humano*), as it does in a similar way in a concordat. In this way the feared dangers of a papalistically unified Church could be eliminated.

Secondly, there is no need to fear that the teaching authority of the pope expressed in decisions *ex cathedra* will be so fully taken advantage of and realised in the future that the conscience of 'sometime' Prot-estant and Orthodox Christians will be faced with the dilemma of having to accept *positively* the Vatican's interpretation of the papal teaching authority as binding on faith, or of having to reject – even in actual content – supposedly 'new' *ex cathedra* papal decisions. For reasons connected with the mental climate and the history of thought (which initially have nothing to do with ecumenical strategy and tactics) we shall not in the future have to reckon with *ex cathedra* decisions by the pope which go beyond the continually reiterated assertion of the basic substance of Christianity in accordance with particular historical situations. In actual fact we shall have to reckon with them even less, as Christians and Christian faiths bring their own weight into a unified Church.

Here we cannot describe and justify in detail this thesis about a material limitation to what the First Vatican Council stated to be the formally unlimited papal magisterium – a limitation conditioned by the historical situation of theology and thought.[11] But if we assume for other reasons that this thesis is sufficiently cogent, then the acceptance of the papal office, even as magisterium, in the sense to which we have narrowed it down, does not need to lead to conflicts with Protestant and Orthodox Christians and Churches which would make such a union of Churches seem inopportune from the outset, or would undo it again. We must remember here that no Christian in any Church at all can be absolved from the hope that the Church to which he is attached (in whatever way) will be prevented from any development that would lead to an absolute conflict between the individual conscience of the Christian and a decision made by that Church itself. So why should we not be permitted to demand this hope in a unified Church, and in the direction of a unified Church? Why should it not be a hope required of all Christians, each in his own way and in accordance with his own historical origins?

Having narrowed things down in this way, and having formulated these provisos and limitations, we can, I believe, answer our original question in the affirmative. We can in fact say: the major Christian Churches of today could unite, even institutionally; their sense of faith presents no insuperable obstacle. If this is correct, then today the ecumenical question is a question for the authorities in the Churches, rather than a question for the theologians. The authorities in the different Churches must not behave today as if they could do nothing at all for the present, because the theologians cannot come to an agreement.

[11] On the limitation of the papal magisterium in the light of the history of theology and thought, cf. especially 'On the Concept of Infallibility in Catholic Theology', *Theological Investigations* XIV (London 1976), pp. 66–85.

17

THIRD CHURCH?

CHRISTIANS BETWEEN THE CHURCHES

PROTESTANT and Catholic Christians today can think together about the Reformation and talk about it because, in their
different ways, they have been determined by this tremendous
event in church history and world politics for more than 450 years.[1]
Christians may disagree about the deeper theological interpretation,
but they are all affected by it, because they all confess Jesus Christ as
the centre of their faith and the Lord of their lives.

But the antecedents of Christians in their unity and disruption are
only comprehensible in terms of an abiding task, as a future for which
all are responsible and which all have to recognise as the charge laid
upon them by their common Lord. Under this aspect one must take
an especially questioning look at those Christians who in fact, or at
least in some kind of religio-sociological way, stand *between* the institutionally constituted Churches, and who seem to form something
like a third Church.[2] In using the expression 'third Church', however,
we must always remember the question mark that follows the title.
But to say this gives us the starting point for a genuine question.

NEW PARTNERS

In recent decades, new partners have joined the controversial theological and ecumenical discussions between the different Churches of

---

[1] The present essay is based on a lecture given on Reformation Day, 1972,
in Munich. An extract was published in *Evangelische Kommentare* 6 (1973),
pp. 14–17.
[2] The essay 'Is Church Union Dogmatically Possible?' pp. 197–214 above,
takes more account of the theological aspects of this subject.

the West. These partners did not exist earlier, and to exclude them, or overlook them, would inevitably make the dialogue we are seeking an antiquated affair. These new partners are the secularised, secular and pluralistic world; its widespread and sometimes militant atheism; the modern secular sciences; the forms of Christianity which have developed outside Western civilization and culture; rational or rationalistic postivism, with its new horizons of understanding; and so on. But, partly as a result of the new dialogue situation we have described, one of these new partners in the discussions between the Christian Churches is what we may call the 'third Church'—although we still have to explain what we mean by the term. We shall go into that first, and then consider the question of how the Churches themselves ought to react towards this new phenomenon in the sociology of religion.

What does this catchword mean? Let us ask first of all: what used to be the position? Then the reasons that have led to the emergence of the 'third Church' will become clear by themselves. Until well into our own century, the Christian Churches of central Europe had almost everywhere their own clearly defined geographical areas, in which they lived. Generally they had political, governmental powers assigned to them which offered protection to the particular denominational Church in that area, through a kind of symbiosis between Church and the public life of the secular State. Different territories had their own denominational character, and this helped to determine public opinion prevailing in that particular area. Moreover, in the existing structure of society, it was almost unavoidable, in terms of secular and religious education, that the determining religious convictions of a particular territory should have depended more or less on a social élite, which sustained both public power and education. In concrete terms where Christians views were concerned, the spokesmen of the élite were the Church's ministers and theologians. The convictions of 'the upper echelons' were passed down to the rank and file. Here, too, exceptions only prove the rule. It may remain an open question whether the identification of a territorially limited society with a particular denomination was especially Christian or not. At all events there were reasons enough for this trend, and without these reasons the denominational homogeneity of such a society (and hence its separation from other groups with a different denominational character) could not be explained.

But nowadays the secular sociological reasons for the earlier homogeneous denominational Churches and their ties with a particular territory no longer exist. The Churches in question have slowly been transformed into the confessional communities which are usual today; and in the course of this development what evolved too, almost by itself, was the phenomenon of 'the third Church'.

For in Europe today other Christian denominations and Churches are to be found on what was once the territory of one particular Church, even if the discrepancy in the percentage of members generally still betrays something of earlier conditions. But even if we take that into account, conditions are levelling out. So today the Christian who belongs to a particular Church has to live in the *diaspora*—the dispersion—[3] even if the extent to which this is true still varies very much.

Modern pluralistic, secularised and largely atheistical society, at all events, no longer offers the Christian Churches any support by means of public opinion, or state religion, or accepted models of individual and social life. At least where these supports still exist at all, they are in the process of being torn down.

Under the influence of this situation, earlier assumptions belonging to a particular stage in the history of thought, earlier ways of living and of looking at life, all of which led to, or were connected with, confessional doctrinal differences, are, of course, also receding into an ever more remote past, in the awareness of modern men and women. They are, largely speaking, no longer realised at all, so that the modern Christian can hardly enter into the problems of controversial theology that used to exist, or feel in any way personally touched by them; and so he is bound to remain largely uninterested in the settlement of these questions, unless he clings out of pure loyalty to the denomination which has been passed down to him and to which he belongs as a simple matter of fact. Generally such questions seem to him one aspect of those historically conditioned distinctions which exist between the old denominational Churches but

---

[3] The present author has been concerned for years with an analysis of the *diaspora* situation' of the modern Christian. But he still has the impression that it is even now too little understood and accepted in its pressing reality and challenge. Cf. 'The Christian Among Unbelieving Relations', *Theological Investigations* III (London 1967), pp. 355–72; 'The Christian in this World', *Theological Investigations* VII (London 1971), pp. 88–99; and above all *Strukturwandel der Kirche als Aufgabe und Chance*, Herder Bücherei 446, 3rd edn (Freiburg 1973).

which are really a matter of culture and folklore, having no actual theological significance which could be constitutive for the Church.

For ultimately the whole consciousness of modern men and women (even from a Christian and theological standpoint) is co-determined today by innumerable new influences which used not to exist at all for the individual and collective consciousness. Nowadays these influences are almost inevitably shifting the content of traditional theological awareness, or giving it a different—and in fact a lesser—importance.[4]

What we have called the 'third Church' can now be seen against this background. These are people who, in what they see Christianity to be, in their style of living and their interpretation of themselves, hardly differ from one another; and moreover they do not want to be distinguished from one another, in spite of their religio-sociological adherence to this or that denomination.

PEOPLE BELONGING TO THE THIRD CHURCH

Of the group we have named, we must pay special attention, in the framework of our subject, to the people who more or less think and live *only* in terms of the 'common Christian' ground, without therefore also wanting to leave their traditional denomination publicly and decidedly. For their intention is by no means to live as Christians outside the major 'denominational' Churches. They do not want to live completely without any Christian community, nor as members of a group which, from the point of view of the major Churches, could be classed theologically or in the sociology of religion as a 'sect'. The 'third Church', as we see it here, grows up *within* the traditional Churches—for the moment, at least. Its members ascribe no importance to the traditional doctrinal differences between the Churches, while for themselves they do not see that differences of this kind provide a sufficient reason for forming a separate Church. Perhaps they cannot even formulate these differences, or do not know what they are. When Christians of this kind none the less give their own Church a preference over others (and with a certain emphasis) it is for reasons which the officially valid *theology* of the Churches, on the other hand, does not judge as dividing one from another. This

---

[4] On the notion of the 'pluralism' of the modern mental and spiritual situation, cf. for example 'The Faith of the Christian and the Doctrine of the Church', *Theological Investigations* XIV (London 1976), pp. 24–46.

kind of choice between the Churches is in fact rather like the decision of two Catholics, one of whom prefers High Mass with music by Mozart, whereas the other prefers a modern Eucharist in the vernacular.

But it may be that these 'third Church' Christians even *explicitly* consider that the controversial theological differences which divide the churches are unimportant, theologically and for faith. They generally go on to demand that the different denominations should be united as quickly as possible; or they emphasise firmly that the differences between the various Churches are only of a historical, cultural, sociological or institutional kind, and have no real theological importance. This means, they say, that the real unity of the Christian Church in faith and theology has as such existed for a long time and does not have to be re-created. They have the impression that they have long possessed a common creed, which reaches beyond the limits of the separate denominations: belief in God, the hoping conviction that God has promised himself to them, forgivingly and savingly, in Jesus Christ, practical experience of the meaning of prayer, hope for eternal life.[5] This creed could undoubtedly be differently formulated, and then differently interpreted, but that is not of decisive importance. At all events, beyond a fundamental, simple confession of faith of this kind, these Christians discover nothing which really absolutely plays a part in their own decisions of faith, and which would really essentially distinguish them from the great majority of Christians belonging to other denominations. If they are, in addition, a little better instructed theologically than the average, they believe that they are right in their impression that the old differences of controversial theology between the Christian Churches have been eliminated by the theologians in their ecumenical dialogue. The interpretation of hitherto disputed points of doctrine which is aimed at convergence seems to confirm this; and so does the discovery that denominational differences of opinion are no longer given the importance which used to be taken for granted.

The phenomenon of the 'third Church', of course, displays highly varying degrees and nuances, according to the areas in which it is

---

[5] Properly understood, this question touches on a subject often considered by the present author: the short formula of the faith. Cf. 'Reflections on the Problems Involved in Devising a Short Formula of the Faith', *Theological Investigations* XI (London 1974), pp. 230–46. On the discussion about this subject cf. also R. Bleistein, *Kurzformel des Glaubens*, 2 vols (Würzburg 1971).

found, the degree of Christian and denominational education which its members enjoy, and the social and cultural situation in general. What is more important than these variations is the fact that today the 'third' is an indisputable fact.

THE THIRD CHURCH IN THE LIFE OF THE CHURCH AS A WHOLE

The 'third Church' is making itself felt in the Church's own life too. For example, common ecumenical services would be impossible and meaningless if the participants had the impression that *all* and *everything* in the Christian faith of people who are denominationally divided always and unequivocally has a denominational impress. In theory and practice, there is also the problem as to whether it is possible and opportune to have a common Christian religious instruction which—even though bi-confessional—would not merely be confined to information about religion as a scientific study, but which would also be designed to be a common Christian witness. 'Mixed marriages' no longer count, generally speaking, as undesired by both Churches, or as only possible, in human and Christian terms, in particularly favourable cases. They are often even regarded as desirable; and the impediments put in the way by canon law are correspondingly challenged as un-Christian. There is a call for ecumenical wedding ceremonies. People are demanding common versions of the Bible, common liturgical formulas, and common prayers. Intercommunion or open communion is more or less taken for granted by many people, so that the resistance of the official Churches is rejected as incomprehensible and un-Christian. Different revivalist movements of a 'charismatic' kind—the Jesus people, the pentecostal movement, and so on—unite Christians from the most varied denominations. Common undertakings of social action or protest, in shared Christian responsibility for society and the world, are now widely taken for granted.[6] All these signs of unity and common ground between the Christian Churches are, of course, neither theologically nor practically simply conditioned by the phenomenon of

---

[6] The theological presuppositions and basis for the common action of Christians belonging to different denominations have certainly not been sufficiently considered and clarified; indeed the question itself has perhaps not even been seen. The present essay is designed to offer some stimulus in this respect. Cf. also the ideas in 'On the Theology of Ecumenical Discussion', *Theological Investigations* XI (London 1974), pp. 24–67.

the 'third Church'. But the actual power and matter-of-factness of all these ecumenical activities in the Churches, which their 'official' authorities often find a nuisance, are due to the fact that the actual upholders of ecumenical initiatives of this kind largely belong to the so-called 'third Church'.

The question about the correct view of this phenomenon, and the answer to it, must be directed in the first place to the people who, in some form or other, belong to this third Church. But it is also a question for the Church's official ministers and theologians, since these are socially the most obvious representatives of the distinction between the different denominations. According to the description we have given, that means nearly everybody, though in different degrees, corresponding to their theological training, the particular character of their attitude to faith and the closeness of their relationship to a particular denomination in its institutionally tangible form.

What should we say to the Christian who more or less belongs to the third Church? Of course to lump these believers together is a problem in itself, because they differ considerably from one another. But for the moment let us leave on one side the question whether these Christians simply experience and live by what is common between the denominations—whether this is what they feel the Christian faith to be—or whether in addition they basically judge denominational differences to be meaningless for faith and theology, seeing them as purely historically conditioned, external circumstances. Of course here we can only address ourselves to the people who preserve and cultivate some concrete link or other with their traditional denomination. To these people alone, but to all of them, let me say the following.

The ecumenical features of Christianity and the Church will not be realized solely by a third Church which simply by-passes the existing Churches and their history, their traditional institutions and specific offices—a third Church which tries to arrive at unity between Christians through complete indifference toward the Churches that have existed hitherto. Complete indifference towards the authorities in the denominations, or perhaps actual, even state-registered withdrawal*

---

* In West Germany, members of the Roman Catholic and Evangelical (Protestant) Churches register as such, since the State (on the Churches' behalf) collects a church tax from these registered members. It is possible, however, to opt out of either Church, and to pay taxes to neither; but this choice is also officially recorded by the State [the translator].

from the Church cannot do justice to the reality of Christianity. The true way to realise our Lord's charge to live in his one Church and to bring about the unity of Christians, cannot therefore bypass the denominational Churches. A third Church which tried to do so would bring about an increasing erosion in the substance of the Christian faith, right down to the innermost heart of the message about the living God and the one mediator. What has to be united cannot be united simply by dissolving the subjects of the union.[7]

The attempt to establish the third Church as something on its own would lead to this very thing. For the unity of creed necessary even for this Church could be achieved only by continually curtailing more and more of the substance of its own beliefs. Why? Because on the one hand this Church, too, would have to bring out clearly what Christians have in common, if it wanted to sustain the unity of a genuine and living Church effectively. On the other hand, the formulation of a Church creed which was no longer upheld by the beliefs of the 'previous' Churches and supported by the power of their history, would be bound to lead to an ever-thinner and ever more non-committal expression; and in the end the third Church would find itself in the position already occupied by mere humanism of a purely horizontal kind. But if the third Church were to tend towards a churchless Christianity, then—apart from real theological considerations—we can say only one thing, and it is this. Especially in a period when, in order to be able to exist at all, men and women have to overcome a great deal of the individualism which has determined the spirit of the West ever since the Enlightenment, truth and fellowship cannot be preserved and disseminated if people settle down outside institutions.[8] Christians certainly do not all have the same ideas about what the Church is and ought to be; but it has none the less been the permanent conviction of the whole of Christianity, in doctrine and practice, that faith and its liberating power need to be upheld by a fellowship which is also socially institutionalised—in this sense the Church. And the attitude of mind and experiences of our own time do not allow us, of all people, to disavow this conviction.

[7] Cf. 'Basic Observations on the Subject of Changeable and Unchangeable Factors in the Church', *Theological Investigations* XIV (London 1976), pp. 3–23; and 'Does the Church Offer Any Ultimate Certainties?', ibid, pp. 47–65.

[8] Cf. 'Modern Piety and the Experience of Retreats', *Theological Investigations* XVI (London 1979), pp. 135–55, where the post-modern phenomenon of higher forms of socialisation are considered in detail.

The simple, basic elements of the Christian conviction of faith, which the 'third Church' shares as well, can be the innermost centre from which a Christian can live, and should live, in his accustomed denomination. These basic elements do not provide a valid reason for more or less leaving his Church in actual practice. As long as the Churches have not arrived at Christian unity, they are the specific place where the common Christian conviction has to be lived, if it is not slowly to melt away and become ineffective.[9]

That is why the third Church must not by-pass the existing Churches; it must make itself effective in the right way *within* them. Anyone who is convinced of the human, Christian and theological weight of the ideas which lead to the third Church, should also have the courage for the long march through the ecclesiastical institutions, to express it in modern catchword terms. In our contemporary social situation, we cannot overcome old-fashioned traditionalism and outmoded ways of proclamation and styles of living by way of extremely tiny sects. Yet it is these sects which would be the inevitable result of the completely unreal and utopian attempt to found a genuine major Church (parallel to the previous denominational Churches), whose substance would be contributed in every respect by the third Church. If we do not want to lose ourselves in intangible ideas, thereby losing sight of the Church, and ultimately of our own historical character, too, in the process, then Christians of the third Church have only one task. That is: out of the shared Christianity that exists and is lived, and seriously and fairly taking account of official doctrine and the actual history of the denominational Churches, they have to draw even closer to the institutional Churches (and not in theology alone) until they, too, represent and embody the one Church of Jesus Christ, in spite of all their local and particularist differences.

This general principle does not of course solve all the separate problems. Intercommunion, mixed marriages, common and effective witness to the gospel in our contemporary world with its needs – all these things still call for numerous detailed solutions. Under certain circumstances Christians of the third Church should emphatically urge the official ministers of their Churches to find a Christian answer

[9] On the substance of faith which has to be preserved, cf. 'On the Theology of Ecumenical Discussion', *Theological Investigations* XI (London 1974), pp. 24–67.

to these special questions. It is surely self-evident, and needs no special emphasis, to say that in finding these solutions we must keep the unity of the Church in mind; and also that the third Church itself has the right to expect the theological respect it deserves, as well as an appreciation of its sociological position in the existing Church. But there should be no attempt to provoke anarchy in the Church through over-hasty radical cures, which really only mean a relapse into an old-fashioned individualism and can only exacerbate the plight of divided Christendom even more.[10]

Up to now we were really only supposed to be listening to sober, everyday experience, not to learned theological arguments. Anyone who suffers in the Spirit from the Churches within the Churches will not give himself over to the impious utopia of a third Church as an isolated power parallel to the others. On the contrary, he will live actively in his Church and, out of his own immediately apprehensible experience of faith, find the open courage for the greater riches of the Church, which earlier lay in its doctrine and life, and are still to be found there today. We shall not ultimately advance the Church if we become disheartened, or take up an ultimately arrogant attitude towards the Church of sinners and the official ministers who, like the rest of us, fall continually short of the Gospel of Jesus, which always demands too much of us all. It is in love for these Churches, enslaved and poverty-stricken though they are, that we shall make progress. It is not the destructiveness of indifference or purely corrosive criticism that can achieve anything. It is the all-renewing Spirit of the Lord; this is especially true because this Spirit is still alive in us only because the Churches have existed. This all applies in a quite particular degree to the solution of the ecumenical question. But if we look at the results of ecumenical efforts in the last thirty or forty years in the different Churches, then we have really no reason to doubt that the task of the third Church, *properly* understood and lived, has the promise of fulfilment in the Churches.

---

[10] Except in this briefly indicated sense, it is impossible to understand attempts – however well meaning they may perhaps be – such as G. Hasenhüttl's new contribution; cf. his *Herrschaftsfreie Kirche. Sozio-theologische Grundlegung* (Düsseldorf 1974).

THE THIRD CHURCH AND ECCLESIASTICAL AUTHORITY

The fact of the third Church does not only pose a problem for those Christians who feel they could belong to it. It also poses a question to official ministers of the individual Churches,[11] though this is in no way to be seen as an accusation. In this connection a whole series of aspects emerge which these officials perhaps do not always see and appreciate sufficiently.

Officials in all the Churches are always subject to the temptation to identify the faith of their own Church, tacitly and if as a matter of course, with the faith which is formulated in their respective articles of belief, or in the heads and books of the theologians of that particular Church. That is why official ministers and theologians often view the actually existing faith of Christians purely and in every respect as a cruder and more rudimentary version of the faith they know and administer. That is why the official ecumenical dialogue is almost always, as a matter of course and without any further inquiry, a discussion designed to overcome differences of doctrine between the denominations in their *official* creeds. But the question whether these official differences exist at all for the faith of most members of the divided Churches, or whether they play any serious part, simply does not arise. In saying this I do not mean to deny the particular and irreplaceable importance of theologically differentiated faith, as it is expressed in the official doctrines of the Churches. But in the question we have raised here, what is at issue is something different.

Has it really become clear theologically that the faith that saves is not the faith of the creeds and articles of belief, but the faith that actually lives in the heads and hearts of contemporary Christians? If faith really means the salvation of *people*, then we must first of all make this fact clear to ourselves. But in the official ecumenical practice of the Catholic Church, for example, the statement of the Second Vatican Council about the 'hierarchy of truths'[12] even now sounds

[11] Of course we are not considering here the ecumenical interpretation of the official ministries of the Church, which has been under recent discussion; on that cf. *Vorfragen zu einem ökumenischen Amtsverständnis* (Quaestiones Disputatae 64) (Freiburg 1974), where the present author develops his ideas on this subject.

[12] On the 'hierarchy of truths' cf. Vatican II: '*Unitatis redintegratio*' (decree on Ecumenism) n. 11, and the present author's comments in 'The Faith of the Christian and the Doctrines of the Church', *Theological Investigations* XIV (London 1976), pp. 24–46.

like the title for a book that still has to be written.

If we were to take the common faith of the third Church in the divided Churches completely seriously, then we ought surely to ascribe greater importance to it, in our ecumenical dialogues too. Moreover we should have to take into account the fact that today, in the case of many statements if not yet all, *the statements that divide us* have a much lesser logical and existential importance than the statements which express our common, fundamental Christian convictions. This is a fact that has not yet been sufficiently appreciated at the theological level. Epistemologically, many statements have a provisional character. They are hypothetical and hence replaceable by other statements which are better, more subtly nuanced, or have more integrating power. Perhaps all that is meant is that something is not realisable here and now, but does not therefore have to be denied altogether. These and other characteristics of the statements which still divide Christians today must be perceived more clearly. For the official-ministers, what emerges naturally from this is a question: given certain other provisos which we cannot go on to consider here, could the faith of the third Church provide a sufficient foundation for a unity of faith among the Christian Churches? At all events, the theological relevance of the third Church (beyond its mere significance for the sociology of religion) has not yet been sufficiently thought about. And the consequences for the Church's actions and the actions of its official representatives have certainly not been grasped.[13]

Ultimately the term 'third Church' in the positive sense in which we have used it here, is only a term for the great and decisive 'one' in which the Christians of the different denominations and Churches really do already come together today when, each in his own way, they confess the triune God and Jesus Christ as sole mediator. It is not true that the denominational differences – weighty though they indisputably are – divide us to such an extent, and in the different Churches so determine what we have in common, that this common ground is pure illusion – though this is what people on all sides have sometimes maintained in their excessive polemical zeal. Common Christian ground really does exist. It binds us together even now. In

[13] Cf. 'Ecumenical Theology in the Future', *Theological Investigations* XIV (London 1976), pp. 254–69; esp. the section 'Church Christians Without Any Confessional Awareness', pp. 264–8.

all of us it creates salvation for eternity and gives us the power to persevere in the time in which we live. It goes further than mere human solidarity and tolerance. It makes possible and governs everything which already exists today in our ecumenical closeness and our common ecumenical activity. So the ecumenical movement must not peter out and become resigned to failure. What we have in common must become still more vitally realised in all the Churches; it must find new forms of expression and determine the actions of all Christians more forcibly. Paradoxical though this may sound, it must discover its own presence and reality at the very point where there is apparently only a secular world, because the breath of the Spirit who builds the Church also blows through the highways and by-ways of the world. This common Christian ground of the third Church must not be interpreted overhastily, or in too simple-minded a way, as a contradiction and denial of the existing denominational Churches – even though it certainly calls in question the actual existing form of all the Churches and is a breakthrough in the direction of that unity in faith which is laid upon us all. On the contrary, it is that very 'oneness' which God in Jesus Christ gave to all the Christian Churches, the oneness which was accepted by them all, from which they all live, and which is to be the living seed from which the fulness of unity can flower.

18

RELIGIOUS FEELING INSIDE AND OUTSIDE
THE CHURCH

THERE is a kind of piety that springs from the Church, is upheld and sustained by it, and is related to it.[1] By piety we mean here the personally adopted and freely accepted relatedness of a person to God in faith, hope and love; but a relatedness that is Christian, being mediated through Jesus Christ. The faith in Jesus Christ which sustains this kind of piety rests on the Church's message. It knows that it is related to the sacrament of baptism (which incorporates a person in the Church) and to the historical phenomenon of God's salvific turning towards man in Jesus Christ. But though it is this divine turning to the individual person himself which empowers his devotion, the devout person experiences it as having taken place through God's turning to his people as a whole. God's efficacious manifestation of himself in the sacrament belongs to the mutual relationship between God and man. Thus piety, since it is the relatedness of the whole person to God, necessarily has a common and even a social dimension as well. But it is something truly belonging to the Church itself, rather than smothered by external legalism and ritualism, only when all the attitudes and acts which are related to the social character of the Church are really animated by the innermost, free turning of man to God which is sustained by God's grace.

CHURCH PIETY

The church-relatedness of personal piety is highly variable and has its individual and collective history. For man's relatedness to God, and

---

[1] The ideas in this essay grew out of a working paper which the author prepared for a commission of the German Episcopal Synod. It has been extensively revised.

the nature of that relationship as it is related to the Church are certainly connected, but are not identical. There is a piety which effects salvation and is yet outside the Church. (We shall later describe and specify what we mean by this.) But within the piety of the Church, there are quite legitimate different forms in individuals, in social groups, and in different periods. Ultimately all these variations will be parallel to the historical possibilities available.

In piety, both elements, the Church and the individual, are related to each other. The nature of man makes it impossible for either one of them to be fully eliminated; and yet the mutual relationship of these two factors is not rigid and unalterable. The Church's part in piety can be subjectively experienced as the sustaining foundation for its understanding, its certainty and its vitality; but this ecclesiastical form can also be experienced as something secondary, as a kind of merely tolerated appendage of piety in its solitary relationship to God, the certainty and power of which come from within. From what we have said it has already become clear that we cannot expect very much of the contribution of the Church to the piety of the individual. In the practice of the Church and in its edicts there is something like a minimum requirement in this respect (Mass on Sunday, confession once a year, Easter communion, the baptism of infants, etc.). But here almost everything is a fluid, variable offer on the part of the Church, and its pastoral and human expediency must continually be re-assessed. The contribution of the Church to personal piety can also vary in accordance with the picture of the Church which is viewed as the standard and model. This varies between the Church seen as an institute for salvation, and the Church seen as the community of the saved. Accordingly the individual feels himself to be either the guided recipient of the Church's saving gifts, or as the co-sustaining and co-responsible member of the Church's fellowship. The Church's part in piety can also vary according to whether the individual experiences the Church as the Church universal—the Church extending to the whole world—or as the individual congregation of brethren.

In considering the different ways in which piety is related to the Church, we ought not to try to reconcile the variations through an all too hasty 'both—and'. Pastoral life and the life of the Church as a whole must permit these variations and endure the tension between them. It must not, by means of a tactically shrewd—or slick—'both—and' demand all degrees of attachment to the Church from every individual. For in doing this it would force many people, who seem to be less devout in the Church's sense, into the situation of 'fringe' Christians. On the other hand, there can also be new forms of piety in its Church-related form, whose intensity of practically lived brotherly love must not from the outset be measured against the average type of normal church practice.

Piety in its churchly guise can also occur in mistaken forms. The partial debasement of this form of piety may even characterise a lengthy period in the Church's history; though this may not be explicitly thought about, and the collective conscience of the Church may not react to it with sufficient emphasis. There is always a deterioration when church forms of piety are given independent importance, compared with piety itself, so that piety, which is something absolute in itself, is turned into the instrument for binding people to the Church; or when devotion to the Church is judged, clearly and unequivocally, as the criterion for a person's relationship to God; or when piety understands the Church as a sect and tries to turn it into as closed a social ghetto as possible; or when there is triumphalism; or when attachment to the Church degenerates into group egoism, so that freedom of the spirit to see good outside the Church is lost; or when the individual uses his membership of the Church as a protection against God; or when people forget that the Church is there for the world, and not the world for the Church; or when the smooth running of the Church's life and activities is made too much of an ideal; or when the Church's institutions and proceedings cease to be continually challenged by the question whether they really bring about faith, hope and love in the world; or when a brotherly relationship between hierarchy and the faithful remains pure theory; and so on. The struggle against mistaken forms of this kind is important. For experience of them seriously blocks access to an understanding of and true attachment to the Church for non-Christians and non-Catholics.

At all events, attachment to the Church must basically be judged only as a particular and, in the true sense, secondary element in piety. It is particular and secondary because piety and attachment to the Church are so much to be distinguished from each other that there can be a saving piety which is not bound to the Church at all. For fundamentally, even in the Church's own piety, the experience of God and Jesus Christ is more primal than the experience of the Church. This at least is true for the basic structure of the objects of faith and the reasons for faith. It is by no means a denial, either of a mutually conditioning relationship between all the springs of faith (of which the experience of the Church is one), or of the fact that 'normally', devotional experience does in fact generally come about in the fellowship of the Church.

PIETY OUTSIDE THE CHURCH

There is a piety outside the Church, even apart from the plurality of the Christian Churches and the forms of devotion which are specifically related to any one of them. The statement is at first self-evident to everyone who knows the history of the non-Christian religions, which is not yet simply at an end, even in the so-called Christian countries today. But what is meant is also that there is a specific Christian piety outside the Churches as such, and Christian groups or sects—a relationship to God, that is, which knows itself to be in some way or other empowered by Jesus Christ.

This non-church piety can very well be efficacious for salvation. The Christian ought not to see it as a mere human attempt to set up a relationship to God 'from below'. For it is really inwardly sustained by the free grace of God, which is offered everywhere and effects salvation wherever man obeys the absolute command of his conscience, and realises and objectifies this obedience, at least in some form of devotion, as an explicit relation to God. So the Catholic Christian and theologian can basically recognise that in fact all conscientious, honest piety is saving, is sustained by grace, and is in this sense already Christian in the anonymous sense.[2]

The Christian message aims to make real, explicit Christians, and is hence not simply the indoctrination from outside of some hitherto unknown fact. It is the awakening of something which is really already existent through grace and is already experienced, even if it is not the object of explicit reflection. It is in a sense the ontogenetic repetition of a phylogenetic human history, as God's self-communication to the world, which is always already sustained by grace. To give ecclesiastical form to this saving piety as it exists outside the Church means the complete self-realisation of a piety that has always

---

[2] The author has discussed numerous other aspects of the same basic problem under the heading of the 'anonymous Christian'. For further details, cf. 'Observations on the Problem of the "Anonymous Christian" ', *Theological Investigations* XIV (London 1976), pp. 280–94.

existed through grace, in explicit encounter with Jesus and his institutionally constituted community of faith. So incorporation in the Church is not the beginning but the end of the grace which, in its sovereign freedom, calls some people among others. These people form the Church, which is the historical sign of the victorious presence of God's grace in the world, and is therefore (in spite of the universal trend of Jesus' message) an actual, particular sign in human history of the fact that God is present through his grace in all piety, wherever conscience obeys that call than which there is nothing higher here and now.

Even in a piety of this kind, as in every free human act, we have to distinguish between the ultimate, primal, free and grace-sustained alignment of knowledge and freedom towards God, and its material, historical objectification in space and time, and in word and deed. The objectifications we come across in society and history can degenerate to a greater or lesser degree without this necessarily meaning that they have completely lost their ultimate alignment with God and their significance for salvation. Analogously, we might point out here that an objectively erroneous but subjectively good conscience can perform acts which contradict what is actually enjoined by the moral law; yet in these acts obedience to conscience and to God may none the less be realised. Of course we cannot go into the different social and individual shapes and forms of such degenerations. The greater the debasement of the religious act, the more the chance will be diminished that its final subjective intention will after all be related to God himself. In our present religious sub-culture outside the Church, it would be useful at some point or other to give a more precise account of such more or less explicitly religious practices, in their typical manifestations and degenerate forms; because such phenomena are not usually viewed clearly enough for us to form any kind of link with them, whether it be acceptance or rejection.

This piety has, of course, its socially conditioned patterns and origins. We only have to think, for example, of the common forms of supersitition or of popular astrology, and so forth. In our cultural sphere much of this still has a Christian origin and frequently still bears the partial impress of the earlier teachings of the Christian Church.

THE EXPERIENCE OF GOD AS PIETY OUTSIDE THE CHURCH

The most primal and sustaining ground of all piety outside the Church is the experience of God.[3] It is only in the light of this experience that its nature and existence can really be interpreted. We have to distinguish here between a primal experience of God, and a reflective, verbally objectifying knowledge of God. For there is a fundamental difference between personal spiritual experiences (for example, love, joy, fear) and their verbal objectification in reflective form (for instance, talk about the existence and nature of joy, love and fear, which attempts to define these experiences). Of course there is a connection between the two as well. Consequently the verbal objectification of such primal experiences can be inadequate, and indeed wrong.[4] Primal experience can certainly be related in intention to an object different from itself (for example, true, primal love for another person, which precedes any theoretical, reflecting interpretation by the loving person). An 'object' of this kind could exist in an *a posteriori* experience or in information coming from without (for example, the knowledge of a certain beloved person). But it is conceivable that an originally intentional act of this kind, simply through its *a priori* intentionality, is already aware of an object or its necessary structure.[5]

Such a primal experience of God, as distinct from a verbal, objective knowledge of him, really does exist, irrespective of the way this knowledge of God may be considered as having come about. Of course, if we are to avoid ontologism and the mysticism which appeals to particular experiences, the primal experience of God can only be thought of as the experience of God which belongs always

---

[3] Cf. 'Experience of Self and Experience of God', *Theological Investigations* XIII (London 1975), pp. 122–32.

[4] A materialistic anthropologist may very well misinterpret the nature of love, liberty, responsibility, etc., even when he himself genuinely experiences these things. He does not necessarily have to notice the contradiction between his own primal experience and his interpretation.

[5] From the logic of what he knows, which is experienced *a priori*, a person is aware, for example, that every object which he encounters at any time or in any place will correspond to the fundamental conditions of the human act. In this light the difference between a primal experience of God and a theoretical doctrine about God must be comprehensible, at least conceptually. And here it is unimportant that this doctrine is communicated through others and may in certain circumstances be seen as being information about an object which is in this way communicated to the listener for the first time, or whether it is conceived of as the correct interpretation of a primal experience.

and everywhere to man's transcendental nature, as the direction towards which this transcendental nature tends.

The traditional distinction between nature (man's natural spirituality) on the one hand, and grace (his elevation through grace) on the
other, is not of decisive importance here. For if we pre-suppose that
man is always and everywhere (at least potentially, since the offer is
made to him) 'elevated' through grace, because of God's universal
will to salvation, then a primal experience of God can exist and can
be appealed to; there is no need to make a more precise distinction
as to whether a particular aspect of this experience already belongs to
man's natural spirituality, or only occurs (even if always and everywhere) because his spiritual nature has been elevated by God's self-
communication through grace. For grace can only be understood
from the outset as the radical form of the fundamentally unlimited
transcendental nature of human knowledge and liberty, which tends
towards the immediacy of God, and whose culmination and consummation is the direct vision of God himself.

The experience of God we mean here is of transcendental necessity.
It therefore exists always and everywhere, whenever man implements
his spiritual knowledge and freedom, even if this is often not explicitly
formulated. It exists even when he denies this transcendentally necessary relationship to God, explicitly and in objectively verbal form. If
this transcendental necessity were denied, then we should have to
understand God as an arbitrary object, the experience of which could
be either avoided or permitted with equal justification. An appeal to
the supreme objective significance of God would come too late to
legitimise the necessity and the value of the knowledge of God. There
would be simply nothing in the constitution of the perceiving subject
which could oblige us to ask whether a reality such as God exists at
all, especially since he certainly does not belong to the objects of *a
posteriori* experience which force themselves on our attention. Man's
a priori transcendental experience (like everything which is consciously
existent in man) can be present in both modes—as free acceptance or
as rejection. And again, acceptance and rejection can exist without
their being the object of explicit reflection; or they can be parallel to,
or be the result of, an explicit objectification of this transcendental
relation to God. This would be the point from which we should have
to trace the different possibilities of supposed or real atheism.

THE EXPERIENCE OF TRANSCENDENCE

The foundation for this transcendental experience of God is man's own experience of transcendence. Both are expressions in man of one and the same reality, though the first only expressly stresses the ultimate trend and goal of man's transcendental nature. A more precise phenomenology of the experience of transcendence (if this analysis were carried through correctly and more or less exhaustively) should show that its trend does actually reveal an understanding of the real God.

Here we can only describe the experience of transcendence very incompletely. Its essential characteristic is that man's knowledge and liberty always reach out beyond the individual object of inner and outward experience; that this anticipation is the condition that makes objective knowledge and the free act possible, since it is absolutely unlimited, going beyond every declarable object, because every conceivable limitation in the act of being thought of is already exceeded. In so far as the experience of man's transcendental nature really establishes itself, experiences itself as being sustained by the direction in which it tends, and knows that Nothingness is nothing—this goal towards which transcendence tends can only be thought of as the infinite, unlimited reality which remains at root a mystery: that is to say, God. This goal as incomprehensible mystery is—though not as object in the sense of ontologism—really the beginning of the movement of transcendence.

Of course this experience of transcendence, which has God as its direction and its goal, cannot be grasped, in its concrete, specific originality, in the abstract terms we have used to describe it here. A mystagogic pointer to this experience must therefore remember that the person who is not himself trained in philosophy has this experience as a matter of course, but in quite definite shapes and forms. We are not concerned here with the transcendental in absolute and diffuse form, for that is always a given element in the implementation of knowledge and freedom; it is a matter of more intensive realisations which force this experience of transcendence more clearly on the reflective consciousness as well. In this way these realisations make it possible for the 'ordinary' person to reflect upon his experience of transcendence with the help of an explicitly verbal thematic treatment of the subject of God, which is already to be found in the sociological environment.

In the nature of things, these primal experiences always arise where the movement of transcendence allows the finite character of the specific object as such to be experienced.[6] Through them, the finite character of specific objects, as something that can neither be overcome nor fulfilled, can become the express subject of reflection, just as much as the affirmation of a fulfilment no longer finite, which still none the less exists even in a 'negative' experience of this kind. Preeminent experiences of transcendence may be experience of the fear that threatens everything, and experience of surpassing joy; experience of an absolute responsibility, faithfulness or love, which are no longer adequately justified specifically; and experience of the absolute logic which substantiates the individual object but cannot be substantiated by the object itself. We must of course distinguish between forms which coalesce through a free acceptance, and those which come into being in the radical disintegration between the transcendentally necessary affirmation of God, which is not the express subject of reflection, and rejection of God made in an act of human liberty, whether this be the express subject of reflection or not. For one and the same subject experiences himself, knowingly and freely, as being exposed to several experiences of transcendental necessity; and this subject, in his own unity, feels that these have to be reconciled with one another—though the subject himself can never reconcile them.

But wherever someone still unconditionally hopes beyond all empirical hopelessness; wherever a particular joy is experienced as the promise of a joy that is limitless; wherever a person loves with unconditional faithfulness and resolve, although the frailty of such love on both sides cannot possibly legitimise this unconditional determination; wherever radical responsibility towards a moral obligation is maintained, even when it seemingly leads only to disaster; wherever the relentlessness of truth is experienced and unconditionally accepted and grasped; wherever the unsurmountable discrepancy between what is individual and what is social in the plurality of man's different destinies is endured in a seemingly unjustified resolve of hope for the meaning and blessedness which reconciles everything— a resolve which cannot even be given objective form—in all these situations God, as the condition which makes all this possible, is

[6] By a specific object we mean here in the first place the other, finite and immediate 'Thou' – the people with whom we share and experience the world, not simply the environment.

already experienced and accepted, even if this is not expressly and objectively formulated. This is true even if the word 'God' is never heard and is never used as the term for the direction and goal of the transcendental experiences known in this way.

Experiences of transcendence of this kind are not just sporadic. They are more widespread than that, and may occur in any given event of human knowledge and freedom, without so much as the beginnings of an express and objective formulation. As the condition that makes knowledge and freedom in everyday life possible, this transcendental experience of God is experienced in its necessity and inescapability, so that the person is faced with the question whether he will also make this inescapability the centre of his existence, in free, primal trust; or whether he will suppress it by escaping to the surveyable individual realities in his life which he can control.

But this does not mean any depreciation of the explicit doctrine of God, or of objectifying reflection about this experience. Man is not merely a transcendental creature; he is also a creature of history and reflection. The fundamentally highest stage is reached when he reflects on the transcendental conditions of objective knowledge and of historical experience—when, that is to say, he reflects about the trend and goal of man's transcendence in whose framework history is pursued. But the individual cannot legitimately escape from the common awareness of mankind. He must explicitly want to have to do with God. On the other hand, the conscious verbal and social formulation of the primal experience of God in history and society means for the individual a radical possibility of reflecting on his own transcendental experience of God and of entering into the history of this reflection as purely and completely as possible.

All that we have said up to now is inevitably abstract and very general. Of course it must be translated into different language if it is to be effective in religious education or catechetical instruction or missionary work. But people must be warned against demanding today the pure and simple 'concrete', graphically descriptive language that was possible once. The reason why religious language that sounded much more concrete used to be possible was that people felt able to localise God's workings at particular points in the world and history far more unreservedly; and from these points they could talk about God specifically, so to speak. We cannot go into the question here of whether and in what sense a more or less specific experience of God of this kind is still possible today. At all events, in a radical sense, for us God is only conceivable at all as the final ground and ultimate goal of reality; he is experienced within the sensory world at most indirectly. In view of this, contemporary language cannot, ultimately speaking, avoid being abstract to some extent. This abstractness does not need to frighten us, because man is becoming increasingly aware that language which helps him practically to understand and deal with his material environment is also becoming more abstract. This defence of abstract talk about religion is, of course, not meant to suggest that the language used here is the only one possible, if we want to talk about God.

THE POSSIBILITY OF THE TRANSCENDENTAL EXPERIENCE OF GOD

People must be warned against appealing too quickly and without closer inspection to particular religious, more or less 'mystical' experiences, in order to demonstrate that an experience of God is possible. 'Mystical' experiences are either very intensive cases of an experience of God which is basically open to all; or they rouse the suspicion that they are psychological phenomena which can be explained by particular psychical causes. The grace of a transcendental experience of God that is given essentially radical form by his elevating grace is open to everyone, at least in the sense of an offer which a person can freely accept or reject. That is merely a translation of the binding Catholic doctrine about the universal and efficacious divine will to salvation. It is probably true that not everyone has the grace of free acceptance and love at every moment in his life. But we can hope—even though we cannot know with certainty—that the history of every person ends in perfected salvation, and that therefore the effective grace freely to accept the transcendental experience of God will be given at some time or other.

But the grace of acceptance is something which in everyone cannot be reflected on with certainty. Proper reflection on the transcendental experience of God in a knowledge about God which is consciously formulated is certainly again grace, which experience teaches us is not given to everyone. According to the conviction of Vatican II, it does not even have to be given as offered and sufficient grace to every person in every social and historical situation. But this only means that the particular person, in his own psychological and social situation, is not actually in a situation when he can sufficiently reflect on his existing transcendental experience of God, and recognise it again in what is said to him about God from outside. This basically happens, however, even when an intelligent person in his own particular situation finds it impossible to understand calculus, for example, even when it is explained to him by a mathematician. The claim that the grace of experiencing God has not been given must not assume a mystical-psychological misunderstanding of this grace; nor does it dispense us from a continually renewed attempt to help others to a reflective understanding of their own transcendental experience of God, and thus to make theists of them, even in the dimension of objectifying awareness and of religious society.

A definite mystagogy in the individual's reflection on his personal transcendental experience of God would admittedly have to be slowly developed, in a better way than hitherto. We do not have to think that the word 'God' has to stand at the beginning here. In a situation in which religious language no longer enjoys undisputed rule in society, the word 'God' will be more likely to come at the end. But this allows a concept of God to be formed which will not later produce a highly dangerous crisis of religious consciousness because of its infantile nature. This mystagogy in the self-realisation of the transcendental experience of God must of course link up with experiences which the consciousness declares are clearly and existentially important and which bear in themselves the transcendental experience of God in such a way that they compel the person to a conscious formulation of this experience. These experiences are always embedded in the whole of existential human experience. Where this perhaps more or less miscarries in early childhood—because the experience of love, faithfulness and security between people, and so forth, is not adequately attained—conscious formulation of the primal experience of God is of course very difficult too. Only where life is freely accepted in general as having a sheltering significance, in an ultimate primal trust, will man in his freedom be also prepared to carry out the conscious formulation of this primal trust in the direction of God. The awakening of this primal trust does not take place effectively merely through words. It comes about through participation in the life of another person who, in his serenity and love, may be able to provide a fruitful model for this primal trust.

From this standpoint we can also acquire an understanding of the connection between the experience of God and man's relatedness to Jesus Christ. Christ is the 'fruitful model' *per se* for a committed reliance on the mystery of our existence, which we call God. The

believer calls the absolutely radical form of our transcendental relatedness to God, the Spirit of Jesus Christ. It is in looking at the history
of Jesus that the Christian finds the historical legitimisation for committed reliance on God, whom Jesus called his Father. Transcendental
experience of God and the historical experience of Jesus come together
in a mutually conditioning relationship; Spirit and history are a unity
in which God is at once man's origin and his end.

It is of course also conceivable for someone to have been indoctri-
nated about God by the religious society, without himself being able
to enter very clearly into this expository process in the light of his
own personal transcendent experience of God. He too can of course
let the philosophical and theological dynamic that is also part of this
objectified concept of God work on him, so arriving at an ever more
purified and more subtle concept of God. On the other hand, he does
not need to be pestered with the difficult expository process at all,
unless his individual or social situation makes such an attempt necessary. In people with a sound philosophical training, this expository
process is not necessarily always facilitated by their education; it can
actually be made more difficult as well, so that in certain circumstances they stop short at a 'troubled atheism' in the reflective dimension, where the horror of being without God is seen, admitted
and suffered, and yet this state cannot be specifically overcome on
the level of knowledge about which they can reflect.

THE ONENESS OF PIETY IN THE CHURCH AND OUTSIDE IT

History is the material on which every transcendental experience
works. This applies even to the transcendental experience of God.
Church piety is therefore nothing other than the fulfilling completion
of the transcendental experience of God that is given everywhere, and
which is reflected upon in the contemplation of the historical fact of
the dead and risen Jesus of Nazareth. The historical contingency of
this material gives church piety its obvious tangibility and concreteness; but it also lays it open to attack.[7] This means that today the
piety of the Church must always be clearly 'fed back' into that primal
experience which is its basic material and which it interprets. Other-

---

[7] The material could even be different and would still in any case retain its
contingent origin. This is necessary, but it is hard to endure, precisely because
it is supposed to be, and is, the concrete form of a transcendentally necessary
relationship to God that is universally valid.

wise it cannot be lived without reservation in its historically contingent form (in the human word, and in the worship and law of the Church); nor can it stand up to its openness to attack from atheistic humanism or from people who point to the many other existing religions.

The question here is not whether there is or can be a transcendental experience of God which is reflected upon without the mediation of any specific object. An intensive transcendental experience of God will certainly be possible where the mediating, finite object recedes: where the nameless reality of God is experienced in quiet recollection, in silence, where the conditions of space and time recede, where emptiness is experienced as plenitude, where silence speaks, where death is seen as the life that presses forward to meet us, and where earthly reality is pure, unalloyed promise. Here religious life has an immeasurable field of profundity, down to the phenomena which we usually call mystical. For the Church to make this experience again its own, in a fundamental sense – that is to say, to make it part of its life in the Spirit, for which everything else is merely the instrument – means completing the unity between piety within the Church and piety outside it. Initiation into meditative experience ought to be an art in which the spiritual adviser, the 'director of souls', is proficient. It is one aspect of the contemporary priest's uncertainty about the role he has to play that there is so little understanding of this in the Church. Today's priests have nothing to say about the experience of God.

Against these ideas, the objection may be raised that here everything is too much based on theologumena which are open to dispute and are, at the very least, not generally accepted. This might be countered by saying that no dogma can be preached without the use of theologumena. But if we take seriously God's universal rule for the salvation of all mankind, if we presuppose that a person cannot find salvation without some encounter with God, and if we do not make this into some sort of mystical miracle which can just as well be denied as affirmed – then every Christian is bound to assume that everyone has had some encounter or other with God which already precedes God's proclamation in the Word; for even the person who has not encountered this proclamation in the Word in an effective way, or at all, is to find salvation. Every preacher must say what he thinks about this experience of God, which inevitably precedes his preaching, and must explain how he thinks he can appeal to it. But the question remains whether an answer which is really different in fact from the one we have given here can be formulated in a different terminology.

19

SOME CLARIFYING REMARKS ABOUT MY OWN WORK

Although a number of difficulties are involved, I should like to say something here about the relationship between philosophy and what I have written and published over the years.[1] I myself aim to be a theologian and really nothing else; simply because I am just not a philosopher, and am under no illusions that I ever could be one. Not that this means that I despise philosophy, or consider it unimportant. On the contrary, I have a dreadful respect for it.

It is true that I was once meant to hold a chair in the history of philosophy in Pullach.[2] As a result, for two years I attended Martin Heidegger's lectures and took part in his seminars in Freiburg, after I had finished my normal training as a Jesuit. But in the first place a professor of philosophy is not necessarily a philosopher; and secondly, it was precisely after my time in Freiburg (1934–6) that I became a theologian; not because my philosophical thesis for M. Honegger was turned down, but because a theology teacher was needed in Innsbruck, and my superiors in the order thought that I would be no worse than anyone else. At all events, I am not a philosopher; and

[1] The text was originally written to accompany P. Eicher's book, *Die anthropologische Wende. Karl Rahners philosphischer Weg vom Wesen des Menschen zur personalen Existenz*, Dokimion 1 (Fribourg 1970), IX–XIV. Remarks bearing on the particular situation in which the essay was written have been eliminated in the present version, and some slight stylistic improvements have been introduced.

[2] Reference is to the Philosophische Hochschule Berchmanskolleg Pullach, near Munich. It was here that the German provinces of the Society of Jesus gave students of their order their basic philosophical training between 1925 and 1971. Since that time the Institute has been moved to Munich under the name of Hochschule für Philosophie München – Philosophische Fakultät S.J. It has now been made available to other students as well.

yet philosophical books have been written about my work. That is a curious fact. And it is no excuse to say here (though it may be perfectly true in other cases) that a philosopher can write very philosophically about what is not philosophy at all – so that Heidegger, for example, could write about a poem by Trakl or Hölderlin. That is not what I mean here. So how can anyone write something philosophical about an unphilosophical work, if this work is simply not intended to be the object of philosophy at all?. Philosophy can and must think about the whole of reality – except about other work (in this case my books) which is supposed to be philosophical (that is the assumption) and is not (and of that I am convinced).

The problem that I see here will perhaps become clearer if I at once try to formulate an answer which I think might be given to the question. I would maintain that a new literary genre is developing, because it simply has to develop. This genre is neither theological nor philosophical scholarship; nor is it literature; nor is it the popularisation of theology and philosophy as scholarly studies; it is – yes, what is it? At all events, it is the case today that if one works on philosophy in a specialised and scholarly way, thereby trying to bring one's own ideas face to face with all the opinions and stimuli which are to be found in the history of philosophy (and this is what one must do as a student of philosophy), then nowadays one ceases to get anywhere at all. That is to say, one does not arrive at any definite opinion at all, or only gets drawn into questions which are ultimately unimportant. The philosophy of expert, specialised scholarship becomes a philosophy that is existentially empty and ineffective. Itself moving in circles round its own axis, it moves no one else at all. I am talking here about philosophy *to the extent to which* it aims to be exact and scholarly – scholarly to the extent that is normally demanded of it as a scholarly study today. I am not saying that all philosophical works which actually appear and which one is usually accustomed to think of as being specialised philosophy in the scholarly sense have no power to move existence. Not at all! But what I would maintain is that, *if* they have this power, they have it in the very degree to which they are *not* scholarly; or – to put it rather more profoundly – to the extent that they have the courage for that non-reflective quality which *as a scholar* one ought not to possess at all. Of course this is a dangerous view. It seems to suggest that the people who 'talk a lot of hot air', and the prejudiced and over-emotional are quite right to avoid the trouble of reflection, and to lay down the law instead of thinking.

All the same, I would maintain that a person has the right and the duty to state his convictions without having subjected them to a process of reflection down to the very last detail, and without having translated them into science or scholarship – whether that scholarship be philosophy or theology. I would maintain this simply because an adequate reflection, which completely objectifies the whole of personal awareness, is quite simply impossible and in a finite consciousness is in fact contrary to a transcendental necessity. There will be no need for me to explain that in more detail here.

Now, it is of course clear that no book was ever written which was 'purely' scientific or scholarly, and which *only* presented arguments which had been made the subject of reflection. This is not the case even in mathematics or natural science. For at the very least the choice of subject is never adequately reflected upon, or legitimised by a process of reflection. And we all know that the foundations of mathematics, on which this strict science is built up, are anything but clear – which is to say that even the mathematician does not exactly know, in an adequate process of reflection, what he is really saying. To that extent we can say that the literary genre I am aiming at must always have existed, and has in fact existed; that is always exists and exists everywhere, in every book; and that I am simply tilting at windmills. But this is to see matters in too abstract a light. The scholar used to have the impression – and rightly so – that when he wrote he could get as far as one can, and must, by means of his reflections; so far, that is, that no one else could get any further either, essentially speaking. He therefore did not reflect at all, generally speaking, about the fact that between what he stated, through a process of reflection and objectification, and what he really meant (but had not sufficiently objectified) there was a difference. He, the individual scholar, could reach the heights of the objectification that was possible *at all* at that time. He knew that there was much that he did not know; that he knew little, or even nothing, about fields of knowledge other than his own. But a 'top' scholar, when he was writing on his own subject, put on paper everything that was to be said. And what he did not know with regard to his own subject was part of the lack of knowledge common to all; it was a not-knowing that was not related to a declarable object, but which was only the 'transcendental' vacuity which of course surrounds all knowledge to an infinite degree. Things are quite different today. If today anyone works and writes in the way that scholars worked in earlier times, or in their style, the subject can only be so limited that it is unimportant and a matter of indifference, once it has been related to existence in some way or other. We are becoming like the man who, so as to achieve exact knowledge, specialised more and more until he knew everything about nothing.

What really has to be said today can no longer be said any more with scholarly exactitude and complete reflection. One knows that one says a great deal which one ought to know more about, and which, moreover, one *can* know more about today, because studies exist which one has not read. One is perfectly conscious that it would be quite easy to draw up an exact programme of research to discover all this, and that a learned critic probably knows a great deal which he can put into a 'scathing' review, in order to show the amateurish way in which one has skated over the pitfalls of the problems without even noticing. I claim to say something about the subject and yet know nothing about all this. Nor shall I ever know it, simply because (for reasons of time, and so forth) one finds personally impossible what really ought – and must – be possible if one wanted to say anything that is both scholarly and existentially significant.

I write about the question of transubstantiation and know very little indeed about the history and problems of 'substance' as a concept, although I am perfectly aware that there are books about this, which I have not read and shall not read – not because I despise them, or am too lazy, but because I am simply unable to do so. Perhaps I may write about the Trinity, and have not even studied what has been said by Thomas Aquinas or Ruiz de Montoya,[3] though this has a bearing on the subject. I talk about the relationship between the pope and the episcopate and realise that I ought really to know all about the philosophy of law and about constitutional law; and realise, too, that I am versed in neither and never shall be. Measured against what is 'actually' possible in the scholarly field today, and what I myself see to be possible in a general way, what I write is the work of a dilettante.

This means that the '*haute vulgarisation*', the high-class popularisation of earlier times, is no longer merely a secondary by-product of scholarly theology and philosophy. It is more or less the only way

---

[3] Diego Ruiz de Montoya, s.j. (1562 – 1632), Spanish philosopher and theologian; cf. J. P. Grausem in *DThC* XIV/1, pp. 163–7, and LThK IX, 2nd edn, pp. 94f.

in which someone who wants to write something important in this field can write at all, quite apart from the degree in which this is an exact science or study. Is it gradually becoming clear what literary genre I am talking about? It is a statement made in the definite awareness (i.e. not merely in the indefinite, 'transcendental' awareness of not-knowing) that one is talking about something which 'really' could be, and ought to be, considered more precisely – historically, speculatively, and so forth – without one's being in a position to do so.

Of course as a scholar one starts with the highest intentions and ends up with a statement which – as one is all too painfully aware – falls short of being scholarly. The paradoxical thing about this is then that one makes this less-than-scholarly statement in such a way that, even so, a good proportion of one's readers do not understand it, because it is again, or still, too scholarly. Of course I am well aware that what I have said can be misinterpreted as meaning that 'scholarship' must be the highest standard and ideal; and that all other kinds of utterance have to make this their yardstick and their standard of judgement, only to be recognised as something 'lower'. But this is not what I mean. Only, if one writes long books, this gives the impression that one is writing as a scholar. And so it seems useful to say clearly that this is not really the case, and that one knows it.

Apart from a few essays on the history of penance[4] (which belong to the history of dogma) nothing I have written can be called theological scholarship, let alone (professional) philosophy. It is all far too amateurish for that – but rightly so, in the modern situation we have described; I am not ashamed of the fact. I do not believe that a judgement of this kind involves a depreciation of what I have written. I even believe that when one talks to people today who want to know something 'existential', it is the only way one can talk and write. Of course that does not mean that one could not do it in a thousand other ways, or a thousand times better than I have succeeded in doing. But I would still maintain that it can only be done nowadays in this unscholarly way.

If that be the case, then I can only hope that all the people who ask about a philosophical anthropology in my work will be merciful.

---

[4] Collected and revised in 'Frühe Bussgeschichte in Einzeluntersuchungen' *Schriften Zur Theologie* XI (*Theological Investigations* 15). On the importance of this work for the work of the present author as a whole cf. K. H. Neufeld, 'Fortschritt durch Umkehr – Zu Karl Rahners bussgeschichtlichen Arbeiten', *StdZ* 192 (1974), pp. 274–81.

And a reader should be lenient and remember that he ought to listen more to what I wanted to say than what I actually did say. For in matters of theology and philosophy, he must not forget that today the difference between what is said and what is meant is greater that ever before. It is an ancient piece of insight that the person who fails to recognise the genre to which a piece of writing belongs inevitably misunderstands the work itself. Today there are writings which inevitably give the impression of being scholarly, because they are long and difficult to read – or because they try, as far as they can, to make an intellectual effort and demand the same effort of their readers. Yet they are at once much more and much less than scholarship. They are less because the dimensions of the reflections which are collectively possible today are beyond the reach of any individual; they are more because an attempt has been made to say something which may minister to salvation.

LIST OF SOURCES

CHRISTMAS IN THE LIGHT OF THE IGNATIAN EXERCISES
Hitherto unpublished text of a sermon preached at Christmas 1974
before a Jesuit community; slightly revised for print.

JESUS' RESURRECTION
The text is based on hitherto unpublished material used for a lecture
which the author gave on the occasion of receiving an honorary
doctorate from the University of Louvain. The original character has
been retained in spite of some revision and expansion for print.

CHRISTOLOGY TODAY?
The text is based on a hitherto unpublished lecture given at the
University of Saarbrücken in December 1973. It has been revised for
the present edition, and notes and cross-references to other work of
the author's have been added.

JESUS CHRIST IN THE NON-CHRISTIAN RELIGIONS
Published in *Offenbarung, Geistige Realität des Menschen. Arbeitsdoku-
mentation eines Symposiums zum Offenbarungsbegriff in Indien*, ed. G.
Oberhammer (Vienna 1974), pp. 189–98.

THE THEOLOGICAL DIMENSIONS OF THE QUESTION ABOUT MAN
Lecture held before those responsible for the Religiösen Schulwochenarbeit in Westphalia on 9 Sept. 1972, in Dortmund. The original
text was published in a collection under the same title as the present
contribution (Donauwörth 1972), pp. 9–28. It has been revised for
the present edition.

THE BODY IN THE ORDER OF SALVATION
Originally published in K. Rahner and A. Görres, *Der Leib und das
Heil (Probleme der Praktischen Theologie – Festgabe zum 60. Geburtstag
von Weihbischof Josef Maria Reuss)*, vol. iv (Mainz 1967), pp. 29 – 44.
Stylistic improvements have been made for the present edition; and
above all notes have been added.

MYSTICAL EXPERIENCE AND MYSTICAL THEOLOGY
Revised text of the preface to C. Albrecht, *Das mystische Wort. Erleben
und Sprechen in Versunkenheit*, H. A. Fischer-Barnicol (Mainz 1974),
pp. vii–xiv.

THE LIBERTY OF THE SICK, CONSIDERED THEOLOGICALLY
Published in *StdZ* 193 (1975), pp. 31–40. Notes and cross-references
have been added for the present edition.

THE INTERMEDIATE STATE
Written for a Spanish periodical. Here published for the first time in
German.

OPPOSITION IN THE CHURCH
Originally published in *StdZ* 192 (1974), pp. 812–20. Notes and
cross-references have been added for the present edition.

'MYSTERIUM ECCLESIAE'
First published in *StdZ* 191 (1973), pp. 579–94. Matter of purely ephemeral interest has been omitted. Notes and cross-references linking the material more closely with the author's other work have been added.

THE AREA BISHOP: SOME THEOLOGICAL REFLECTIONS
Originally published in *Weltkirche, Festgabe für Julius Kardinal Döpfner*, ed. H. Fleckenstein, G. Gruber, G. Schwaiger, E. Tewes (Würzburg 1973), pp. 478–87.

TRANSFORMATIONS IN THE CHURCH AND IN SECULAR SOCIETY
The text is based on a hitherto unpublished lecture, given in spring 1974 in Madrid at a symposium. It has been revised and notes have been added for the present edition.

THE ONE CHURCH AND THE MANY CHURCHES
The article is the revised text of a lecture held in June 1968 in Münster, published in *Orientierung* 32 (1968), pp. 155–9, and in expanded form in *Philosphia. Festschrift für J. I. de Alcorta* (Barcelona 1971), pp. 477–89.

IS CHURCH UNION DOGMATICALLY POSSIBLE
Originally published in *ThQ* (1973), pp. 103–18. The text has been slightly revised and cross-references have been added.

THIRD CHURCH
Lecture held on Reformation Day 1972 in Munich. Already published in shortened form in *Evangelische Kommentare* 6 (Stuttgart 1973), pp. 14–17. Revised for the present edition.

RELIGIOUS FEELING INSIDE AND OUTSIDE THE CHURCH
Based on a working paper for the German Episcopal Synod. Originally published in *StdZ* 191 (1973), pp. 3–13.

SOME CLARIFYING REMARKS ABOUT MY OWN WORK
Originally written to accompany P. Eicher's book, *Die anthropologische Wende. Karl Rahners philosophischer Weg vom Wesen des Menschen
zur personalen Existenz*, Dokimion 1 (Fribourg 1970), ix-xiv. Some
purely personal remarks by way of introduction and conclusion have
been omitted in the present edition.

INDEX OF PERSONS

INDEX OF SUBJECTS